THE
ROOTS
AND FUTURE
OF MANAGEMENT
THEORY

THE
ROOTS
AND FUTURE
OF MANAGEMENT
THEORY

A Systems Perspective

WILLIAM ROTH

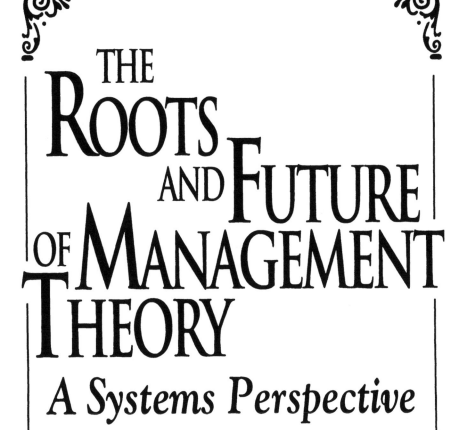

ISBN: 1-4610-2308-4
ISBN-13: 9781461023081

Dedication

This book is dedicated to Russell L. Ackoff,
my teacher, my friend,
the person who has done the most to shape
my contribution.

With love and respect

William Roth

BIOGRAPHY

William F. Roth is currently a professor of Management Sciences at Kutztown University in Pennsylvania. He is also a Senior Fellow at The Wharton School, University of Pennsylvania. He earned his B.A. from Dartmouth College in Economic Geography, his MSW from the University of Pennsylvania School of Social Work, and his Ph.D in Management Sciences from The Wharton School, University of Pennsylvania. Professor Roth has six books on management theory, ethics, health care, and quality improvement in print and over fifty articles published in a wide range of both national and international journals. At the beginning of his career he worked with The International Paper Company as Corporate Manager of Organization Design. Later, he consulted on management systems with Anheuser Busch, The Mars Corporation, ALCOA of Tennessee, Mack Truck, The Cities of Philadelphia, Charleston, S.C., and Allentown, P.A., the governments of Saudi Arabia, and Mexico. As a member of the Association of Quality and Participation Doctor Roth designed an effort to train people in the "systems" approach to Quality Improvement. He later took the lead in setting up a global network of systems thinker. More recently, he was asked by The Deming Institute to facilitate integration of the ASQ, AQP, and Deming Institute community development models. Currently, Professor Roth is leading an effort involving more than eighty health care professionals from twelve different countries to design an ideal health care system. One result of this effort is *Comprehensive Healthcare for the U.S.: An Idealized Design* published last year.
,

Contents

Preface

The Roots and Future of Management Theory has been written as a history of management theory with "feeling." This means the text contains not only dates, names, and descriptions of events, but also an interpretation of their significance from a variety of perspectives including philosophical, religious, scientific, economic, sociological, and psychological.

The Roots and Future of Management Theory is a "systemic" offering that it attempts to break down the boundaries between disciplines and to integrate the range of viewpoints presented in a way that gives life and comprehensive meaning to events, not only in terms of their individual moment in time, but also in terms of key historic trends, both workplace and societal.

The book's major theme is humanity's ongoing quest for the resources necessary to implement the *development ethic* on a society-wide level, and how this quest has shaped the workplace. It offers concepts that have materialized during our struggle for these resources and over these resources, some new, some well known, some supportive, some intended to be supportive but then perverted, some nonsupportive — the scarcity mentality, the Protestant work ethic, laissez faire economics, the economic man, the growth ethic, Social Darwinism, scientific management, the systems approach — and the names of key players as road signs on our journey.

The book also identifies key societal conflicts that have helped shape the workplace and still rage today — the trade-off between physical security and emotional security; the struggle between Machiavellian humanism and Christian humanism; the struggle between the mechanistic, engineering school and the human relations school of management theory.

The book explores the role of technology in workplace evolution and how, on the most obvious level, technology has sometimes been our friend, sometimes our enemy. Nevertheless, it has always kept us moving in the right direction, forcing us to overcome ingrained workplace habits no longer cost effective. Technology has increasingly freed us from physical labor, allowing us to contribute more with our minds than just with our hands.

Finally, *The Roots and Future of Management Theory* tries to project the direction that management theory is headed, the direction management theory is helping society as a whole to move in our historic drive to "round that corner." The aim is to make the *development ethic* the primary force in our culture, to make it possible, through work and its rewards, for every individual to develop his or her positive human potential to the fullest possible extent, and, in turn, to contribute to the development of others.

Good reading, and good luck.

William Roth

THE PRE-INDUSTRIAL REVOLUTION ERA

1

The Pre-Industrial Revolution era began at the end of the Dark Ages, roughly around A.D. 1000. It includes the later Medieval period, the Renaissance, the Reformation, and the Enlightenment. This last provided a bridge to the early Industrial Revolution. But the supports for this bridge, its pilings, were shaped over the previous 700 years by a wide range of socioeconomic institutions and by individuals.

What happened during the Pre-Industrial Revolution era depended little upon technological innovation. The primitive technology available during this time changed little and remained secondary in importance to the skills of workers. Neither was the era influenced greatly by changes in the size of businesses. Most were small and remained relatively small. Finally, the era was not guided to a major extent by marketplace pressures. Such pressures existed, to be sure, but, for the most part, they were heavily regulated.

The Pre-Industrial Revolution era world of business, therefore, received its character and direction primarily from socioeconomic forces — the Church, feudalism, the state, then the church again, then the state. It was also molded by a progression of larger-than-life individuals — ambitious businessmen, bold explorers, innovative thinkers, and courageous change agents — who defined key concepts upon which modern-day management theory continues to feed. These concepts, despite their age, are at the core of most of our current business successes, as well as most of our current management problems.

In order to understand the secret of these successes and the real causes of these problems and to put them into a clear context so that we can deal effectively with them, the place to start is with their historical roots.

1 Medieval Period and the Renaissance: Developing the Basics

After Reading This Book You Should Know

1. How, during the Medieval period, the three major forces shaping European society were the Catholic Church, the nobility, and the craft guilds.
2. How guilds kept the economy in balance.
3. The role the Crusades played in the development of the European economy.
4. How the new merchant class built its power on the new concept of "profit."
5. How increased wealth became the objective of individuals, nations, and the church.
6. Why, while life improved tremendously for those with power, the situation of the working class deteriorated.
7. What the origins of Machiavellian humanism were and why it became a driving force in the economic world.
8. How and why Christian humanism evolved as an alternative to Machiavellian humanism.

Medieval Europe: A Tightly Bound Society

While the Roman Empire, under Julius Caesar and his successors, was still the dominant influence in Western Europe (up to around A.D. 500), economic development remained an objective. A network

3

of well-built roads was laid to link the various regions. Towns were erected to serve as focal points for commerce. Protection while traveling was provided for those involved in trade.

Once the Roman influence disappeared from this region, however, the tribes that regained power allowed the road system to deteriorate and the towns to crumble. Craftsmen and peddlers traveling any distance usually had to provide for their own protection. Those in control had no desire to integrate the economy or to develop a centralized government, characteristics that had been the strength of the Roman Empire. Rather, kingdoms remained loose federations of extended families that lived off their own lands, independent and self-sufficient, sometimes trading with each other, more frequently fighting.

This was the societal model that persevered through the Dark Ages and into the Medieval period. By that time, around A.D. 1000, the wood and thatch hut of the headman had evolved into a stone fortification; family members had become the local nobility; the amount of land controlled and cultivated had grown; and "serfs," nonfamily members who worked the land and swore their allegiance to the local lord in return for his protection, had been brought into the fold. The serfs paid for the lord's protection and for the Church's blessing by giving part of their harvest to each. Also, they were required to spend time working in the fields of each. Self-sufficiency remained the rule and survival the major concern of most.

As the Medieval period progressed, life began to improve. One reason for this was a population explosion. During the Dark Ages, largely because of the continual wars waged between feudal lords, because of the nobility's attitude toward the common people, because of the generally harsh living conditions, the population of the continent had decreased. But now, in England, for example, the population tripled in a span of 300 years, thus creating more production power and a larger market for goods and services.

This was both a blessing and a problem for those in power. While more crops could be planted and harvested, there were also more people to control. Peasants had begun voicing a desire for more than a life of simple servitude. The nobility responded the only way it knew, with force, which had traditionally been its major policy-shaping vehicle. Male members of the nobility had been trained since childhood in the arts of warfare. They now used those arts not only to protect, but also to control their serf populations.

The Church was initially subtler. It tried to keep the population dependent. Peasants were not allowed to learn to read. Curiosity was considered a sin. The church promised that it would provide the right answers to any reasonable questions that peasants might have. In the middle of the 13th century, however, with the Inquisition, the Church took off its gloves, making it painfully clear that those who questioned its authority would suffer for their indiscretions, for their lack of obedience.

But change, despite all efforts, was inevitable, as it always has been. Perhaps the most significant driving force was the reestablishment of trade. By the 11th century, regions of Europe had begun exchanging goods again. Flanders, for example, began producing excess woolen cloth which it traded to Norse sailors for honey, furs, and other goods from the north. The French began exporting wine to England. The British began exporting tin, the Italians glassware, and the Spanish horses.

Also, as settlements around the castles of lords and the establishments of the clergy expanded, an obvious need arose for organization of the crafts industries so that supply would meet, but not exceed, demand. The guild system evolved in response to this need. The first guilds included a mixture of all the craftsmen of a town, as well as merchants who were originally street peddlers buying here and selling there to gain a few pennies.

The original mission of these guilds was not so much to regulate trade as it was to negotiate with the local lord concerning what part of profits would be taken in taxes, what the trade laws would be, who would make the legal decisions, what warehouse and shop space would be made available, what protection would be provided. These initial guilds, therefore, could be considered early versions of our present-day unions, representing the workers in negotiations with owners.

As guilds grew in economic strength, some were eventually able to wrest the power of community governance away from the local lord. The lords were in a bind. They no longer owned the source of production outright; as they had when land was the wellspring of all wealth and power. They no longer possessed the skills necessary to control the economy. They were fighters and rulers, not businessmen. And their quality of life was improving rapidly due to the contributions of the local craftsmen and merchants. So, from at least one perspective, trying to stop this shift in power did not make much sense.

Towns were becoming, as in Roman times, centers of trade. Their inhabitants, however, were a new breed. They were not serfs working the land, not nobility, not clergy, not professional soldiers. Instead, they were mainly the producers and providers of an ever-growing range of goods — houses, carts, candles, rope, cloth, shoes, tables, rugs — some brought in from other regions, some, even, from other countries. These citizens were called "burgers" which means, literally, "townspeople," and they were the beginning of a new middle class.

By the 1200s, the Church also had begun to realize the value of this new class and had grudgingly sanctioned it. Still, in its desire to uphold traditional values, in its concern for the general welfare, in its ongoing effort to maintain control over the lives of its flock, the Church made an effort to stifle the greed that might erupt from newly evolving economic opportunity. The Church said that the merchants were allowed to ask only a "just price," a price that enabled them to maintain a reasonable standard of life, but no more. The Church resisted development of the banking industry so critical to business growth and commerce and banned related practices that it considered un-Christian including speculation and usury (the loaning of money for profit).

As things progressed, friction arose between the two key factions in the guilds, the local craftsmen and the merchants. The latter, because of their expanding reach and greater opportunity for profits, also because of their ability to manipulate the craftsmen, were becoming wealthy and powerful. The craftsmen, however, still limited by the fact that they could sell directly only to local markets and by the fact that they were dependent on the merchants for access to markets outside the local sphere, were not doing as well. Suspicion and resentment grew.

Eventually, the guilds broke up, merchant houses going off on their own. Because of their success, they no longer needed the security that the "togetherness" of the guilds had provided. The various crafts also broke away, forming independent "subguilds" that focused on the welfare of their specific trade.

The Crusades End Europe's Isolation

Another major contributor to change, progress, and to the development of the middle class was the Crusades, initially mounted by Pope Urban II for three reasons. The first was to stop fighting among Europe's lords by giving them a common objective, a common enemy. The second was to unite the European and Western Catholic Churches under papal leadership. The third was to reclaim the Holy Lands, specifically Jerusalem, from the Moslems.

Less religious, more pragmatic people also saw the Crusades as an opportunity to regain control of shipping routes in the eastern Mediterranean from the Moslems and actually to reopen trade relations with those they were going to fight, as well as with cultures lying beyond the Holy Lands to which Europe, up to this point, had been denied access.

Militarily, these Crusades, lasting until almost the 1300s, were a disaster for the European forces. Commercially, they were a success. They did, indeed, allow merchants to find new trading partners, to discover and bring home new technology and products. Marco Polo, perhaps the most famous merchant of that period, traveled during the late 1200s overland all the way to China and developed trading relations with the clan of the great warrior Genghis Khan whose armies dominated the Asian continent and, at one later point, threatened to overrun even Europe.

Back on the home front, the craft guilds were moving steadily to solidify their position in the local market. Each community of any size now had its own well-organized guilds. These organizations had several key responsibilities, the most important of which was to protect members from outside competition and to restrain members from taking unfair advantage of each other. Guilds also controlled the training of apprentices and set limits on the number of craftsmen producing any one product.

Although guild-controlled craftsmen had no geographic mobility, almost no social mobility, and little chance to improve their economic situation, they generally enjoyed job security. People, during the Medieval period, had little opportunity to develop individual potential. Emphasis, as we have said, was on surviving. Group effort, rather than individual effort, offered the best chance of doing so. Craftsmen were members of closely knit communities, their efforts meshing with those of everyone else in the community.

The economic conduct as well as the personal conduct of guild members was bounded by the rules of morality and, to a large degree, by the laws of the Church, which housed God's representatives on Earth. Most guilds built their own chapels. The guild's major purpose, from a religious perspective, was to help members gain grace and, therefore, gain salvation through "good works," deeds that contributed to the welfare of the community. They charged their "just price," a share of any business profits going to glorify God.

It was during the Medieval period that many of the great cathedrals of Europe were raised, sometimes several generations of craftsmen contributing to the same structure. In any village, the largest and handsomest building was usually the stone church that was, in turn, often surrounded by the thatched huts of the local people.

Guild-controlled businesses, like all other organizations, were hierarchical in structure. This model mimicked the chain of command of the Church, the original hierarchy in the Western world, and the system of feudal lords. The Church had the pope, bishops, archdeacons, and clergy on descending levels. The feudal system had the king, barons, lesser lords, and knights. Guild shops had the owner/boss (called the "master craftsman"), "journeymen," and "apprentices."

No other way of structuring organizations was even considered at this point. Because of the ceaseless turmoil and warring, because of the unstable nature of kingdoms and boundaries, because of the sometimes violent confrontations between church and state concerning supremacy, emphasis was on clarifying the lines of authority and power; the hierarchy provided the best vehicle for accomplishing this.

Although the management *structure* of the guild shop mirrored that of church and state, its management *philosophy* did not. Church parishioner and state subjects, on the one hand, were children to be controlled, guided, and taken care of. They were expected to contribute when called upon without question, but were allowed little input into decision making. On the other hand, while guild members were to be controlled, guided, and taken care of, they, unlike parishioners and subjects, were also expected to contribute to the solution of problems. As a result, the decision-making aspect of guild management was frequently a group exercise. And this was something new.

Several good reasons existed for this novel approach. First, craft shops were relatively small. A large craft shop during this period might include 10 or 12 employees and might produce a limited range of products, frequently only one. Such smallness of size and simplicity of technology facilitated participation. Those who controlled the workers of the organization knew the expertise of each worker and could utilize that expertise advantageously. Opinions could be gathered and a consensus shaped without slowing production.

Second, guilds encouraged craftsmen to share innovations and to pass knowledge on to apprentices. Guild training programs turned out new craftsmen familiar with every aspect of the item produced. Because local sales were made directly from the shop to the customer, with no middleman or merchant involved, workers could take part in all phases of the business — planning, production, sales — along with the owner/boss and frequently the customer. By gaining the necessary overview from such involvement, each could make meaningful contributions.

Third, utilization of employee expertise in decision-making situations was facilitated by the fact that an adversary relationship had not yet evolved between management and labor. The ethic that guided boss–employee relations, at least during the "glory years" of the guild movement, was cooperation. "Cooperation" occurs when the efforts of both the boss and the employees enhance the chances of the other to fulfill work-related needs and desires. The journeymen and apprentices helped the master to get the work done and to gain profit, most of which the master kept (apprentices were not even paid, receiving only room and board), and the masters provided training and experience so that the others, journeyman and apprentice, could eventually become masters themselves.

Fourth, because of the "family" nature of businesses, which was encouraged by both the church and the guilds, grievances could be worked out informally and immediately. The Church provided the family model. Church leaders were benevolently paternalistic, and business leaders were encouraged to emulate this model to gain grace.

Finally, from a more pragmatic perspective, there were not many job opportunities available to craftsmen in a town, not many chances to become an entrepreneur. The skills of individual craftsmen were limited and focused, as was the market. It was usually to their benefit, therefore, to cooperate, to "pay their dues," to get along with their boss, and to maintain a good reputation with the guild.

The Existing Order Breaks Down

As the Medieval period drew to a close, however, the seeds for drastic change were sown. Progress had been slowed dramatically and, in some instances, had even been reversed by two catastrophic events. The first was the advent of the bubonic plague. This "Black Death," as the plague was called, was carried by fleas on the bodies of black rats which first arrived at the Sicilian port of Messina in the year 1347 aboard ships from the Russian Crimea. The disease spread north from there and, in approximately 4 years, killed off one third to one half of the total European population.

The plague struck especially hard in the continent's cities. Some of these, London, for example, now housed over 100,000 people. As a result of lack of planning, most city residents were crowded into unsanitary conditions, the narrow streets serving as the main conduit for the disposal of waste of all types. As a result, city streets supported large populations of rats.

The second catastrophic event was the Hundred Years' War between England and France which began in 1337. This was basically a struggle for the French throne and over territory in that part of Europe. Armies lived off the land, looting and destroying villages. Famine and sudden death became the common fate of the peasants, who had no protection.

In terms of traditional institutions, the Church was in decline. Internal politics and corruption were splitting it. The plague had decimated its ranks of priests, and the peasants, in their frustration, fear, disgust, had, in some instances, renounced it.

The status of the ruling nobility was also eroding. The political control of the nobility continued to slip away as power struggles similar to those that caused the Hundred Years' War sapped its strength and turned increasing numbers of people against it.

And in the business world, the guilds and the order they had gradually brought to the local marketplace were dying. One problem, of course, was the sudden, sharp decrease in the consumer population brought about by pestilence and war. Internally, however, guilds suffered from another disease, one even more lethal and long lasting than the plague, one that has stalked humanity from the beginning of recorded history.

In essence, the problem was that the master craftsmen got greedy. As the opportunity grew to gain more wealth, to improve one's individual situation, so did the realization that the fewer master craftsmen there were to compete, the more each would profit. Eventually, then, it became almost impossible to move beyond the rank of journeyman. The only way to do so was to inherit a relative's business, or to marry into the family of a master craftsman who had no son waiting in line.

The alternative, if one aspired to the master craftsman level or, now more importantly, to the owner level, was to leave the guild and to set up shop on one's own, luring away other apprentices and journeymen with promises of a salary. This, of course, is what began to happen.

A third problem was that, as a means of preventing competition and advantage-taking between member shops, the guilds had adopted an increasingly rigid set of standards for the products they manufactured, as well as an increasingly rigid definition of manufacturing procedures. While these measures did, indeed, reduce competition, they also stifled innovation. Any improvement in the product, any new technology, for example, had to be approved by all guild members before it could be incorporated. Someone, of course, was always threatened, so that very few improvements were allowed.

So the guilds, which during the early Medieval period had been a driving force for change, now, in their efforts to protect membership, to maintain their preeminence as an institution, to maintain a comfortable status quo, had joined the church and the nobility in opposing change.

The end of the Medieval period, then, was the beginning of a time of "breaking away" and of individualism in Europe. People were starting to question the authority of the traditional powers. John Wycliffe, an Oxford scholar, taught in the mid-1300s that the Church did not have the right to

come between a man and his God, and that the Church should not be allowed
to involve itself in civil government. The state fared no better; on several
occasions the peasants rose up against unpopular rulers. One well-known
incident was the Peasant Revolt which occurred in England in 1381; three
peasant armies eventually marched to London to parley face-to-face with
King Richard II.

In the business world, the banking industry, so critical to economic
growth, despite the continuing qualms of the Church, was by this point well
established. The governing guild system, on the other hand, which had originally dominated the marketplace and had been obedient to the Church, was
being swept away by those eager to compete openly, to take the chances
necessary to improve their individual fortunes. Emphasis was shifting from
self-sufficiency, a feudal concept based on survival economics, to *surplus production,* a means of accruing wealth.

The only group that, despite the hardship and slippage in the late Medieval
period, prospered and grew stronger was the merchants. For merchants,
opportunity continued to increase, no matter what was happening on the
local level. And that brings us to the Renaissance, a period dominated and
shaped by the power of the merchant class more so than any other in the
Pre-Industrial Revolution Era.

The Renaissance: Individuality and the Profit Motive

Although idealistic values, defined by scholars and other thinkers as well as
by the Church, continued to play a major role in shaping the reality of life
at this point in history, a split between desire and reality, between ideals and
pragmatism, started to occur. The Renaissance, which began approximately
in the 1400s, was shaped by several key influences. The most important of
these, as we have said, was the steadily increasing power of the merchant
class. A second influence was the wave of adventurers and fortune seekers
that issued forth from Europe to establish contact and to begin mining or
plundering the wealth of distant cultures and continents. A third influence
was the movement toward centralization of governmental power in many
countries. And a fourth influence was the steadily declining power of the
Catholic Church over both the spiritual and daily working lives of the people.

Renaissance means *rebirth.* This period saw the rebirth of capitalism, of a
profit-driven society, which had largely been dormant in Europe since the
decline of the Roman Empire. It saw the rebirth of education for nonclergy,

of inquiry into the nature of man, whereas the only type of inquiry previously encouraged had been into the nature of man's relationship with God. It saw the rebirth of the arts; practitioners — painters, sculptors, writers — began expanding their perspective, breaking away from the Medieval period's almost total focus on religious figures and themes to begin celebrating man and his accomplishments. And, as is reflected in all of these areas, this period saw the rebirth of individualism, of the quest to fulfill individual potential, as opposed to simply trying to fit into a community in order to survive and submitting to the will of God as defined by the Church.

As has been historically true with every period of impressive societal advancement, the cornerstone of the Renaissance was a tremendous increase in the amount of wealth generated. Credit for this accomplishment went mainly to the merchants, initially to those in the great trading cities of Italy — Venice, Genoa, Milan, Florence. Especially significant were those in Venice, the city that dominated the trade route to the Levant, to the lands of the Turks, Arabs, Indians, Chinese, the trade routes along which flowed spices, silk, porcelain, a wide variety of goods increasingly popular in Europe.

Other European cultures, however, reacted rapidly to the advantage enjoyed by the Italians and to the heavy tolls charged by both the Venicians and the Turks in Constantinople on goods passing through their territory. Explorers set sail to find new, nonland routes to the ports of the new trading partners. Spain and Portugal took the lead. Vasco da Gama sailed east in 1498. He rounded the horn of Africa to open a route to India and the Far East, allowing the Portuguese to bring clover, nutmeg, pepper, and other valuable spices and goods back at less cost than that incurred by overland travelers.

A little earlier, in 1492, Christopher Columbus, under the sponsorship of the Spanish king, attempted to reach these same spice-producing nations by sailing west instead of east. He encountered West Indies first because they lay in the way, and he stopped there. This "failure" led, during the following century, to the acquisition of great stores of gold and silver through the conquest of the Aztec and Inca by adventurers and explorers who followed Columbus. The wealth brought back to Europe helped to fuel further economic development.

Eventually, the countries of northern Europe — France, England, Belgium, Germany, the Netherlands — also became seriously involved in the Renaissance. The generation of new wealth again provided the foundation for desired change. As economic opportunity increased, the merchants again led the way.

Life, however, was not so optimistic for everyone during this period. In fact, a relatively small percentage of the population benefited from the increasing wealth. A majority of the craftsmen, for example, did not benefit. Many, in fact, saw the quality of their lives deteriorate. The concept of a "just price" still applied to the local market because the church was there to oversee. So guild shop master craftsmen were rarely able to reap the benefits of supply and demand.

Also, craft shops were rapidly being swallowed up by the merchants so that production could be better monitored and related to the demands of the marketplace, both in Europe and abroad. It was more profitable for merchants to control the process of turning the raw materials they imported into the products they exported, than it was to first sell the raw materials to a guild shop, then afterward to buy back the finished product. This practice deprived the craftsmen of much of the control over their work and economic lives.

Also, there were taxes. The centralization of government in most European countries had been made possible by the generation of excess wealth. Because there was little excess wealth during the Medieval period, governments had needed to stay local, small, and, therefore, relatively inexpensive. For example, most legal decisions made during Medieval times were rendered by the local lord based on the testimony of the complainant and defendant with no appeals, no record of proceedings. The legal system, therefore, during the Medieval period, was basically a one-person show. Now, during the Renaissance, there existed a system of state-supported courts. Now there were lawyers and judges and court recorders and courtrooms to support.

The development and maintenance of a centralized government costs a lot of money. The most powerful merchants, because the government was dependent on them, were able to avoid paying their share of the costs. A very heavy part of the tax burden, therefore, fell on all other businesspeople, on the middle class, as it does today, and for much the same reasons.

Another serious blow to the general public in its quest for improved quality of life was loss of its greatest ally, the church. The Catholic Church was eventually overwhelmed by the rate of change and lost its perspective. The church, during the Medieval period, had been the most powerful institution in Europe. It had been the only thing binding together the wide range of kingdoms and cultures spanning the continent.

In this role, willingly or not, the church had become increasingly political and had gained great amounts of temporal (everyday life) as well as spiritual power. Eventually, it had openly declared its right to guide the fate of the kingdoms under its aegis in all matters and to enforce its decisions by whatever means necessary. This was done formally through the codification in Canon Law of the Doctrine of Papal Supremacy (final say) in the temporal as well as in the spiritual sphere.

Part of the perceived power of the Church came from the fact that, while it claimed the right to control the lives of its flock, its representatives stood apart from and above that flock, as intermediates between God and His children. An example of this exclusivity was the fact that the Church had its own courts. No member of the clergy was allowed to be tried by local lords or by centralized governments.

The Church had become accustomed to exercising this degree of control. When the city-states of Italy and the centralized governments in France, England, and the other northern countries began wresting away temporal powers, began communicating directly with each other, began demanding that clergy no longer be immune from the legal jurisdiction of the state (the French, at one point, actually attempted to arrest an Italian pope on charges of heresy), and, finally, began demanding that the Church pay taxes to the state, the church became deeply troubled.

The power of the state was built on taxes and, in the final analysis, on the success of the merchant class and bankers who had generated the economic foundations which made taxation possible. *Wealth*, not grace, not land, but monetary wealth had become the key to power. The Church, in desperation, also went after wealth. It began to collect taxes. It began to court the same merchants and bankers it had previously railed against. In its darkest hour, it even began to sell pardons, dispensations, sacred relics, indulgences, and, although perhaps not as directly, even positions, sometimes very high positions in the Church hierarchy, to raise money.

But as the Church became increasingly wealthy, as it became increasingly conspicuous in its displays of wealth, the people began to protest. The validity of the Church as a spiritual leader had come into question. The clergy had proved itself too mortal, succumbing to the very temptation, to the very greed it had for so long fought against in others and from which had tried to protect its parishioners.

The Church was sending out a double message, one that could no longer be trusted, and the faithful did not like it. The people felt totally exposed to exploitation now. With the guilds dominated by the merchants, with the church questionable in its commitment and the state busy trying to establish its preeminence as a governing body, there was no one left to protect them.

The Rise of Machiavellian Humanism

And this brings us to the *humanism* movement which set the tone for, or perhaps provided the necessary rationalization for, what occurred during the Renaissance, especially in Italy. The humanists were philosophers (those concerned with the meaning of life) who rebelled against the Medieval focus on the afterlife. They rebelled against the belief that God had preordained everyone's place in nature, everyone's station in this life, and that man's duty was to humbly accept God's decisions. Again, like Wycliffe, they said that no group, specifically not the clergy, should be allowed to impose itself as an intermediary between an individual and God. They rebelled against the Medieval period's stress on obedience and on the maintenance of order.

The humanists set about to revive the glorification of the human spirit and of earthly affairs that had been so important during the classical Greek and Roman periods. They believed that, as part of this celebration of the secular, individuals should strive to develop their potential to the fullest possible extent, this being a concept derived from the Greek theory of human development.

But the original Italian humanists added something new. They said that *pilgrims needed to be strong of heart during their quest for self-development, letting no one stand in their way, no matter what the cost to others and to society.* In Italy, this became known as the concept of *virtu* which, while similar in etymology to our modern-day "virtue" was almost directly opposite in meaning. Machiavelli's book, *The Prince*, which remains popular today in certain circles, was a guide for those willing to do what was necessary to demonstrate *virtu.*

Niccolò Machiavelli made his contribution to society in the late 1400s when Italy was a collection of city-states — Florence, the papal state in Rome, Naples, Venice, Milan — that spent most of their energy struggling against each other for increased power and, at the same time, battling to keep lesser cities under control. The air was thick with intrigue, assassination, and war between ever-changing factions. The most powerful family in Florence, where Machiavelli's family lived, was the Medici. One of his ancestors had opposed and alienated these "mildly despotic" rulers. Machiavelli, as a result, did not receive the chance to take a position as a public servant until 1494 when the Medici family was finally forced from power.

For the next 13 years, while Secretary to the Second Chancery of Florence, Machiavelli worked skillfully as a diplomat in the areas of foreign and military affairs, mingling and negotiating with the great rulers of Europe. When, however, the Medici eventually returned to power, Machiavelli was immediately exiled from his native city to a country home where he wrote *The Prince*. He did not write the piece for publication. Rather, he saw it as a means of regaining favor with the Medici rulers. The manuscript was not, in fact, published until 5 years after his death in 1532.

Machiavelli was a realist of the first order. His lessons were entirely antithetical to those being taught by the Church at the time (although the Church was obviously not always practicing what it preached). His basic thesis was that if all men were good, the best course would be to proceed in a respectful manner, keeping one's word and telling the truth. But all men were not good and, therefore, if one wished to stay in power as a ruler it was necessary to do whatever one must to win, holding no promise as inviolate, seeing no man as a friend. Machiavelli believed that he who was the least predictable ultimately won.

In Machiavelli's own words, "A man who wishes to make a profession of goodness in everything must necessarily come to grief amongst so many who are not good."[1] He continues later:

> The experience of our times shows those princes to have done great things who have had little regard for good faith and who have been able by astuteness to confuse men's brains, and who have ultimately overcome those who have made loyalty their foundation.[2]

Also, he adds:

> One ought to be both feared and loved, but as it is difficult for the two to go together, it is much safer to be feared than loved.... [M]en love of their own free will, but fear at the will of the prince, and a wise prince must rely on what is in his power and not on what is in the power of others.[3]

Finally, he says that appearances are more important than actions, image is more important than content because "everyone sees what you appear to be, few feel what you [actually] are, and those few [who do so] will not dare to oppose themselves to the many."[4]

The leaders of the Italian Renaissance, in their move toward humanism, no matter what form, were reacting to the restrictive bonds that had held society together during the Medieval period. They were breaking those bonds and swinging as far as they could in the opposite direction. Instead of a total focus on community, on fitting in, there was now a growing focus on individualism, on taking control of one's life, on achieving self-defined objectives.

As the Renaissance progressed, then, due at least partially to what we shall label *Machiavellian humanism*, the plight of the common folk, of the small craftsmen and businessmen, who were now almost completely at the mercy of the increasingly powerful merchants, princes, and merchant-princes, continued to worsen. Gradually, as a result of their increasingly hopeless economic situation, their increasing powerlessness, they returned to the Church.

The Church, however, at this point, not understanding the social transition occurring, or, perhaps, not wanting to understand it, was still trying to reclaim its former role in society, its former pivotal position. In Italy, achievement of this objective was relatively easy. No central government, as we have said, existed. The city-states were eventually taken over by military dictators called *condottiere* who were constantly battling each other. The situation there resembled the situation found during the Medieval period with its feudal kingdoms, so that the church could once again establish itself as the only force binding everything together.

The church also began a campaign to stamp out the individualism, the free thinking, and the lack of respect for ecclesiastical authority bred by the humanism movement. While, once again, this effort was relatively successful in Italy, the northern countries were not as receptive. In the same way that the rise of the merchant class had begun in Italy, based on contact with the Levant, and had spread northward with the rounding of the African horn and the discovery of the Americas, humanism also found its roots in Italy and then crept slowly northward. As it spread, however, it changed, so that the northern version differed greatly.

The Challenge of Christian Humanism

The northern version, called *Christian humanism*, instead of focusing entirely on the rights of the individual, sought a way to respect and celebrate the rights of the individual while, at the same time, preserving the social virtues taught by the Church. Rather than turning their backs on the Church's teachings as the Italian humanists had done, the northerners sought reforms based on cutting through dogma and ceremonial practices. Their objective was to focus once again on fundamental Christian values that respected the individual without compromising the church's basic spiritual message. Desiderius Erasmus, whose *The Praise of Folly* is still appreciated today, was the leading spokesman for this movement. He did not want to destroy the Catholic Church, but simply to reform it.

The move toward individualism at any cost was obviously less intense in the north than in Italy. Perhaps this resulted from the late start of the merchant class there, which had not yet succeeded in overpowering both the economy and society in general. Or perhaps it was because the centralized governments in these countries felt more responsibility for and to the general public, and did not rely as much on one segment for support as Italy's city-states did. Perhaps it was because the Church's bonds had not been as tight here during the Medieval period, because of the distance from Rome. Or perhaps it was due to the growth of secular education, to the establishment of universities that taught law and medicine as well as philosophy and theology.

No matter what the causes, the result was that the "little people" in the north, the craftsmen and other businessmen, did not feel as threatened. It was not because life had improved that much. It was still pretty miserable. Population levels were again declining steadily as a result of constant warring and disease. Markets were collapsing. The feudal lords, in order to remain solvent, were beginning to focus on one cash crop, so that the serfs no longer had direct access to many of the foods needed to survive and had begun rebelling, killing the lord and his family, burning down the manor, then wandering off. Unemployment and starvation were rife.

But the citizens of the north were much less eager to huddle once again under the wing of the Church, especially when the Church stubbornly refused to take into consideration the requests of the Christian humanists; especially when the church seemed bent, instead, on reestablishing its traditional control over the secular as well as the spiritual lives of followers. The individuals, the cultures, the governments of the north had changed too much to accept the Church's demands, and began looking for an alternative.

During the Renaissance, therefore, despite great growth in the amount of wealth generated, changes occurred which affected the worker adversely. Emphasis had swung toward battling over the profits then being generated. This inspired individualism and conflict, as opposed to the sense of community and cooperation found during the Medieval period.

The Renaissance also saw a split between Italy, with its "either/or" stance in the dispute between individualism and the church, and the northern countries which were trying to find a way to accommodate both. This split, with its pivotal economic as well as religious implications, helped set the stage for the upcoming Protestant Reformation.

Topics for Discussion

1. What was the role of the guild in the Medieval economy?
2. Why did the Catholic Church begin to lose power over the economy during the Renaissance?
3. What were the major factors supporting the rise of the merchant class?
4. Why was the achievement of a centralized government important to economic development?
5. Why did the guild system break down?
6. Why did the working class begin to lose power?
7. What was the difference between Machiavellian humanism and Christian humanism?

Notes

1. Niccolò Machiavelli, *The Prince*, New York: Mentor Books, 1952, p.84.
2. *Ibid.*, p. 92.
3. *Ibid.*, pp. 90–91.
4. *Ibid.*, p. 94.

2 The Reformation: Opening the Door to Opportunity

After Reading This Chapter You Should Know

1. The difference between the Catholic concept of "good works" and the Protestant concept of "work" and how this difference legitimized the struggle for profits.
2. Why the Protestant Reformation was as much an economic movement as it was a religious one.
3. How Calvin's theory of "predetermination" became an excuse for exploitation in the workplace.
4. Why "cottage industries" developed and how this shift affected the situation of craftsmen.
5. How René Descartes and Sir Francis Bacon provided the philosophical foundations that allowed us to progress economically.
6. How, using these philosophical foundations as a basis, modern scientific method was developed.
7. How the empirical, science-based approach to understanding and improving life allowed tremendous progress, but, at the same time, by excluding values, set the stage for modern-day problems.

Critical Changes in Social Systems

The Protestant Reformation, which began in the early 1500s, is considered by many a religious movement that took place during the later part of the Renaissance. The reason we are including it in our discussion as a period in itself is that social changes generated during the Reformation, changes in thinking facilitated by this religious revolution, have had far-reaching effects on management theory and the workplace.

A second, less important reason is that the Reformation provided perhaps the first instance in history when a new technology played an immediate, decisive role in fomenting social change.

The Protestant Reformation began with a single event that crystallized the population's increasing uneasiness and resentment toward the activities of the Catholic Church. Martin Luther, a priest, in the year 1517, posted on the door of the castle church at Wittenberg, Germany his now famous "97 Theses." The theses concerned the need to reform the Church's practice of granting indulgences, nothing more.

An "indulgence" was a forgiveness that released a sinner from punishment. According to the Catholic Church, a sin had two repercussions — guilt and the necessary penalty (punishment). The guilt could be forgiven by God if the sinner repented. But the Church believed that it was still required to name a penalty and to see that the sinner paid it.

In the early days, for a serious sin, the penalty could be extremely severe. Thus, we had the torture chambers of the Inquisition. Thus, we had people, even kings, being whipped for lesser offenses, or whipping themselves. Penalties could also take a long time to work off. They could take a lifetime. They could frequently take an additional period of time after death, which was spent in purgatory.

Eventually, however, the Church mellowed and began granting indulgences to the contrite, which removed all or part of the penalty for both the living and the dead. Those who received an indulgence promised, in return, to complete a "good work" or several good works which could take the form of a monetary contribution. Such contributions were then used to help build cathedrals and hospitals, to care for the poor.

But as the Renaissance progressed, proceeds from the indulgences, instead of being distributed to benefit society, were increasingly held back by the clergy and used to improve their own lives. This latter practice, along with the pressure being put on people of all classes to buy the now notorious indulgences, was what Luther decided to protest. He remained a good

Catholic. He wanted only to reform what he saw as a weakness that was hurting the Church.

The Church, however, by this time was too corrupt and too entrenched. It reacted to Luther only as a threat. Instead of listening to his warning, the Church immediately began trying to silence him, eventually threatening death. And it probably would have succeeded in the end except for two factors, and for some very good timing.

The first factor was the new technology, the printing press, introduced by Johannes Gutenberg in 1455. Nailed on the door of a church, Luther's "97 Theses" had little impact. They caused a stir in the local community. That was about all. But then, unfortunately for the Church, someone sent a copy of the "97 Theses" to a printer. Within half a year Luther's thoughts had been circulated throughout Germany, and had created a sensation.

The second factor was that businessmen interested in practicing and expanding capitalism were seeking ways both to cast off the strictures of the Church and to neutralize it as a competitor in the marketplace. They believed that Luther's movement might provide the desired opportunity.

In terms of casting off the Church's strictures, Luther offered three basic teachings. The first was that salvation was earned through faith alone, rather than through faith combined with good works. By this he meant that showing one's faith in God was by itself enough to earn passage to heaven. What one did otherwise, what good works one accomplished, what gifts one made, were no longer as important. People who became Protestants and accepted Luther's teachings could now shed the requirement of paying the penalty part for their sins, of paying indulgences. This saved the merchants time, money, and aggravation.

Luther's second teaching was that all true believers automatically became priests themselves, thus gaining the power to deal directly with God. This cut out the middleman, eliminating the traditional role of the Catholic clergy. Luther's belief, in effect, threatened the Church's very existence. On the other hand, it freed merchants and others in business from the right of the Church to judge their activities and to call them to task for practices considered unethical.

Luther's third teaching was that the scriptures, not the Church's interpretation of them, held all the necessary answers. This teaching is not important to our discussion.

Concerning the neutralization of the Church as a competitor in the marketplace, for one thing, the Church was the largest landowner in Europe during this period. In Germany alone, mainly though bequests and legacies, it owned up to one third of all the real estate, much of which was in cities, in marketplaces. It could rent these spaces, but did not have to pay taxes. This put a tremendous financial strain on the cities. One city, Freiburg, complained that religious holdings were more of a threat to the economic survival of the city than war costs or imperial taxes.[1]

Also, many of the religious orders had actually gone into business themselves, manufacturing textiles and clothing, opening up breweries, bakeries, mills, wineries. Their business philosophy seemed to mirror that of the Machiavellian humanists (*virtu*) more so than that of the Christian humanists. Due to the availability of a relatively free workforce which always showed up on time and was easy to control (monks and nuns), production costs were lower. The Church, as a result, could, and did, underprice the competition, driving it out of business and creating monopolies.

Also, the Church businesses did not have to obey local ordinances. Their manufacturing facilities could, for example, stay open on Sundays while everyone else had to shut down (to go to church?). Also, if Church businessmen got caught breaking the law, governmental courts could not touch them. As we have said, they had to be tried by officials of the Church. Also, when war broke out, as it frequently did, monks were not forced, like most other able-bodied men, to join the army and fight. They could stay home in the shop and continue producing goods.

Finally, and perhaps most important, these religious industries had the financial backing of the wealthiest institution in Europe, the Church, which, at that point, was actually practicing what we now call communism. As we know, "communism" is an economic system that is at the opposite end of the spectrum from capitalism. In capitalism the individual owner(s) controls the means of production, adjusting them in ways that will produce the most profit. Employees, in capitalism, work for wages supposedly tied to their productivity. The government benefits from their efforts through taxes, taking a percentage of the business profits and providing services in return.

On the other hand, in a communistic economy the government (Church) owns businesses and controls their production. It also collects the profits generated, then distributes them in ways that it considers best, based on its interpretation of individual and societal need, rather than on individual productivity.

The Church, during the Renaissance/Reformation, had the final say whether a monastic order should build a winery or not. The Church financed the venture. At the same time, due to their vows of poverty, the monks and nuns working in these businesses were not as interested in salary. Most profits, therefore, went into the Church coffers for distribution by officials.

But the Church, as a result of its growing corruption, slipped into the same destructive habit that modern-day countries practicing communism, at least up until recently, have demonstrated. Most of the profits derived from the economic ventures were supposed to be spent on good works, to be used to improve society. But, in fact, Church officials, just like members of the Communist Party, began holding back an increasing share of the wealth generated for themselves and their own purposes.

The Protestant Alternative

The Church was obviously playing by its own rules. It was showing increasingly flagrant disrespect for those it supposedly served, many of whom began looking for an alternative. Martin Luther, with his new way of thinking, provided that alternative. He had eventually realized that reform was impossible. So he began moving toward a doctrinal change, toward the creation of a new religion, although he did not see it that way.

The Catholic Church had actually become schizophremic. It now housed two personalities, the traditional good one and the corrupted one. We have discussed the characteristics of the corrupted personality. The good personality continued to preach virtue (not *virtu*), social responsibility, the Golden Rule, that man was responsible for his neighbor as in the Medieval period and for "good works," and that the clergy were God's watchmen sworn to monitor the flock's behavior and to help strays get back into the fold.

Businesses during this era continued to be labor intensive. The only way to increase productivity was to work longer hours. Organizations were not yet large enough for improvements in management practices to have much impact. Technology, as we have said, with the exception of the printing press, new milling techniques, and, of course, improvements in weaponry, had not changed much in the last 1000 years. Basically the same hand tools were being used. Power to drive the few crude machines that existed was provided by the worker, by animals, or, in the instance of mills, by running water or wind. So improved technology was not yet a source of increased productivity either.

From the owner's viewpoint, therefore, the only way to add to his fortune, beside buying and selling wisely, was to work his employees longer hours and to pay them less. While the traditional, caring personality of the Church obviously frowned on such greedy, self-centered behavior and had fought it since the Medieval period, Luther's new pronouncements, if interpreted in a certain way, produced a rationalization that opened the way to exploitation without fear of repercussion.

First, Luther, not unlike the Catholic Church, believed that man was born in evil and had to free himself from it. The only way to do this was to gain God's forgiveness, which was given freely to the contrite. The trick was to show one's contriteness, and this was done through hard "work."

The key to this argument is the realization that Luther's concept of *work* differed greatly from the Catholic concept of *good works*. While the Catholic concept, no matter how corrupted it might have become, concerned making a contribution, helping to improve society, Luther's "work" had to do with the more mundane, with one's occupation, with being a farmer, a tailor, a stone mason, a teacher, or a serf. As Wenzerlaus Linck, one of Luther's close friends and fellow rebels said:

> Work is medicine given man after the fall, through which he should atone and return to God, avoid and stay away from evil.[2]

Both Linck and Luther believed that "man must labor in the temporal world in order to live according to the will of God." Work, therefore, was required to make the necessary impression on God and, as a result, to reach heaven.

With this new religion, the Catholic insistence on good works was no longer there to encourage a sense of selflessness, of community and cooperation. Rather, the focus was now more on the individual, on an individual's direct relationship with God, on an individual's personal efforts to gain grace. If I, as an owner, made my employees work longer hours, was I not, indeed, helping them to improve their chances of reaching heaven? And was I not, through my actions, earning merits as well by showing my understanding of the spiritual value of work?

It was during this time that the concept of *work* formally became tied to the concept of *sacrifice*. Work, itself, now became time and effort sacrificed willingly in order to gain grace. This change, for the worker, actually made the pain of being exploited more bearable because sacrifice, by definition, usually involves suffering of some sort.

As happens so frequently in history, Luther unwillingly, while trying to put into place a vehicle (Protestantism) for fighting what he thought to be one serious human corruption, helped open the door to another, the corruption of *exploitation*.

The Reformation rapidly spread through Europe, dividing it into many camps. Martin Luther was not the only leader. One other, important to our discussion, who came after Luther, was John Calvin, a brilliant, dogmatic man whose work was done mainly in Geneva, Switzerland. Calvin was the person who in his writings pulled the pieces of the Protestant religion together into a cohesive whole. He was, however, more radical than Luther, more severe.

Calvin believed strongly that "discipline" was the key to developing godliness in the individual and in the community. He eventually demanded that the Protestant Church in Geneva be self-governing and have the right to discipline anyone it believed to be acting unacceptably according to his interpretation of the scriptures. He set up a "big-brother" system, a watch committee structure similar to the religious police found today in some Islamic countries, which was called a "Council of Elders." Each elder was charged with staying in touch with the families in his district and was responsible for reporting such unacceptable behaviors as failure to go to church, suspected shady business dealings, card playing, dancing, quarreling with one's mate, telling dirty jokes. The offender would then have to appear before the council and be chastised. More serious crimes were turned over to the civil authorities for judgment.

What we see, then, is that Luther, and especially Calvin, were by no means Christian humanists. Rather than focusing on the development of individual potential, they were interested mainly, as were the Catholics, in monitoring and shaping the individual's relationship with God. Calvin, in fact, with his extreme emphasis on discipline and church control over every facet of community and individual life, probably put even more of a damper on individual development than had the Catholic Church, whose controlling behaviors he was supposedly rebelling against. When upper-class members, the merchants, and educated people of Geneva protested his tactics, Calvin simply drove them out of town.

Most important to our immediate discussion, however, was Calvin's introduction of the concept of "predetermination" or "salvation by election." Calvin also stressed that saving faith comes not by the acts of man (penalty paying, "good works," even "work"), but as an "unmerited gift" from God to those God had "eternally predestined for salvation."

Although this might sound similar to what Luther had said, it was very different in a very critical way. In Luther's scheme of things, the way people lived their lives was still critical to their reaching heaven. In Calvin's scheme, quite simply, it was not. The way people lived their lives was, instead, only a sign whether they were predestined for heaven or hell.

Calvin apparently stressed this concept of predetermination in order to free his followers from concern about the afterlife so that they could spend their time on Earth concentrating on their real job, serving and glorifying

God.[3] But if Martin Luther had earlier opened the door to exploitation, John Calvin, with this declaration, again unwittingly, might have opened the flood-gates. The obvious reaction of those interested only in personal gain, of the Machiavellian humanists to Calvin's logic was: "Gee whiz, hear that? Everyone messes up. So there's no use worrying about the afterlife. That little issue has apparently already been decided. The only thing that I still have any control over is my life on Earth, so I better make the most of it. Make as much money as I can. Live as secure and enjoyable a life as I can. And, when you think about it, the fact that I might misuse other people in order to get what I want doesn't really matter."

People, therefore, during the Protestant Reformation were gaining more control over their lives on Earth, but they were losing whatever say they might have thought they had in what transpired after death. Under such a system, as would be expected, focus began shifting away from eternity and toward generating prosperity in the here and now. Both Luther and Calvin encouraged hard work as a means of improving one's immediate individual situation and benefiting the community. Both said that making money was a good thing because it showed that you were trying. Both men, at the same time, naively warned against exploiting the less fortunate in order to increase one's personal wealth.

The *Protestant work ethic*, the name given this philosophy concerning economic development, was probably the Period's most critical contribution in terms of future impact on management theory. It was not spelled out in the writings of Luther and Calvin. Rather, the term was coined by later historians. The emphasis on hard work and sacrifice implicit in this ethic, coupled with the concept of salvation by election, gave strength to, or excused, the continuing trend toward individualism and the quest for *virtu*.

Critical Changes in Economic Systems

Meanwhile, concerning the large-scale European economic scene, as opposed to the social scene, drastic changes were also occurring which strongly affected management practices. *Mercantilism* had become the buzzword of the day as centralized governments grew steadily stronger and began attempting to develop national economic policy. International trade was booming. Governments regulated and profited from this trade through tariffs, international trade agreements, production regulations, bounties on both production and exportation.

The center of commerce shifted northward from Italy to Antwerp, then to Amsterdam, and eventually to England and France. The bankers were taking over from the merchants as the major force driving the economy. Their largest loans were made to governments to finance wars, growth, and the expensive tastes of royal courts. Loans were also made to monopolistic, government-created associations of merchants formed to control all transactions involving a single product, such as raw wool, lumber, slaves, or formed to control all trade with a certain geographic area, such as India, Africa, parts of North America.

Such associations were modeled after the guilds, which had made a comeback under Protestantism because they provided a convenient vehicle for both societal and economic control. The guilds, however, were now dominated by an old-boy network of wealthy burghers that was almost impossible to penetrate, so that craftsmen still had little opportunity to improve their situation.

Guilds now also served a different purpose. During the earlier Medieval period guilds answered to the Church and had been created to provide security for members by controlling the production and distribution of their product, as well as to protect the community by setting "one fair price." Their modern counterparts answered mainly to the state which supported them because monopolies were easier to tax than individual enterprises. The one fair price concept, as well as that of a fair wage, had been swamped by the tidal wave of individualism and capitalism washing through the continent. The purpose of owners now, encouraged by increasingly tax-dependent governments, was to do what was necessary to make as much money as possible.

The only serious constraint that remained to the growing greed of owners was the wrath of the working class, which flared with increasing frequency. Uprisings occurred, but were squashed rapidly by the government with support from the burgers and frequently the church, be it Catholic or Protestant. However, these uprising continued because the common people, at this point, had less and less to lose.

Such uprisings were costly to the government, growing more so as increasing numbers of people got involved. And increasing numbers of people did get involved because the cities were growing again, the population in most countries expanding rapidly. Things began to unravel. Despite the income generated by mercantilism, and the bounty brought back from the colonies, governments found themselves sinking ever deeper into debt and having to borrow more and more from the great banks, doing so with no intention of ever repaying the loans.

Inevitably, the banks failed. This collapse of Europe's main economic drivers contributed to the inflation which was already severe, and which was another major cause of social unrest. Most people in the cities were living in a survival mode, and when the price of bread increased fivefold in England and sevenfold in France as it did during the last half of the 1500s, their very survival was seriously threatened.[4]

The workers, of course, reacted. They went on a rampage and destroyed businesses. Such desperate measures, however, only made the situation worse. The destruction contributed further to shortages and, therefore, helped increase inflation. Also, governments had to send out troops to quell the disturbances, which cost money, which resulted in more taxes, once again increasing inflationary pressures, especially on the poor.

One alternative to this lose–lose–lose scenario, from the owner's viewpoint, was to move businesses out of the cities, to begin contracting with rural people to do the work. Country people grew their own food and had their own homes, so they were less volatile.

Thus began the cottage industry era. In many parts of Europe small "domestic" shops replaced guild operations and eventually dominated production. Merchants brought the raw materials to craftsmen in their own homes and picked up the finished pieces. Workers were no longer familiar with markets or marketing procedures. Craftsmen from several different regions might be supplying goods to the same capitalizer. These goods might then travel across borders or even across oceans to markets.

Businesses increasingly became networks rather than "families." The element that connected all the strands was the owner/capitalizer. He alone now understood both the production and marketing aspects of the operation. Because he possessed important information that his employees lacked, like that concerning changes in the prices of raw materials, or that concerning changes in the value of goods on the market, he could improve his share of profit at their expense. Also, this lack of information prevented employees from contributing meaningfully to management decisions.

Critical Changes in Philosophical and Scientific Systems

Changes that occurred in the related fields of philosophy and science during this period also helped set the stage for the future of management theory. Up to this point, philosophy had been built around the search for ultimate truths that would provide the foundations for our explanation of human reality. *Ultimate truths* had traditionally been the domain of the church. But now, as part of the trend toward individualism, which was growing stronger, the value of this quest as well as the authority of the church in philosophical matters was being questioned.

Eventually, a school of philosophical thought called *skepticism* was revived from ancient Greek writings. Skeptics argued that man was incapable of reaching valid conclusions rationally. He was too limited. There was no way that the ultimate truths upon which the previous *rationalistic* school of thought had been built could be proved through the use of reason.

The revival of skepticism was supported by the world of science, which was going through a revival of its own. Nicolas Copernicus, a Polish priest educated in Italy (which had once again taken the lead, this time in the development of secular education, its universities shaping many of the period's great contributions in the fields of philosophy and science) published his revolutionary belief that the Earth was moving rather than standing still and, more important, that it was not the center of the universe as had been presumed up to that point. He proclaimed that the sun, instead, was the center of the universe. The Earth and other planets revolved around the sun. This discovery directly contradicted the church-espoused belief that God, the primary force, had made man in His image and had centered the universe around man. It also obviously decreased man's importance in the scheme of things. It made man part of a much vaster, more complex reality, one more difficult to understand and to explain.

While society in general was not ready to accept Copernicus's radical hypotheses, neither could it ignore them. Traditional "truths" had already been sorely challenged by the philosophers. In philosophy, after much fumbling around, two thinkers, René Descartes, a Frenchman, and Sir Francis Bacon, an Englishman, had emerged to lead the way toward developing an acceptable means of getting beyond skepticism. In essence, they said that instead of expending (wasting?) our time and energy trying to address universal, ultimate questions (Is there a God?), which we probably do not have the ability to answer, philosophers should focus on the things we can answer. They believed that the purpose of philosophy and science, with this narrower perspective in place, should be to enrich human life and to encourage the development of both individual and societal potential, once more getting back to the development theory of the humanists and, ultimately, of the Greeks.

Descartes still believed that "truths" existed upon which we should build our reality. But he said, "The judgment of truth was an individual and internal process....[K]nowledge comes from within by the use of rational intuition which reveals the indubitable truth."[5] Descartes' approach was significant to our present study in that it empowered individuals to develop their own understanding of reality, their own approach to science, releasing them from dependence on any "external authority."

Francis Bacon represented the other philosophical pole. He was one of the first to begin resurrecting the empirical school of thought developed also by the ancient Greeks in their prime. This school assigned the quest for truths to the realm of science. It said that any truths discovered would be found through scientific investigation, through the medium of experience, rather than through "rational intuition." For example, we know that the sun will rise tomorrow morning in the east not intuitively, but because we assume man has seen it do so since the beginning of recorded history.

One other important point has to be made concerning philosophy. Descartes, Bacon, and others in these new, or reborn, schools of thought made critical contributions, key contributions that facilitated economic development. At the same time, however, due at least to the approach of the empiricists, seeds were planted which would create serious problems in the future. Again, they were sown unwittingly. In fact, what the empiricists proposed was unavoidable in light of their mission and their frame of historical reference.

Bacon and others in his school said that their approach to discovering useful truths through experience could only be effective if it focused on the *quantifiable*, on data that could be defined and manipulated arithmetically. Such concepts as human values, ethics, and quality, so critical to the earlier rationalistic arguments of the Church and later to the Christian humanists and still later to Descartes and his school of individualistic rationalism, were obviously not quantifiable and, therefore, could not be included in the equation.

In the interest of improving man's situation, therefore, the early empiricists were the first in modern history to separate the quantitative from the qualitative, the numbers from human values. This separation, although critical to their contribution, has returned to cause serious problems in the modern-day workplace.

In the realm of the physical sciences, during the same period Bacon and Descartes were doing their work, three astronomers — a Dane, Tycho Brahe, a German, Johannes Kepler, and an Italian, Galileo Galilei — were developing *modern scientific method*, the practical application of Bacon's experience-based approach to discovering useful truths. They did so as a means of testing Copernicus's hypotheses concerning the Earth's relationship with the sun.

Brahe's contribution was the development of methods to gather relevant data through observations. Kepler, who started as an assistant to Brahe, used these data rigorously to discover new principles, providing a model for objectivity. Galileo showed how experimentation must be used to provide corroborating data and to help prove hypotheses. But Galileo's most important contribution, as relates to our interest in management theory, was his effort to prove that the universe, in fact, resembles a machine driven by physical forces understandable to man. Thus began, on the grandest scale, our love affair with the concepts of order and technology, setting the stage for what occurred during the Enlightenment and, ultimately, the Industrial Revolution.

Topics for Discussion

1. What is the meaning of the statement; "The Protestant Reformation loosened many of the constraints that had been impeding economic development"?
2. What rationalizations for "exploitation" were shaped during the Protestant Reformation?
3. Why did the advent of "cottage industries" at the same time benefit workers and put them at a disadvantage?
4. Do students feel that the "work ethic" still has the same relevance in today's workplace that it had during the Protestant Reformation?
5. How did the philosophical contributions of René Descartes and Sir Francis Bacon affect economic progress?
6. How is the scientific method used in today's workplace?

Notes

1. John Dolan, *History of the Reformation*, New York: The New American Library, 1965, p. 216.
2. Lawrence Buck and Jonathan Zophy, Eds., *The Social History of the Reformation*, Columbus: Ohio State University Press, 1972, pp. 42–43.
3. Charles Nauert, *The Age of Renaissance and Reformation*, New York: University Press of America, 1997, p. 165.
4. *Ibid.*, p. 245.
5. C. West Churchman and Russell Ackoff, *Methods of Inquiry: An Introduction to Philosophy and Scientific Method*, St. Louis: Educational Publishers, 1950, p. 18.

3 The Enlightenment: Cornerstones for a New Socioeconomic Order

After Reading This Chapter You Should Know

1. Why the Enlightenment is considered to have shaped modern society.
2. The key principles upon which Adam Smith's "laissez faire economics" is grounded.
3. Why laissez faire economic theory was considered by some to be naïve.
4. Sir Thomas Malthus's theory concerning the relationship between economic growth and population growth.
5. The effects of the "division of labor" on productivity.
6. The origins and purpose of "manufactories."
7. Why the Industrial Revolution began in England.

The Rebirth of Reason

During the Enlightenment major changes occurred in the nature of the workplace and, correspondingly, in management systems. These changes resulted from advances in technology, from growth in the size of businesses, and from increasing marketplace pressures as government-sponsored competition between countries grew. But mainly they resulted from continuing changes in the socioeconomic sphere and from continuing changes in the way people thought and inquired.

The Enlightenment was called the Age of Reason. René Descartes' famous quote, "I think, therefore I am," provided the slogan. Man discovered, or rediscovered his mind and the powers of rational thought. It was as though, from the Dark Ages on, the mind had been tucked away, locked in an attic closet, and guarded by overly protective nannies who considered it too advanced, too dangerous a thing for the children they watched over to play with.

But now the old order was crumbling. Religious forces were losing their power to dominate and dictate in several Western European countries. And the new order, the state, while it sought in many instances the same intense level of control, was too busy with wars over religion, territories, and succession rights to immediately fill the void. The intellectual set, during this period, enjoyed an unusual amount of freedom and took full advantage of it, turning the Enlightenment into possibly the most progressive period ever.

Emphasis was not only on individual development, but on societal development as well. The involved frenzy of learning was led by such men as Rousseau in France, David Hume in England, and Benjamin Franklin in the British American colonies, men who called themselves "cosmopolitanists" because of their wide range of worldly interests. Their desire was to become well rounded, to cultivate expertise in many fields rather than in just one.

The Enlightenment thinkers, with scientific method as their vehicle, delved into every corner of reality — the universe, the world of plants and animals, philosophy, economics, government, technology — frequently making serious contributions in more than one field. For example, Immanuel Kant, the philosopher, was also a student of physics and astronomy. Rousseau, the writer, was also a botanist and chemist. Thomas Jefferson, a statesman and eventual president of the new United States, was a linguist who also studied and practiced architecture and agricultural science.

Their search, based on the application of scientific method, was for "order" in the natural world, for Aristotle's "unchanging natural law pertaining to all men."[1] They believed that once such order, such laws were discovered or defined in some specific sector, that sector would become increasingly understandable, manageable, and open to investigation. Not even God was exempt from this new mind-set, so beneficial were the ideas proving themselves to be to the fortunes of humankind. God, according to Jonathan Mayhew of Boston, "...needed to be guided by the external laws of truth and equity and the everlasting table of right reason."[2]

The list of contributors to the advances made during the Enlightenment is long and impressive. The two most important, however, the two Englishmen who set the stage, were John Locke and Sir Isaac Newton. Once again they represented the fields of philosophy and science. John Locke, born in 1632, is considered the father of *empiricism* as we know it today. His message was that all human knowledge results from observations gathered through our senses, which are then combined with intuitive reflection to produce *simple ideas.* Human reason, the source of all knowledge for the earlier rationalists, is introduced in Locke's system only at a later stage. It is used to manipulate already formed simple ideas in order to produce more complex ones.

In the realm of astronomy and physics, Sir Isaac Newton is credited with rounding out the work of Copernicus and Galileo, with generating a totally scientific, comprehensive explanation of the mechanics of the universe based on an understanding of the gravitational relationship between force and mass. His work lifted such studies out of the realm of mysticism and opened the mysteries of the universe totally to an assault by the powers of reason. As Ackoff and Churchman later say,

> Indeed, in the [following] 19th century, many physicists thought that Newton's [revised] mechanical theory had once and for all found the secret of the laws of the natural world, and that all that remained was to work out the details of his system.[3]

Most important to us in terms of management theory was Newton's belief that the universe was not just any old piece of machinery, as Galileo had said, but a finely tuned clock, its workings understandable through mathematical analysis. Newton said that the clocklike universe had been designed by God and built by God to do His work.

Thus, Newton was able to open outer space and the things that filled it to scientific investigation without turning his back totally on the church. Rather than an "either/or" situation, he was able to create an "and" situation, an acceptable synthesis, keeping God in the equation (clock creator), but on a higher, removed level which would allow man access through scientific investigation of workings of the clock.

While Newton was "ordering" the universe, Linnaeus of Sweden and Cook and eventually Darwin of England were working to discover "order" in the natural world of Earth, in the world of plants and animals. Linnaeus was best known for his efforts to develop universal classifications for the domain of plants which would allow naturalists from all countries to speak a common language. Captain James Cook, whose original mission was to explore and chart the regions of the Pacific, sailed around the world, visiting both the Arctic and Antarctic, and brought back thousands of specimens, both plant and animal, for study.

Charles Darwin, born in the early 1800s, after the two others had completed their work, eventually developed and offered, in his 1859 book entitled *On the Origin of the Species*, a scientific, orderly explanation concerning humanity's origins. He said that we started not as full-blown humans placed on Earth by God, but as a "lower" life-form. He said that this lower form had evolved, had changed for the better through natural selection over several million years until our present state was reached.

By "natural selection" Darwin meant that those specimens of our ancestors with the most advanced abilities — physical, intellectual, emotional — had been better able to adjust to changes in their environment (such as the coming of the glacier age). They had survived to bear possibly more progressed progeny who were even better able to adjust and survive, while those whose abilities were weaker had died out.

In the realm of societal governance, the belief that the traditional "order," that rule by kings, princes, condottiere, or other protectors, was unnatural because it inhibited societal development was discussed and debated at length by great thinkers including John Locke and David Hume in England, Rousseau and Voltaire of France, Ben Franklin and Thomas Jefferson in the colonies. The British philosopher, John Locke, once again led the way declaring that, according to the concept of human order derived from the mind of God, "All men were equal and independent [so that] no one ought to harm another in his life, health, liberty, or possessions."[4] When those in positions of power did harm, citizens had the right to "dissolve the social compact" with their governmental leaders and, presumably, to pick new ones who would reestablish the correct, natural order of respect and tolerance.

Countries that remained Catholic such as France, Austria, Spain, and Italy retained the autocratic form of government. This was not unexpected. King Louis XIV of France exemplified their attitude with his pronouncement, "I am the State." On the other hand, countries like England and Holland which had turned Protestant had grown more moderate. They eventually began taking power away from the king, who was no longer considered divine or connected in any special way with God, and gave much of the power to a representative (although in a very limited sense of the word) parliament.

It was during discussions of Locke's and other philosophers' beliefs in the clubs of England and the salons of France that the concept of democracy (according to which those being ruled have the power to replace their rulers by peaceful vote), as the most effective and natural form of governmental order, blossomed. It was also during these discussions in both France and England that support for trying out democracy in the British North American colonies, which were pretty much a "greenfield site" at that point, grew. This support eventually enabled the future United States to win the Revolutionary War with help from sympathetic members in the British Parliament as well as from the French state and military.

Finally, and most important to our discussion, is the realm of economics. Here, Adam Smith, a Scot, took the lead in spelling out the natural order of things. Smith was preceded by the French physiocrats who said that, according to the natural order, allowing individuals to follow their own selfish interests would in the end result in the greatest general good.

The physiocrats, like Smith, were disturbed by the constraints which nationalistic mercantilism put on the development of commerce, by the taxes, tariffs, and agreements, by the amount of stifling bureaucracy involved. In his famous book, *Inquiry into the Nature and Causes of the Wealth of Nations*, published in 1776, Smith expanded on the hypothesis that natural laws existed in the arena of economic theory as well as in those of nature and government and that, if not disrupted by government activity, these laws would regulate the economy effectively.

The most important of these natural laws, according to Smith, was *supply and demand*. This law kept the market in balance in terms of the supply of the product available, the marketplace demand for it, and the price charged. For example, if I were the only person on the block manufacturing widgets and they became popular so that demand exceeded supply, I could raise my price and keep raising it until demand decreased, or until enough other manufacturers started manufacturing widgets that supply outstripped demand. Then, I would have to drop my price in order to remain competitive, and continue dropping it until enough other manufacturers stopped manufacturing widgets that demand again exceeded supply. At that point I could, once more, begin raising my price and keep raising it until demand decreased or until enough other manufacturers... and so on until the end of time.

Conceptually, Smith's theory made good sense. It still does, from an economic point of view. Smith was an idealist, but at the same time he was not totally naive. He realized that human motivation was also a key factor. When asked what would keep industrialists and merchants from focusing entirely on improvement of their individual situation with no concern for employees or for the general welfare, Smith initially replied that there were two reasons this would not happen. The first "internal" reason was man's *inherent good* that would keep owners from taking unfair advantage of their workers. The second "external" reason was that while in a laissez faire economy the individual "intends only his own gain," he is also "led by an *invisible hand* [the law of supply and demand] to promote an end which was not part of his original intention."[5] The working of supply and demand would help ensure that the general public as well as the individual owner benefited from Smith's proposed self-centered pursuit of wealth.

Eventually, to his credit, Smith admitted that he had been overly optimistic concerning the character of man. He changed his opinion and said that merchants and manufacturers, "being born *Monopolists* [monopolists, I assume, being the Enlightenment version of the Renaissance Machiavellian humanists], must be subject to public supervision."[6] This statement contradicted his original thesis. But it also showed him to be on the Christian humanism side of the fence. He wanted to improve society in general and saw laissez faire economics as the best vehicle for doing so. But he realized, at the same time, that a need did indeed exist for some degree of societal control over those who gained economic power.

Smith's logic concerning the distribution of wages further demonstrated his end objective. He said that:

> No society can surely be flourishing and happy of which the far greater part of the members are poor and miserable. It is but equality besides that they who feed, cloathe, and lodge the [population], should have such a share of the produce of their own labour as to be themselves tolerably well fed, cloathed, and lodged.[7]

He went on to say that wages were the "encouragement of industriousness" in workers, that employee industriousness improves as the "encouragement" improves.

Two of Smith's contemporaries, Thomas Malthus and David Ricardo, lacked Smith's conviction that, because the logic of his reasoning was so obviously beneficial, members of society would be sure to follow it. Both agreed that laissez faire was the best alternative. Both also believed, however, that the undisciplined society created by the lack of regulation and by rapidly increasing wealth would eventually self-destruct.

In Malthus's mind, the problem was the laboring poor, who had too many babies. The population in most European countries was now growing again. The plague had finally subsided. War was still taking its toll, but living conditions and nutrition, for most, had improved. As the situation of the laboring poor grew better, Malthus reasoned, their reaction would be to have still more babies, just as lower-level animals do when their living conditions improve. His fear was that, while the food supply was growing only arithmetically (1,2,3,4,5), population was growing geometrically (1,2,4,8,16) and would eventually outstrip ability of society to feed everyone. Famine and ongoing poverty would be the result. The only way for society to forestall such blights was to regulate family size. Society should not help feed large families of the poor. This would only make the problem worse.

David Ricardo's pessimism was also based on an interpretation of the human psyche, but, in this case, on an interpretation of the "monopolist" psyche. His concept was *The Iron Law of Wages*. In a society were each man is encouraged to pursue his own selfish interests, Ricardo reasoned, owners would take from Smith's model only that which was directly beneficial to themselves. They would seek to find a way around any attempt by government to regulate them and would pay employees as little as possible so that they could continue to increase their own wealth. As a result, "The natural price of labor [would be] that price which is necessary to enable the labourers...to subsist and to perpetuate their race without either increase or diminution."[8] Wages would provide nothing more. According to Richardo's probably more realistic reasoning, therefore, the increased wealth generated by the laissez faire system would not do much to improve the situation of the public in general.

Meanwhile, Back in the Workplace

Machiavellian humanism and Christian humanism evolved during the Renaissance as a quest for individual liberty from *church* domination. Their major impact was in the economic sphere. The later eruption of basically the same type of thinking during the Enlightenment resulted from a quest for individual liberty from *state* domination and affected the workplace possibly even more drastically. On the positive side, it set the stage for the tremendous economic advances made during the Industrial Revolution. On the negative side, it showed the dark face of a society blinded by unbridled greed.

The Industrial Revolution began to take shape during the Enlightenment mainly as a result of major advances made in technology. One of these advances involved the harnessing of new sources of power by British inventors and technicians. It must be remembered that previously the power to drive the simple machines that existed came from man himself, from animals, water, or wind. The first two sources produced an extremely limited supply of power; the last two were location-specific and, although more constant, were still limited in terms of the amounts of power they could provide.

In the early 1700s two Englishmen, Thomas Savery and Thomas Newcomen, independently developed the same "atmospheric" engine, run by steam and atmospheric pressure. They invented it to meet a specific need, to drive machinery designed to pump water out of deep mine shafts. James Watt was credited with later refining this engine to run solely on steam and to produce a rotary motion which would drive a great variety of machines.

Another critical advance made during the Enlightenment that shaped the Industrial Revolution, which we need to discuss, was not in technology, but in production theory. Adam Smith, besides clarifying the value of laissez faire economics on the macrolevel, contributed to the definition of and encouraged the introduction of the *division of labor* on the microlevel. The division of labor differed from the traditional approach to production in that employees, or craftspeople, instead of producing a complete product individually, now contributed only one section of that product. For example, instead of producing an entire shoe, one person might cut out the leather sides, another might sew them together, a third might cut the sole for the shoe, a fourth might sew that on.

This change, in effect, was the beginning of efforts to increase productivity through reorganization of work, rather than by simply working harder or longer hours. It added a whole new dimension which was much appreciated by merchants. At that point, rather than the small, largely local market of Medieval times, merchants faced a relatively unlimited market where they could sell just about everything produced.

The division of labor succeeded for three basic reasons. The first was that it forced employees to focus on one simple activity, rather than on a range of activities. This allowed them to develop expertise and "dexterity" more rapidly. The second was that less time was lost while the individual passed from one activity to another, from one set of tools to another. Only the finished parts were now passed along, and the next worker and the next set of tools were immediately ready.

The third reason was that the change sped up the development of workplace technology. When a manufacturing process was divided into steps, the machines and tools necessary to complement each individual step were obviously simpler and easier to design. For example, designing a machine that helped stamp out shoe soles was obviously a much easier task than designing a machine that produced completed shoes.

From a societal perspective, this workplace change also provided the laboring poor with an opportunity to improve their situation, to become more employable. Building a whole shoe properly required much expertise and training. Simply stamping out a shoe sole, however, did not. Almost anyone, therefore, could be brought in off the street and taught how to do it in a matter of minutes. As a result of this advance in production theory, the laboring poor suddenly became eligible for the industrial workforce.

Smith used a pin-making operation to demonstrate the increase in output made possible through the division of labor. He said that while an untrained workman individually would be lucky to produce 20 pins in a day, a team of 10 workers cooperating in a shop where the labor had been divided, where "one draws out the wire, another straightens it, a third cuts it, a fourth points it... and so on, can produce upwards of 48,000 pins in a day."[9]

Smith, however, talked about the downside of this advancement as well, about how with it, although society as a whole would benefit from the increase in wealth and goods generated, the actual work itself would become sacrificial in the extreme, how it would become deadening, numbing, in no way developmental. He noted specifically that such labor "tended to make human beings as stupid and ignorant as it is possible for a human being to become."[10]

Obviously, this new, more efficient but more labor-intensive approach to production encouraged the growth of operations. One would think that the birth of the "factory" would be a natural result. But, in fact, the first legitimate "manufactories" were textile mills built for a different reason. Up to this point most textiles had been manufactured by people spinning or weaving in their own homes as part of the cottage industry system. As the market expanded, however, and increasing numbers of spinners and weavers became involved, serious management problems arose. The coordination of employee efforts as well as the transport of both raw materials and finished goods to meet schedules proved increasingly difficult.

As we have said, most of the craftspeople involved lived in the country and farmed on the side. They were not entirely dependent, therefore, on the money earned from the goods they produced for survival. Employers could introduce bonus systems or make threats. They could not, however, truly control their employees. The individual craftspeople continued to decide their own daily rate, retaining a large degree of power over their working life.

The obvious solution, from the owner's point of view, was to bring the individual workers together under one roof where the owner could gain more control over their time and efforts. This solution fit neatly with the move toward mechanization and the trend toward the division of labor. Soon manufactories producing a growing range of good were appearing. These manufactories were powered increasingly by steam rather than by running water or wind, giving them greater latitude in terms of location and size.

It should be obvious from the number of British people we have named who made critical contributions in all fields and from the fact that manufactories appeared first in this country that the British forged ahead of their European competitors in terms of economic development during the Enlightenment. This advantage resulted from the country's greater willingness to incorporate innovative technology and management techniques. This willingness was encouraged, at least partially, by the lesser degree of religious, governmental, and guild regulation found in Britain. Craft guilds, unable to compete with mass production, were now rapidly disappearing, their power to protect members and markets by blocking change was completely gone.

The laissez faire approach to economic development was also accepted more openly in Britain. Businesspeople and businesses were left pretty much on their own with no government support and few government controls. At the same time, Britain had become the greatest naval power in the world so that commerce with her colonies and other sources of raw materials flourished. Finally, due to the power of the British parliament, taxes were relatively low, so that businesspeople had money to invest in new ideas and improvements.

Tremendous economic progress was obviously made during the Enlightenment. But despite it, once again, most people in Europe remained at the subsistence level. Cities were being flooded by poor from the countryside fleeing food shortages caused by population growth. In Britain they were also driven there by "enclosure" laws passed by parliament. These laws allowed wealthy landowners to enlarge their holding by taking over what used to be common lands. New agricultural technology had given estate owners the ability to work more land with fewer people, to grow larger crops, and to make more money.

So the serfs were, at the same time, losing their jobs on the farms and losing the opportunity to survive by growing their own food and raising livestock on the common lands. The same was true for people in the cottage industries. These people, however, were losing their work, instead, to the new manufactories. Both groups had no alternative but to move to the cities in search of employment.

In the cities, relatively few of the low-skill factory jobs that Adam Smith talked about as yet existed. Those that did, as Richardo had predicted, while perhaps keeping workers from abject poverty, did little to improve their situation. Textile mill workers in Britain, for example, who were at the upper end of the pay scale, survived mainly on a diet of potatoes and oatmeal, a far cry from the lifestyle that spinners and weavers in the cottage industry had enjoyed.

Highly skilled craftsmen were still in demand — apothecaries, silversmiths, scriveners, drapers, ship chandlers, potters, masons, bricklayers, glassblowers, furniture makers. But these, again, constituted a relatively small percentage of the worker population. The majority, who had traditionally labored in the fields, were suited in this new urban culture mainly for work as servants, as beasts of burden, or as miners. Children joined their parents in this work by the age of 6, or begged, or stole, or prostituted themselves.

In summation, although the Enlightenment was a time of great ideas and revolutionary changes in almost every sector — philosophy, science, government, economics — the implementation of these ideas and changes was not yet far enough along to benefit the majority of Europe's population, to benefit the laboring poor who were labeled "the common sort" and "the mob."

Charitable efforts by churches as well as small-scale efforts by some governments to help the laboring poor were swallowed up and relatively ineffectual. Two such efforts, however, deserve note. The first was the development of schools to give poor children practical skills which would help them find jobs (perhaps the first trade schools?). The second was the development of government-sponsored public works projects as a means of employing the laboring poor.

Topics for Discussion

1. What contributions made during the Enlightenment have helped shape modern society?
2. What are the strengths and weaknesses of laissez faire economics?
3. Has Sir Thomas Malthus's theory concerning population growth proved correct?
4. How did "division of labor" benefit the unskilled worker?
5. How did the advent of "manufactories" both improve productivity and increase profits?
6. What are the factors that allowed the Industrial Revolution to get off to the quickest start in England?

Notes

1. *Time Magazine: Special 1776 Issue on Thomas Jefferson,* "Independence: The Birth of a New America," p. 12.
2. Henry Steele Commager, *The Empire of Reason,* New York: Doubleday, 1977, p. 3.
3. C. West Churchman and Russell Ackoff, *Methods of Inquiry,* St. Louis: Educational Publishers, 1950, p. 79.

4. *Time Magazine, op. cit.*, p. 12.

5. Sidney Fine, *Laissez Faire and the General Welfare State,* Ann Arbor: The University of Michigan Press, 1966, p. 7.

6. Peter Gay, Ed., *The Enlightenment: A Comprehensive Anthology,* New York: Simon and Schuster, 1973, p. 576.

7. *Ibid.*, p. 598.

8. Fine, *op. cit.*, p. 8.

9. Gay, *op. cit.*, p. 578.

10. David Jenkins, *Job Power,* Baltimore: Penguin Books, 1973, p. 23.

4 Bringing the Pre-Industrial Revolution Era into Perspective

After Reading This Chapter You Should Know

1. The major changes in socioeconomic theory that occurred during the Pre-Industrial Revolution era and why they occurred.
2. Why people, beginning with the Renaissance, were willing to sacrifice "emotional security" for increased "physical security."
3. The importance of the "scarcity mentality" as a societal and economic shaping force.
4. How and why the quest for "grace" was replaced with one for "profit."
5. The key rationalizations that set the stage for what happened during the Industrial Revolution.

Making Sense of the Past

The Pre-Industrial Revolution era was one of great economic fermentation. It began placidly enough. Europe had been sunk into the depression of the Dark Ages. The tribes that dominated the Continent had destroyed the economic and the social stability enjoyed under the Roman Empire and now spent their time battling each other. A feudal system had slowly evolved, a loose network of small kingdoms constantly fighting over boundaries, bound together only by the Catholic Church, which was as much a political force as it was a religious one.

Life during the Dark Ages was very simple. The vast majority of the population received no formal education. Peasant farmers and craftsmen had only the skills passed down from generation to generation. Most people were born in a small town, grew up in that town, married in it, and died there after a relatively short life without traveling very far beyond its borders, except, perhaps, as members of the local lord's army.

Changes in this scenario came about mainly as a result of the aggressive, warlike nature of these kingdoms. Their eventual marches beyond the borders of Europe brought them into contact with new ideas and new opportunities. The church lost its power over social evolution to the new merchant class. Focus shifted rapidly from spiritual matters to temporal considerations, from preparing for the next life to improving one's situation in this life.

Wealth and the things it purchased became more available to greater numbers, and, therefore, became the focus of activities as Europe moved through the Medieval period where guilds dominated the economic world to the Renaissance where they began collapsing under the pressure of merchant-driven free enterprise. Government also began to play an increasingly important role as kingdoms were joined together and evolved into economic blocks. Governments required financial support, which meant that they encouraged the development of the merchant class. The rate of workplace change began to pick up, driven by opportunity.

The major contribution of the Protestant Reformation was to make this opportunity available to the general public rather than just to the upper classes, by beginning the reorganization of the philosophical underpinnings of society and by encouraging people to focus more on their own, immediate self-interest. This trend came full flower during the Enlightenment, one of those rare moments in human history when a group of great minds come together to provide the conceptual changes necessary to allow humankind to make a tremendous leap forward in almost every sector.

The most important sector, from our perspective, was the economic sector, although the others, because of their influence, must be taken into account. The economic sector had become dominant, and had changed from a sector of almost total stability during the Medieval period to one of increasing instability. While this change increased opportunity, it also generated greater risk, especially for the workers who had lost the protection of both the church and the guilds.

Workers were increasingly on their own, at the mercy of those for whom they worked. The hope of Adam Smith, the father of laissez faire economics, and of the other Christian humanists whose goal was the advancement of society as well as that of the individual, was that those with growing economic power would understand the long-term benefit to themselves as well as to society of sharing their new wealth. The reality of the situation, however, was unfortunately quite different. The desired redistribution did not occur. Exploitation became the accepted, or perhaps I should say, the expected attitude of the day. Machiavellian humanism, the early Italian modification of ancient Greece's vehicle for individual and societal development, prevailed.

At this point, several battles broke out which continue to this day. The most basic, of course, was the battle between the Christian humanists and the Machiavellian humanists. The efforts of both sides are an ongoing theme in this book. Another battle was between those who practiced laissez faire economics in its most selfish form and those who favored various degrees of socialism. A third battle was between people who wanted to maintain spiritual values as the force that governed societal change and people who preferred to depend on the scientific method when searching for answers.

And then there was technology, which, by the end of this era was evolving more rapidly than workplace values, much more rapidly than ownership and management systems. Major technological barriers to increasing productivity were finally being overcome. The most important of these advances was the development of the technology necessary to generate increased amounts of machine-driving power. Such advances, however, while increasing the amount of wealth available and while improving our ability to turn natural resources into goods that benefited their owner, were negatively affecting the situation of the majority of people in the workforce. It was becoming increasingly obvious that although progress was being made, serious problems loomed.

Reaching into the Future

The question is, "What does all this history have to do with current and future management theory, with our current and future workplace culture?" The answer we must offer is, "a whole lot." Improvements in technology have, overall, probably played the most important role in forcing workplace changes. But during the Pre-Industrial Revolution era technology still played only a bit part on the stage of life. Toward the end on that era the steam engine provided a major breakthrough in the generation and availability of power. The printing press, indeed, changed society. Other important improvements occurred in agriculture, the steel industry, textiles. But they were relatively minor compared with what was to come. With the inventions of the Enlightenment, the age of technology was just beginning.

The importance of the Pre-Industrial Revolution era, as we have said, lies mainly in the realm of socioeconomic theory. Foundations were laid which have not changed much since. During this period we watched workplace motivation and the relationship between employees and employer change radically. We watched the *profit motive* take hold and felt the tremors as it rippled through society, cracking the veneer of tradition. We watched the birth of rampant *individualism*. We met the predecessors to the union movement, the guilds, which failed for much the same reason that unions are in trouble today.

We witnessed the emergence of a strange contradiction, that the more economic freedom society gained from church and state, the less economic freedom a majority of citizens, namely, the working class, seemed to enjoy. We watched the working class lose the minimal security it had clung to during the Medieval period and fall into a state close to that of slavery during the Enlightenment, despite the fact that ideas were being hatched in the fields of science, economics, government, education that developed into some of the greatest advances in all of history.

But why? Why did the promise of these advances turn sour? Why did what should have been societal progress turn, instead, into backsliding?

In order to understand what happened, we must begin at the beginning, at the most basic level possible. We must start by examining the psychological forces that drove people during this era, that destroyed the sense of community which had originally prevailed, citizens sacrificing the sense of well-being and respect derived from being part of a well-integrated whole in order to seek their individual fortunes.

Obviously, during this era, the chance to gain wealth, despite the risks involved, was more important than the security provided by the church, the government (be it feudal lords or kings), and the guilds. The question is, why did people choose the loneliness of an individual, competitive quest over the assurance of God's blessing offered by the Church in return for loyalty? Why did they spurn the gratitude of a community served? Why, when the opportunity arose, were people willing to destroy the very foundations on which their lives and culture had traditionally been built?

And, again, when the amount of wealth available did increase, why were people unwilling to share it, why did they instead battle each other for it? The vehicles for distribution were in place — the church, the guilds, and eventually the state. But even these institutions proved vulnerable. Instead of sticking with and reinforcing the tradition of sharing, which had been a cornerstone of at least the church and guild, these institutions also got caught up in the frenzied quest for profit, becoming, in some instances, the most ruthless of competitors.

The concept of security is key to answering these questions. In order to explore this concept in a way that is easily understandable, we will divide it into two basic subcategories — physical security and emotional security. Physical security relates to material things in one's environment that influence a person's physical well-being. It centers on the search for "enough," on the quest for the inputs necessary to fulfill the individual's basic physical needs. A list of these inputs includes adequate nutrition and shelter, adequate heath care, sufficient employment opportunity, adequate protection from crime, and so on. The key point to be made here is that *it is possible to gain physical security without first gaining emotional security*. The latter is not a prerequisite to the former.

By emotional security I mean individual achievement of self-respect, recognition, and positive self-actualization as relates to the individual's definition of an acceptable purpose in life. Emotional security relates to nonmaterial things in a person's environment which influence his or her emotional well-being or mental health.

We must realize, however, that, as Abraham Maslow, the modern psychologist who developed the well-known and comprehensive "Hierarchy of Human Needs" theory from which I borrowed most of the above, pointed out, it is impossible to gain ongoing emotional security unless physical security is in place. The components of physical security are foundational. They come first. Without them, emotional security is always tentative. For example, it is pretty hard to be emotionally secure, no matter how well respected you are, if you are starving and do not know where to find food. Or, in a more familiar vein, it is hard to be emotionally secure when you have just lost your job, and do not know if you can find a new one in time to meet your next mortgage payment.

Getting Our Priorities in Place

In terms of physical security, then, almost everyone during the Medieval period still had a long way to go. Famines occurred periodically. Hygiene was abominable, especially in the cities. In addition to periodic epidemics of the plague, people had to deal with a multitude of diseases including typhoid, smallpox, and, soon, gonorrhea. Any wound could prove fatal due to the lack of disinfectants. Chronic dysentery was an accepted fact of life.

People were helpless before these onslaughts, as they were helpless pawns in the power struggles that raged between and within feudal domains. When armies marched, they frequently lived off the land. Neither citizens nor their belongings were safe in the name of causes that frequently reflected the whims of rulers rather than the reality of populations.

As long as there seemed no escape from these threats to physical existence, people sought solace in the spiritual life. They were awarded a degree of emotional security by the Church in return for obedience and loyalty. This reward centered on the promise of God's forgiveness and a better life in the next world. Commoners were willing to subjugate themselves to the powers that offered this security. They were willing to remain a part of the community, to contribute their talents and strength freely if required to do so in order to find some reward in their lives, or at least in the afterlife. There was little alternative.

But emotional security, as we have said, cannot be complete without physical security. Therefore, once the situation changed and the opportunity appeared to make sure personally that one's family did not starve when the next famine came, that one always had enough wood to burn during the cold months, that one's daughter or son was not carried off the next time an army marched through, people were willing to fight for the opportunity, to risk the degree of emotional security they currently enjoyed in order to obtain physical security.

Increasing one's wealth was now key to increasing one's physical security. Early profits had been absorbed by the church and the feudal lords. But no more. As new sources of raw materials and new markets opened, as the economy expanded, as controls were loosened, an increasing number of individuals began discovering ways to carve out parcels of their own. With these new riches, tomorrow became a better day.

The next question was, why did the people during this era not feel more inclined to share? Why did they hoard and continue to increase their wealth even when they had more than enough to meet reasonable desires as well as needs? The key here, I believe, is that although the amount of overall wealth generated did increase greatly, it was still limited. Not everyone was going to be able to get enough to improve their physical security. Somebody had to lose out.

We could say that a *scarcity mentality* prevailed during the last part of the Pre-Industrial Revolution era in terms of the distribution of wealth. Those without would go to any length to gain a share while those with would go to any lengths to protect and, as insurance, to increase their share. If an endless amount of wealth, if an endless supply of the things it could buy had been readily available, if citizens had been able to pick gold coins up off the streets after each rain shower, the desire to continually increase one's share, even at the expense of others, would not have been as strong. It was the limited nature of the supply that was the driving force behind the fierce competition which erupted during the Renaissance.

Another key factor in this argument is population. By the end of the Enlightenment the amount of wealth and of goods available had grown tremendously. But, contrary to expectations, the quality of life, as we said, for most had not improved much. The reason for this shortcoming was that while the wealth had grown, the population had also grown, so that even though more money and goods now existed there were also more people competing for them. Sir Thomas Malthus explained this one for us. It is a problem that has not gone away.

In terms of the broader picture, in terms of socioeconomic theory, something else happened during this era that helped set the stage for today's world. Two major camps of thought evolved and immediately began butting heads. Originally, these camps were called the Humanist School (which we relabeled the "Machiavellian Humanist School") and, its offspring, the Christian Humanist School. Both schools of thought found their roots in the philosophy of classical Greece concerning individual and societal development. The early Italian humanists, however, took the original Greek work on development and added their own Machiavellian twist. This was the part about not letting anyone get in your way. They focused entirely on the individual, made development an entirely selfish endeavor, cutting society as a partner out of the equation. The sentiment was, get as much as you can from society, give as little back as possible. That way your progress will be sped. Adam Smith later labeled businesspeople following this philosophy "monopolists" and said that government intervention was necessary to control their unbridled greed and their lack of respect for society.

The alternative to Machiavellian humanism was Christian humanism, which borrowed heavily from both Judaism and the Moslem tradition, as well as from the ancient Greeks. It simultaneously encouraged individual development and concern for others. It obviously provided a more balanced perspective in terms of societal development.

A series of apologists have appeared through history to excuse the excesses of the Machiavellian humanists, the monopolists, as being, in the long run, in the best interests of society. They have taken concepts from various periods of time and various sectors — religion, philosophy, science, economics — reshaping them or extracting that part of the involved logic which best rationalizes the monopolistic mentality. They have then presented that part as the whole.

Such apologists were not necessary during the Medieval period because individual profit was not a consideration for most. The quest was for *grace* and *self-sufficiency.* Survival was still the major issue. The workplace attitude was necessarily one of cooperation and community.

During the Renaissance, however, the generation of growing amounts of profit allowed more than self-sufficiency. The Church remained a major force in society, so that, at its insistence, the quest was still for grace, but *grace* and *profit* now, rather than grace and self-sufficiency. These two goals sometimes conflicted. The sense of workplace cooperation and community found during the Medieval period was replaced by a sense of competition.

Making It Work

The first serious justification for this increasing degree of self-interest no matter what the cost to others occurred during the Reformation. This movement's leaders very neatly resolved the discrepancy between grace and profit by saying that grace was gained through *hard work* and that the amount of profit earned was a measure of how hard one had worked. Therefore, the amount of *profit* earned was also a measure of how much *grace* one deserved.

Early apologists twisted this logic into a rationalization for making employees work unreasonable hours. They said that by doing so, owners were helping employees gain increased amounts of grace. The apologists also interpreted Calvin's theory of predetermination in a way that benefited monopolists. They said that those being exploited in the workplace had been born to this role, just as the owners/exploiters had been born to theirs. Both were simply fulfilling their destinies.

It was during the Reformation that *work* became synonymous with *sacrifice.* From this point on the amount of control employees enjoyed over their lives decreased until, by the Enlightenment, unskilled labor had none. The quest focused increasingly on profit. The grace part had faded as the power of the church was replaced by that of the revenue-hungry state.

During the Enlightenment new rationalizations for the monopolistic perspective were found in the realms of the physical sciences, economics, and sociology. In the physical sciences, the universe was defined as a great machine built to do God's work. The apologists said that businesses, according to this model, were also machines, but machines built to serve the owner's purpose. Employees were viewed as machine parts, rather than as human beings and were treated as such. Thus, we had the beginning of the *mechanistic* school of thought.[1]

In the field of economics, Adam Smith played right into the hand of the monopolists with his theory of *laissez faire* economics or *free enterprise*. Let businesspeople be guided by self-interest with minimal governmental regulation. The natural law of supply and demand would ensure that society benefited. Actually, Smith, as we have said, was a Christian humanist who was searching for the most effective means of generating wealth through industry so that all of society could benefit. The generation side of Smith's model was and still is powerful and beneficial. The distribution side, his desire to distribute the additional wealth generated equitably, however, was less successful. In most cases, it fell on deaf ears.

In sociology, the work on population growth and its relation to the food supply completed by Thomas Malthus was turned into another popular rationalization. This rationalization went as follows. Population is growing faster than the food supply. The laboring poor will suffer the most when famine occurs. The poor, at the same time, are producing a majority of the new children. Employers, therefore, are doing society and especially the poor themselves a favor by making them work longer hours so that they are too tired to procreate.

Finally, and perhaps most importantly in terms of what is to come, we have to talk about technology. During the Pre-Industrial Revolution era, although it got off to a slow start, technology played an increasingly important role concerning the fate of especially the majority of the population, the working poor. It began as their enemy. It was instrumental in forcing them off the farms, their traditional place of employment, and out of the rural areas where they could build their own homes, collect their own firewood, grow some of their own food, raise their own chickens and cows, where they could retain some degree of control over the basics of survival. It forced them into the cities where that control was abruptly lost, where everything had to be bought with money that now had to be earned through service to others.

But the laboring poor, unlike trained craftspeople, were relatively unskilled and had little to offer as a way to earn money, until technology again entered the picture, this time as the good guy, and rescued them. Technology made the laboring poor employable by facilitating the division of labor and simplifying the resultant jobs so that people with few skills could handle the jobs.

Even with their new jobs, however, most of the people involved did not regain control over their lives, or see much improvement. Emphasis remained on survival, rather than on graduating to an improved scenario. The amount workers could earn when manufactory positions did become available was decided by the owners, and the owners, for the most part, were Adam Smith's monopolists, rather than Christian humanists. As a result, during the early stages of the Industrial Revolution we found David Ricardo's worst predictions proving true.

From a socioeconomic perspective, then, perhaps the key question addressed in our next section on the Industrial Revolution era will be, did technology during this era possess the potential to eventually improve the lot of the laboring poor? Or was it going to make their situation even worse? And, if it did, indeed, make their situation worse, what would be the result in terms of society? For, from this point on, the numbers of the laboring poor would grow steadily.

Topics for Discussion

1. Can emotional security be gained without first achieving adequate physical security? Is the opposite true?
2. Why were the contributions of Martin Luther, Adam Smith, Thomas Malthus, and others twisted to serve purposes other than those intended?
3. Is the "scarcity mentality" still a societal shaping force in the modern world?
4. If society ever gets beyond its quest for "profit," what comes next?
5. What was the role of technology during the Pre-Industrial Revolution era?

Notes

1. Russell Ackoff, *Redesigning the Future*, New York: John Wiley & Sons, 1974, pp. 10–11.

THE INDUSTRIAL REVOLUTION

The Industrial Revolution began during the late 1700s and lasted until the mid-1900s. It changed greatly the way we think as well as the way we work. It was during the Industrial Revolution that technology proved its value by allowing previously unheard of increases in the supply of just about every physical entity, from agricultural produce, to household wares, to the machinery of new industries.

When utilized in societies that had adopted Adam Smith's laissez faire economic philosophy, technology also facilitated tremendous growth in the amount of wealth generated. The Western world quickly fell in love with its new success, with its ability to escape the survival mode, with its wealth facilitating opportunity for increasing numbers of people to gain control over their lives. We celebrated our victory. We reveled in it. We gladly displayed our gains for all to see.

The early Industrial Revolution was even more an age of absolute individualism than the Renaissance. The church as a moderating force had lost its power, sometimes even its inclination. Government was, at least initially, dominated by the moneyed factions. The "scarcity mentality" still reigned supreme, supported by the rationalizations for exploitation provided by Pre-Industrial Revolution thinkers. And the population continued to grow.

With this growth, and with the necessary movement of industries to rapidly swelling, unplanned cities, the number and seriousness of social problems increased dramatically. With no real help being offered by traditional advocates, the workers themselves were eventually forced to take control, to organize into unions, and to begin fighting for a role in shaping of their destiny.

Eventually, as communication systems improved, it became increasingly difficult to ignore the plight of the laboring class. First the academic world, then the government joined the struggle to make social sense of our increasingly bountiful harvest. First in Europe, then in the United States those who had led the rush to wealth were reined in; the arguments of their apologists were refuted; and Western civilization began its quest for the best balance between the interests of self and those of society as a whole.

Section II, then, centers on the Industrial Revolution, defining its great moments and great theorists. It explores the logic and arguments that drove these people, that drove the technological innovation of the period so critical to our modern world. It explores the early attempts at developing a theory of management which worked in organizations where it was now necessary to integrate the efforts of hundreds and sometimes even thousands of employees.

While the Pre-Industrial Revolution era provided the foundational roots for modern-day industrial society, the Industrial Revolution can be seen as its launchpad, although the launch, as we shall discover, went anything but smoothly.

5 | The Early Industrial Revolution: Europe Leads the Way

After Reading This Chapter You Should Know

1. How the textile industry kicked off the Industrial Revolution.
2. How Adam Smith's "monopolists" reshaped the lives of the working class.
3. Why the quality of life deteriorated rapidly for the working class.
4. The relationship between "utilitarianism," "Social Darwinism," and the concept of "economic man."
5. How children were subjected to the cruelest exploitation in mills and factories during this period.
6. How Robert Owen provided the necessary model and began the reform movement.
7. Why the exploitation of labor was not as rampant in France.
8. How the union movement began and then failed in its early days.
9. How "communism" evolved as an alternative to the excesses of the laissez faire economic system.

England Gets Things Started

The Industrial Revolution began in England, but not, as one might suspect, because that country was a leader in scientific and technological development. No polytechnic schools existed here as in France and Germany. England, in fact, at that point in history actually trailed other European nations in developing its ability to train people in technical areas.

The attitude of England toward education was elitist. What schools existed were inferior and were not supported by taxes. Teaching the poor was considered dangerous. The wealthy who wanted to educate their children either brought in tutors or sent the children to school abroad. Oxford and Cambridge were the best England had to offer in terms of "advanced" education. At this point, however, the two universities were more so finishing schools for the elite than the top-level educational institutions they have become.

The Industrial Revolution began in England for two reasons. First, the technical requirements for early machines were not so sophisticated, the scientific principles involved not so subtle that a skilled craftsman could not put them to use. Second, the cultural climate in England was right. The feudalistic power of the throne had been broken. A relatively representative government existed, whose driving principle was economic advancement and private profit. Also, the previously mentioned Enclosure Acts of 1760 to 1830 had accomplished three things. First, they had allowed technology to be used more effectively in the fields to produce the increased yields necessary to feed a growing population. Second, they had made farming more profitable for owners, thus helping generate the investment capital necessary for industrial start-up. Third and most importantly, as we have said, they had driven laborers off the land, out of the fields, and into the previously mentioned "manufactories."

The product that launched the Industrial Revolution was cotton cloth. This industry was triggered at least partially by trade with the North American colonies. England, with the most powerful fleet in the world, had wrested control of the slave trade away from the Spanish and French by the early 1700s. What England needed now was customers. The southern colonies in North American were a prime target. With the assistance of land speculators, England overcame efforts by Virginia and South Carolina to stop the importation of slaves, then played a lead role in development of the plantation system. Slave labor produced cheap cotton. The cotton was sold to England. The resultant cloth was then sold throughout Europe and to England's network of colonies throughout the world, including those in North America, from whence the cotton originally came.

England's Lancashire mill system began growing in the mid-1700s. The mills paid for themselves almost immediately because the machinery involved, the spinning jenny, the water frame, the spinning mule, and later the power loom, was relatively simple and cheap to construct.

The textile industry kept alive and drove the early Industrial Revolution. First, it generated increasing amounts of investment capital. Second, its expansion stimulated related growth in the construction industry, in local transportation systems, in international shipping, in financial institutions.

The initial mill owners made a lot of money. But then, as free enterprise began working its magic, as more competitors got involved, Adam Smith's law of supply and demand took hold and profits fell. Manufacturers had to begin seeking ways to cut costs. The easiest way, of course, was to cut wages, which was done, until workers were pushed to the edge of starvation. For example, the wages of a handloom weaver fell from 33 shillings in 1795 to 14 shillings in 1815 to approximately 5 shillings in 1829.[1]

Owners rationalized the resultant suffering. They said that it was a product not of their own greed, but of the high cost of living. Food, for example, was too expensive. They blamed it on the farmers. The farmers were the greedy ones with their "Corn Laws" or tariffs against agricultural imports put into place by a parliament composed mainly of landlords. However, when the industrialists did finally gain enough clout in 1846 to have these laws abolished, the cost of living, unsurprisingly, did not fall, and the suffering continued.

Coal was another key actor in the early stages of the Revolution. Once England's forests had been cut, coal had become the major fuel for both the country's industrial and domestic sectors. People had been burning coal for heat for quite some time. But only in 1709 was it substituted successfully for charcoal in the iron ore smelting process. This change cut pig iron production costs greatly because of the local availability of great quantities of coal and triggered the transition to coal as the major source of industrial fuel. By 1800 Great Britain produced nearly 90% of the world's total output of coal.[2]

Interestingly enough, the growing popularity of this fuel was also indirectly responsible for the development of the railroad. After the steam-driven engine had been invented it was used to power a winch which pulled carloads of coal by cable out of the mines. The next step was to install the engine directly in the car so that the winches and cables could be done away with and the cars could carry the coal along tracks to destinations distant from the mine.

And it was the railroad, more than any other technology, that spurred the growth of worldwide industry. In 1830, only "a few dozen miles" of track had been laid. By 1840 there were over 4500 miles. By 1850 there were more than 23,500 miles of track laid across the world, most of which had been built with British capital, British iron, British machinery, and British know-how.

The mass production of steel was a natural by-product of the growth of the railroad. A mile of track, for example, required 300 tons of iron.[3]

The Monopolists Have Their Day

At the same time that this tremendous burst of industrial expansion was occurring, the problems of the working class were growing. The challenge to mill and factory management was to recondition the workers, to make them accept the new reality, the new life patterns and values being forced upon them. Up to this point, working hours for most had centered around activities necessary to survival — growing food, building and heating a shelter, raising a family, contributing to a community. Life had been hard. But at least some degree of control had been enjoyed. People had lived mainly by the seasons, by nature's cycles. Once enough food had been grown and harvested, once the roof had been repaired against the coming winter, they had been able to stop, to rest, to celebrate, or to do something else of their own choosing. They had lived by the cycles of nature, by the cycles of family, by the cycles of community and the church.

Now all that had to be changed. For the Industrial Revolution to survive, laborers had to be trained, or forced to live solely according to the all-devouring cycle of work — 12 or more daylight hours in the factory doing the same repetitious, deadening, and frequently dangerous thing over and over. And 12 evening and nighttime hours into which workers had to crowd the rest of their lives, including sleep. Existence centered around and was totally shaped by the job. People lived simply to work now, rather than working in order to live or in order to improve and enjoy life more during their free hours.

And it started early. Although the first mill workers were men, they were soon replaced by women, who proved easier to manage, and finally by children, who were the easiest. Children were expected to begin working in the mills by the age of 5 or 6. They normally put in a 10-hour day 5 days a week. As they matured, this stretched to a 12-hour day, and upon reaching full adulthood, if it was reached and if they still had a job, they were expected to put in 14 to 16 hours. Rarely during this span did the hourly wage improve, so that in order to make more, in order to support a growing family, the only alternative was to work longer hours. Adults, of course, were needed for heavy work, like mining, though children were still used even here. One of their jobs was to sort through the coal as it came out of the mine on a conveyor belt and throw out "clinkers," or pieces of slate.

Activities in industrial communities were structured to reinforce the realization that work was the focus of life. According to J.J. and Barbara Hammond in their book *The Skilled Labourer:*

> The age that regarded men, women, and children as hands for feeding the machines of the new industry had no use for libraries, galleries, playgrounds, or any of the forms in which space and beauty can bring comfort or nourishment to the human mind. The new towns were built for a race that was allowed no leisure. Education, it was believed, would make the workers less passive and, therefore, less useful instruments. Therefore, workers should not be educated, or should be educated only within the narrowest limits. Recreation was waste: the man who was kicking a football or playing a fiddle was wasting time and should, instead, be wielding a hammer at a forge or superintending a spinning machine. In some parts of Lancashire it was the custom to forbid music in the public houses, and parsons and magistrates were found who thought that the worker would be demoralized by hearing an oratorio in a church on a Sunday.[4]

The major complaint of industrialists was that the workers were too slow to adapt to this new cycle of living built around work. They were lazy. It was hard to keep them at it. The industrialists rapidly lost patience and began using whatever measures necessary to improve this attitude — threats, promises, starvation, beatings. But work, for most, obviously no longer had anything to do with improving life, nothing to do with improving the quantity and quality of food available, nothing to do with opening a new field to grow crops or with getting glass windows for one's house, nothing to do with ensuring a better life for one's children. For these reasons — because work, for most, was now solely about survival — the problems did not go away.

Instead, the problems grew steadily worse. Laborers worked now only because there was no other alternative. All control over their lives had been taken away. The situation of the factory hand had reverted, in essence, to that of slavery. Most employees had to work the hours demanded by the owner. They had to accept strict discipline and fines. They often had to live in the owner's housing, buy food from the owner's store, drink in the owner's saloon. Frequently laborers did not receive the wages earned. Instead, such wages were put toward their debt incurred from rent, food, drink, the purchase of tools needed on the job, a debt which never seemed to stop growing.

Chains were not necessary to keep these "slaves" from running away because they had no place to run away to. They could not return to the country, to farming. There was no land left. A second alternative, living on the streets, competing with thousands of other beggars and thieves, dealing with unsympathetic courts, totally losing one's dignity, was even less appealing. So they stayed at their jobs, hoping against hope that somehow life would improve, and allowed themselves to be worked to death. An example would be the razor-grinder's fate. According the S. Pollard in *A History of Labour in Sheffield*, "In 1842 50% of all razor-grinders in their 30s, 79% in their 40s, and 100% of all over the age of 50 wretched out their lungs with the grinders disease."[5] When a grinder died, usually the eldest unemployed son would rush to fill the position in order to keep the family alive, thereby beginning his own dance with death.

Industrial cities grew unplanned into sprawling slums. The owners and middle class residents moved out, building walls and growing trees along the roads taken to their factories so that they would not have to witness the misery of the worker slums. It was estimated that at this point in England's history the peasants who had been able to remain in the country, despite the fact that their existence was still harsh, many surviving on a diet composed mainly of potatoes and thin coffee, lived twice as long as their city cousins.

The Argument for Exploitation

This was the period during which all the rationalizations for exploitation that had been building since the Renaissance were pulled together into an argument that allowed the monopolists to take over and shape society. That Britain was a Protestant culture helped. Her thinkers and politicians relied heavily on Luther's and Calvin's writings in their reasoning, ignoring those arguments that did not fit. They presented only the parts of the work ethic philosophy that suited their purpose, ignoring, for example, Luther's admonition that "we should help [our neighbor] guard and increase his livelihood and property."[6] They did the same with Adam Smith's theory of laissez faire economics, presenting only those parts which sufficed as rationalizations for the ambitions and excesses of the powerful.

Conveniently, in the realm of philosophy, a new school of thought that supported current economic practices had evolved, one which carried empiricism to its extreme. The empiricists, as we remember, had said that rather than indulging in the seemingly endless quest for a universal truth upon which to build our reality, we should use science and experience to define truths useful to the development of society. The *utilitarians*, under the leadership of Samuel Bentham, during the early 1800s carried this logic a step further, saying that *usefulness* was the only standard by which individuals and society should judge moral conduct and that by adhering to such a standard we would produce the greatest good for the greatest number. Thus, the phrase, "whatever works" was born.

Also during the second half of the 1800s there sprang up an entirely new school of apologists offering an entirely new supportive theory, this one with its origins in the natural sciences. The new school was called "Social Darwinism." Its theories were related loosely to the findings of Charles Darwin, the naturalist. The most extreme members of this faction were against public education, government-supported health care services, a federal postal service, and, of course, any kind of support for the poor, working or not. All they were interested in the government providing was military/police protection and a system of courts.

The Englishman Herbert Spencer was considered by most the philosophical leader of the Social Darwinists. Their heyday was the last half of the 1800s. Spencer's main tenant was that the "law of the jungle" should be allowed to prevail in human society as it did in the society of other animal species. He believed that human society was an "organism" controlled by natural laws which overrode any changes or adjustments attempted by humans. The purpose of these natural laws was to ensure perpetuation. As with other animal species, the way nature did this was by allowing the strong to dominate and to gather unto themselves the majority of the resources available.

Spencer had no faith in the State, which, in his opinion, labored under the false assumption that it had the ability to "improve upon the divine arrangement." Taking resources gathered by the powerful away from them to assist the weak not only hampered society's progress, but actually threatened society by draining its energy in order to keep alive those who had the least to contribute.

This belief was set out in Spencer's "law of equal freedom" which said that every man had the freedom to do all that he willed, provided that he did not infringe on the equal freedom of any other man to do the same. Interestingly enough, Spencer was referring not to the exploitation and frequent enslavement of the "weak" when he talked about infringement, but to the fact that the weak, if assisted by a tax-supported state, were infringing on the God-given rights of the strong. Labor, therefore, was invited by the Social Darwinists to "give in to the decrees of fate without a murmur."[7]

By 1840 the newly spawned industrial upper and middle classes of England were well entrenched. They were composed mainly of self-righteous, poorly educated, short-sighted, hard-working, self-made men with little imagination and absolutely no sympathy for the human sacrifice being made in the name of their financial success. They were the most recent version of Machiavellian humanism, of Adam Smith's monopolists. They were the epitome of the utilitarianistic, individualistic, law-of-the-jungle, every-man-for-himself cult heroes still worshiped in some circles today.

Because there were no taxes in England as of yet, the wealth of this group grew rapidly. The concept of "economic man" was soon to come into vogue. It held that man's sole interest, at this point in history, should be the accumulation of wealth; it held that social issues and the importance of redistributing some of that wealth should not be considerations.

The church, which at one time had been able to provide at least some protection for the less fortunate, was no longer a factor. The Protestant Church of England catered to the upper and middle classes. It was supported by these people and, in return, generally supported their position. It stayed out of the industrial slums. In order to soothe its own conscience it did provide occasional band-aid-type remedies to the great wound industrialization had dealt humanity. But it generally refused to confront, even to consider the real issues.

One such "real" issue was child labor. The "poor laws" had been put into place during Queen Elizabeth's reign (1558–1603) to force communities to provide employment for those who could not otherwise find work. These laws were now being used to allow authorities to deliver pauper children "… in batches of 50 to 100 directly to factory owners, making no account for their welfare or even survival." Here they were "underfed on rancid bacon, worked as many as 18 hours a day, put in irons or whipped, kept prisoners. Blindly ignorant, stunted 'infants' as they were called, stood whimpering at their machines from dawn until deep at night with scarce a pause to eat. Their one friend, death, was a constant visitor to the mills."[8]

In the textile mills children usually worked 13-hour days. They were allowed to sit down occasionally so long as it did not interfere with their production. On some days the shifts would stretch to 14, 15, or 16 hours. The children worked 6 days a week, putting in several extra hours on Sundays to clean the machines. All this was endured in a temperature kept uniformly at 80° "with little ventilation, and no facilities for washing or for getting rid of the cotton fluff and dust floating in the air." That "fluff" caused a respiratory infection later labeled "brown lung." The pauper children were housed by mill owners in "unregulated and seldom-inspected barracks where they slept several to a bed and in shifts."[9]

One of the Good Guys

There were also, of course, good guys during the days of the early Industrial Revolution, although, at this point in history they were in the minority. The most notable was Robert Owen, a man whose vision and courage have made him one of the best-known figures of the Industrial Revolution. Although he did not believe in or practice organized religion, being appalled by the slaughter and hatreds it had led to historically, Owen was a Christian humanist in the truest sense. Although extremely intelligent, he was a relatively simple man driven by simple values which he practiced without deviation through his entire life. His core message was that *the condition of mankind would improve if people would be willing to replace competition with cooperation as the driving force in both economic and social life.*

In 1781, at the age of 10, Owen left home to apprentice with a linen merchant in London. By the age of 20 he had become master of one of England's most modern mills in Manchester. By the age of 30, he had become part owner and manager of the New Lanark Mill in Scotland that employed approximately 2000. It was here that Owen made his most serious contributions to management and economic theory. He refused to hire any child under the age of 10. He added a second story to each company house, thus giving families two rooms instead of one to live in. He provided cheap coal, free medical attention, and a store where decent clothing and good food could be purchased at reasonable prices. He strove to improve the health of his employees and to attract families to replace the orphaned pauper laborers.

In the community Owen cleaned and paved the streets, built community centers, and instituted a public education system for both children and adults, beginning with a nursery school. Instructors taught natural history, geography, chemistry, sociology, economics, ancient and modern history, dancing and singing. School came before work for young employees.

In terms of economic theory, Owen foreshadowed Henry Ford by insisting that the best way to stimulate economic growth was to pay a reasonable wage, so that employees as well as owners could afford to buy the widgets being produced. In terms of employee motivation, he believed that the best way to increase productivity was to treat employees well, which he did at New Lanark, staking his own future and fortune on his beliefs. As a result, the operation became one of the most profitable in England, drawing the attention of industrialists, economists, and statesmen from all over the Western world.

In 1815, reform-minded members of British parliament tried to introduce a factory bill modeled on Owen's efforts. The bill declared that children under the age of 10 should not be employed in factories. It said that those under the age of 18 should work no more than 10½ hours a day, not including the meal break and time spent being trained. It said that no one should work between the hours of 9 P.M. and 5 A.M. It said that young employees should be allowed to go to school during the first 4 years of their employment. It said that factory inspectors should be appointed by local government.

A fact-finding committee was formed to gather supporting evidence for this bill. Members found in some large factories that one fifth to one fourth of the children employed "were either cripples, otherwise deformed, or permanently injured by excessive toil and brutal abuse. They found that the younger children seldom held out more than three or four years without severe illness, often ending in death."[10]

The factory owners, in response, gathered their own evidence and wrote their own report. In it, they ultimately concluded that

1. "The bill was unnecessary in that the owners were already doing of their own volition all that it proposed;
2. Cotton mills were extraordinarily healthy places and — on the word of several medical men — it was very beneficial for children to work at night, to stand for 12 hours a day breathing in cotton fluff;
3. If the children were not put to work they would all become criminals."[11]

The bill was eventually passed in 1818, but had been so altered, so watered down as to be useless. The reforms Owen and others sought did not seriously begin taking shape in England until the early 1830s.

Robert Owen eventually broadened his perspective to address national rather than simply local problems. He proposed the construction of new agriculture-based communities in the countryside to deal with unemployment when the Napoleonic Wars ended and soldiers came streaming home. He helped start cooperative communities, New Harmony in the United States being the most famous. He became an important figure in the fight to legalize unions. He traveled extensively, lecturing, offering his ideas.

As he aged, Owen, in the tradition of the East, became more of a guru, a teacher, than a businessman. In terms of socioeconomic theory, although little of what he offered was accepted during his lifetime and although some of what he offered was unrealistic, many of Owen's contributions are recognized as basic to the evolution of modern-day management theory.

France Takes a Different Road

France, the other major European power during this period, chose a different route that also strongly affected the evolution of European and eventually of world management theory. During the late 1700s, while Britain was gearing up for the Industrial Revolution, the French were dealing with another kind of revolution, one in societal and governmental philosophy. While the British, in their entrepreneurial fervor, had forgotten the grand developmental schemes of the Enlightenment thinkers, the French had not.

The French could easily have followed the course of the British in terms of economic development. They had the resources. For example, at that point in history one out of every five Europeans was French. They had the philosophers, the scientists, the technicians. A majority of the innovations upon which the Industrial Revolution was built were developed, at least conceptually, in France.

But the French were still governed by Europe's most powerful traditional monarchy, rather than by a parliament driven by laissez faire philosophy similar to that of England. And the monarchy was still tied closely to the Catholic Church, so that change came slowly.

The French Revolution of 1789 was triggered partially by the expenses of the royal household. It was triggered partially by the expenses of supporting the Revolutionary War in North America. But it was triggered mainly by financial mismanagement. Life for French nobility had become increasingly expensive. These people were not allowed to learn a trade. This left only two sources of income for them. The first was rent gained from peasants farming their lands. But as the nobility continued to raise these rents, the peasants grew rebellious. The second source was salaries earned from governmental posts. Aristocrats soon filled most such posts, forcing professional administrators out. The untrained and often corrupt nobility rapidly brought the country to bankruptcy.

This bankruptcy, as might be expected, exacted the greatest toll from the peasants and small shopkeepers who made up most of France's economic world in the late 1700s. These, then, were the people who took to the streets of Paris, who stormed the Bastille, and eventually brought the monarchy crashing down during the French Revolution.

Their leaders built the resultant new society on three overlapping Enlightenment ideals represented by the tricolors in the French flag — liberty, equality, fraternity. They said that all men should be free, should have control over their lives. They said that all men should have equal opportunity to develop their potential. They said that all men should be brothers with no discrimination based on race, religion, class.

But more important to our question of why the French did not industrialize as rapidly or to the extent that the British did was the fact that the members of the new governing body of France, the Constituent Assembly, also produced Enclosure Acts. The French version of these Acts, however, had an intent and effect that was exactly opposite that of the British version. The French Enclosure Acts, rather than turning the common lands over to the landed gentry to cultivate, divided these lands among the peasants, giving them private ownership. It did the same with the confiscated lands of the Catholic Church and of the nobility who had fled the guillotine and moved abroad during the Revolution. The Constituent Assembly also outlawed guilds so that small shopkeepers could survive and compete.

This was probably the first instance in modern European history where a government put the needs and interests of the common people before those of the upper classes. At the same time, however, by making people comfortable in their traditional situation, by not forcing them to change their lifestyle and their way of thinking as the British had done, this revolutionary social philosophy slowed France's industrialization efforts to a relative crawl.

The French people, however, did not seem to mind "crawling." Despite the fact that by 1884 only one out of ten French citizens worked in a factory, their country remained a major world power with a much higher overall quality of life than that of most of their neighbors, including the British.

The Workers Fight Back

Meanwhile, back in England, all of labor was not placidly accepting its situation. In 1811, for example, the destructive "Luddite" movement began in the textile manufacturing center of Nottingham. It was ignited by the introduction of a new technology, the "stocking frame," which produced hosiery (or what we today call socks). The new technology threatened the livelihood of stocking weavers, most of whom were men at that point, by producing hosiery more inexpensively and more rapidly, and by enabling women to do the work.

The chief tactic of the Luddites was to destroy this offensive machinery. The movement spread rapidly from Nottingham to other areas, adding new targets such as the power loom which also threatened the economic existence of hand weavers. As the destruction increased and grew more general, rioting occurred. Eventually, manufactories were burned. Mill owner homes were looted and also burned. The police intervened, then the military. Armed clashes occurred; rioters were fired upon. Finally, suspected leaders were captured and sentenced to be hanged, exiled, or imprisoned.

The Luddite movement changed very little. It did, however, help to bring home the realization that technology had once again become the enemy of labor. Due to ever-increasing levels of competition, owners were forced continually to seek ways to cut costs. They had, as we have said, reduced wages to the survival level and frequently below. No more juice could be squeezed from that turnip. The next step was obviously to replace employees with more cost-effective machines. So while technology had initially made it possible for the unskilled to find work that provided at least a survival-level living, it was now taking that work away as well.

Unionizing was obviously a more reasonable and more long-term approach to stopping the deterioration of the labor situation. The first effort to develop unions had begun in England around 1818. The logic was simple. There was no point in arguing ethics with the owners. The only thing they understood was the bottom line. The only way to force change, then, was to threaten that bottom line. While workers had been spread out across the countryside during the cottage industry era, there was no chance of this happening. But once industrialists began bringing them together in factories and mines to witness each other's plight, to share grievances, the one way workers had of improving their situation became obvious. Through trust or fear the entire workforce had to be convinced to walk out. At the same time, through persuasion, threat, or the use of force, others had to be convinced not to try to replace the strikers, so that the owners would begin losing money, and would continued to do so until the owners were willing to negotiate.

The pressure for change in the British workplace was growing more rapidly now. The working class began finding an increasing number of supporters among the upper classes. By the 1830s men like Edwin Chadwick, whose interest was public health (clean water for towns, waste removal); Jeremy Bentham (Samuel Bentham's son), who focused on the penal system (decrease the amount of violence in it); and John Stuart Mill, who attacked the current economic philosophy, began laying the foundations for turning British parliament into an instrument of social welfare.

John Stuart Mill was born in 1806 to a father who, as head of the British East India Company, strongly advocated the utilitarian philosophy. One of the younger Mill's tutors was Samuel Bentham. Mill, however, was increasingly troubled by what the utilitarians taught. He believed that society could not reduce all the problems of human conduct to the simple dimension of "self-interest."

Eventually, Mill wrote a book entitled, *Principles of Political Economics*. In it he voiced his support for the laissez faire approach to economics as opposed to state control. At the same time, however, he said that no sector should be allowed to stifle actions on the part of the state that would benefit society as a whole. He declared that while the law of supply and demand should regulate the generation of wealth, government should involve itself in the distribution of that wealth. The state should institute income and inheritance taxes. It should take a portion of profits away from the successful, and use these revenues for such things as the development of a free, universal education system and the provision of assistance for the poor.

By 1833, the first child labor laws with real teeth had been passed by parliament, beginning with the Anthorp Act which regulated conditions for employing children in textile mills. In 1847, a 10-hour limit was placed on the workday of children and women. Such laws, however, were still difficult to enforce. What was lacking was the watchdog factory inspectors Owen had earlier called for.

The union movement had been legalized in Britain by 1825, and by 1830 there were fledgling unions in the ranks of cotton spinners, artisans, and coal miners. The first serious attempt at consolidation was made in 1830. The Grand National Consolidated Trades Union was formed under the leadership of none other than Robert Owen.

As businesses grew, so did the unions. The first union members were mainly skilled employees — engineers, builders, textile workers, printers, etc. — the employees who earlier would have belonged to guilds. It was not until later that common laborers were also accepted into the fold, swelling membership and focusing attention on the basics — better pay, shorter hours, healthier working conditions. The real unification of unions in Britain did not come until 1868 with the Trade Unions Congress. Then, in 1913 the International Federation of Trade Unions unified the movement across Europe.

The major obstacle to change in England had been that the working class had no vote. In 1838 a movement called "Chartism" evolved partially out of the early failure of unionization efforts. The unions had failed, the Chartists said, because parliament made the laws and union members, lacking the vote, could not influence their representatives. The Chartists strove to gain universal male suffrage. In 1839, a petition with 12 million signatures on it was presented to parliament. It was rejected. Riots and insurrections followed, but parliament, dominated by the industrialists, held fast, and the vote was not gained for nearly another 30 years.

Seeking the Middle Ground

The concept of *socialism* was also revived around 1820. It was spelled out in Robert Owen's book *Utopian Socialism: A New View of Society*. Owen said that the community rather than the individual should once again become the focus in terms of development, as in the Medieval period. He said that society should pool at least some of its resources, and that government should redistribute the resources to facilitate the greater good — to provide education and health services, to provide assistance for the unfortunate. Owen and John Stuart Mill obviously thought along the same lines.

Louis Blanc, a Frenchman, talked about the type of support this radically new approach to societal management, "utopian socialism," would need to succeed. He said that the approach would have to be introduced and supported by the state, for, "if the State is not used as an instrument, it will becomes an obstacle." Blanc believed that the state must guarantee "the right to work" and must use its power to protect the weak and the poor. The state must intervene to see that businesses are run correctly, and that they are eventually run by the workers.[12]

So now the economic pendulum had begun swinging toward the extreme opposite from laissez faire. This extreme was reached in 1848 when, after the worst economic depression in European history, Karl Marx's *Communist Manifesto* appeared, offering a doctrine and strategy for social revolution, for "the forcible overthrow of the whole existing social order" and for the rebirth of that order as a classless society devoid of "exploitive bourgeoisie" and guided by the previously exploited proletariat, guided by the working class that would see the value of Marx's highly idealistic but thoroughly unrealistic entreaty, "From each according to his abilities, to each according to his needs."[13] What Marx called for was total government control of both the production and the distribution of wealth, and for the proletariat to control the government.

The *Communist Manifesto* initially attracted little attention and had little to do with the social revolutions that rocked Europe as the workers continued to strive for and, in many cases, began to gain increased political power. But through the years the Manifesto gained momentum, eventually influencing and helping to shape the economic fate of major powers, Russia being the foremost.

As a result of the excesses of the early Industrial Revolution and as a result of the radical reaction to these excesses, Europeans during the last half of the 1800s had begun the task of searching out an acceptable middle ground, one that lay somewhere between the extremes of laissez faire economics and communism. They had begun the quest, which continues today, for an economic arrangement that keeps incentive alive but that, at the same time, provides the services and opportunity that allow all people who contribute to realize their potential and to enjoy their lives.

One might say that Europe had begun to mellow a bit after its initial industrial frenzy. This "lull," however, would not last long, for Germany, under Bismark, was soon to supersede England as the major European economic power and was beginning to build her war machine. This war machine would, in turn, after another great flurry of economic progress, incite two terrible wars, the first affecting all of Europe, the second affecting all the world.

The most important result of these wars, in terms of our history, was that they would cripple Europe's economy for several decades, allowing the United States to take the lead as the world's major economic power.

Topics for Discussion

1. Why did the Industrial Revolution begin in England? Why was it most "successful" there?
2. Why did the leaders of society allow the working class to be treated the way it was?
3. Why did we "progress" philosophically from "rationalism" to "empiricism" to "utilitarianism"?
4. What do you think Charles Darwin's reaction to "Social Darwinism" would have been?
5. Why did other owners not attempt to learn from Robert Owen's experiments and successes?

Notes

1. E. J. Hobsbawn, *The Age of Revolution 1789–1848*, Cleveland: The World Publishing Co., 1962, p. 41.
2. *Ibid.*, p. 41.
3. *Ibid.*, p. 45

4. J. J. Hammond and Barbara Hammond, *The Skilled Labourer 1760–1832*, New York: Harper Torch Books, 1970, p. 5.

5. S. Pollard, *A History of Labour in Sheffield*, London: Ashgate Publishing, 1960, pp. 62–63.

6. Hobsbawn, *op. cit.*, p. 201.

7. Sidney Fine, *Laissez Faire and the General Welfare State*, Ann Arbor: The University of Michigan Press, 1966, p. 44.

8. Miriam Beard, *A History of Business*, Vol. II, Ann Arbor: University of Michigan Press, 1965, p. 127.

9. Margaret Cole, *Robert Owen of New Lanark*, New York: Oxford University Press, 1953, pp. 47–48.

10. *Ibid.*, pp. 98–99.

11. *Ibid.*, p. 101.

12. David Thomson, *Europe since Napoleon*, 2nd ed., New York: Alfred A. Knopf, 1962, p. 178.

13. *Ibid.*, p. 179.

6 The Early Industrial Revolution: The United States Catches Up

After Reading This Chapter You Should Know

1. Why the United States was "born into" the laissez faire tradition.
2. How the robber barons gained power, how they built the country, and at what cost.
3. Why the robber barons were not true advocates of laissez faire economics.
4. How the Knights of Labor began the first serious effort to organize workers in the United States and generated a set of objectives that helped define modern social policy.
5. How the robber barons fought and defeated the labor movement, but could not stamp it out.
6. How government became an increasingly powerful force in the struggle to improve the situation of labor.
7. How President Theodore Roosevelt turned the tide against the "Monopolists" and "Social Darwinists" and took the lead in creating a "Welfare State."
8. How Andrew Carnegie defined a third alternative to either laissez faire economics or socialism.

New Kid on the Block

While the colonies in North American were still owned by Britain, the plan was that they should provide raw materials for Britain's growing industrial sector and then provide a market for what she produced. England was against the development of any large-scale manufacturing facilities in her colonies. She did not want colonists competing with her industrially. She did not want them processing their own raw materials into finished products to be sold directly without her making a profit.

Therefore, before the Revolutionary War, what the colonies had in place in terms of nonagricultural production was mainly craftsmen working in small shops similar to the guild shops of Medieval Europe. In terms of distribution, it also had a growing class of merchants that was rapidly gaining wealth and political power (much of the wealth being made through smuggling because of the restrictions imposed by Britain) the same way that the European merchants had during the Renaissance. Ester Forbes' book, *Johnny Tremain*, written about the life of a silversmithing apprentice in Boston during the 1770s, is an accurate portrayal of work and business in most colonies cities during this period.

After the Revolutionary War in 1776, of course, things changed. But it took time for the new country to organize its immense resources. The Industrial Revolution did not really get started in the United States until around 1860, nearly 100 years after it started in England.

Economically, the new United States was a child of the laissez faire school of thought. Revolutionary War leaders spoke of man's inalienable right to pursue his own self-interest guaranteed by nature and/or God which no government should intrude upon, but, rather, which government should protect and preserve. England's supposed reluctance to honor this "inalienable right" was a major rationalization for the rebellion, which merchants like Samuel Adams and John Hancock played a lead role in fomenting.

Though now free of England's control, the United States continued to model itself more on England in terms of economic development than on France. Most early governmental leaders were advocates of laissez faire economics. Thomas Jefferson, the third president (1801–1809), following the lead of Adam Smith, believed this approach to be the best for developing the potential of both individual citizens and the country as a whole. However, Jefferson thought that the United States, due to the great amount of fertile land available, would become an agricultural nation. He did not believe industry would flourish, and, therefore, did not take into account many of the issues that might evolve.

Alexander Hamilton, the first Secretary of the Treasury (1789–1795), reflected more the school of Machiavellian humanism. He was a monopolist at heart. Unlike Jefferson, Hamilton wanted government to become very much involved in setting economic policy. His concern, however, was not protection of the common folk, the workers. For these he had little respect. Rather, Hamilton advocated government support of and aid for business owners. His theory was that as the prosperity of industrialists grew, benefits would eventually trickle down to the working classes.

With Hamilton's proposed policies the United States probably witnessed the birth of the "trickle-down" theory revived most recently by President Ronald Reagan. Hamilton, along with Henry Clay, also called for tariffs to protect home businesses against competition from the far more advanced British industrial sector.

Andrew Jackson, the country's seventh president (1829–1837), was perhaps the first to advocate government intervention as a means of restraining the unbridled quest for personal economic improvement unleashed by the laissez faire approach. He mounted a serious effort to limit the power of the monopolists, especially in the banking industry, as a hindrance to the open competition upon which free enterprise thrives.

In the U.S. Congress, during this same period, a confrontation between landowners and fledgling industrialists, similar to that which had raged earlier in the British parliament, was growing. The landowners, in this instance, were the established southern plantation-owning gentry. The industrialists were from the north. The industrialists, of course, wanted the cotton and other crops grown in the south sent north to feed their factories, rather than being shipped abroad. They tried to pass laws that would force this change. The plantation owners, who originally enjoyed a great deal of power in Congress, balked.

While the British confrontation between landowners and industrialists had been settled mainly through debate and voting, the Civil War (1860–1865), the most bloody war in U.S. history, was necessary to settle it in the United States. The industrialists won due largely to their greater wealth and their ability to manufacture the tools of war instead of having to import them. With this victory, the industrialists gained control of government as well as of the economy.

The Robber Barons Take Charge

It is interesting to note that when the United States was formed following the Revolutionary War, it was kept a loose federation of states, the various states retaining nearly all powers of governance in order to help ensure individual rights. Many of the men who signed the Declaration of Independence in 1776 believed this approach would succeed because citizens would realize the need to be "virtuous." As we remember, this was also Adam Smith's sentiment when he introduced laissez faire economics.

Cynicism set in rapidly. By 1787, when the Constitutional Convention was held to save the new country from civil war over trade issues, George Washington said, "We have, probably, had too good an opinion of human nature in forming our country." The other delegates now agreed that "people were, by nature, selfish," and tried to shape a government which controlled this selfishness, not allowing it to harm the general good, while, at the same time, putting the fewest possible restrictions on individual liberties. Thus, the United States has, in addition to the Constitution that creates and empowers an effective central government, the Bill of Rights which continues to protect individual liberties.

The U.S. system of governance is a precarious balancing act, but it works. The framers of the Constitution, led by James Madison, did a good job. Still, as we see even today, whenever the constraints are loosened, the Machiavellian humanists in society move quickly to take advantage. Thus, we recently had the Savings and Loan scandal materialize as soon as President Reagan loosened restrictions on the banking industry to encourage individual incentive. The same type of thing has happened whenever a "soft spot" has been found in the law.

The *robber barons*, however, were probably the best example in U.S. history of what happens when the power of the central government is corrupted and rendered ineffective, when pure laissez faire economics holds sway and the Machiavellian humanist faction is allowed to gain control.

Following the U.S. Civil War, which ended in 1865, the Republican Party, the party of the industrialists, dominated politics and, following Hamilton's lead, continued to coddle the wealthy manufacturers. These manufacturers rapidly turned the "laissez faire" approach into a rationalization for exploitation. William Graham Sumner, a Yale professor, played a lead role in introducing the concept of Social Darwinism to U.S. society. Though Sumner disagreed with Spencer on specific points, he was also a strong advocate of "the law of the jungle" and of the Social Darwinist version of laissez faire economics.

Sumner saw the main struggle as that between man and nature. Man's role was to overcome or to "beat" nature, playing by her rules. Sumner was more of a purist than Spencer. He did not believe that man had "natural rights" which differed from those of any other animal. The rules were the same everywhere in nature.

Sumner also said that human intellect was not adequate to deal positively with social problems and, therefore, that man should leave the solution of these problems to nature, which would solve them in the most effective manner.

Although by the latter part of the 1800s it was becoming increasingly obvious that Spencer's and Sumner's logic did not, in fact, reflect reality, supporters were eager to believe that because Spencer had borrowed his core theories from those of the great and thorough scientist, Charles Darwin, his conclusions possessed the same validity. Actually, very little scientific evidence had been gathered to support Spencer's hypotheses. Actually, what relevant evidence did exist had begun increasingly to refute them. The European countries enjoying the most rapid economic progress at this point in history were those in which government had assumed the most social responsibility.

Spencer and Sumner, however, never admitted to any doubt concerning their convictions. And despite the growing amount of proof that their arguments were extremely naive, the two spokesmen remained wildly popular with modern-day monopolists and would-be monopolists. In the United States, people flocked to their banner, businessmen defending the two with unceasing vigor.

The Social Darwinists were quick to point out, for example, that by 1887 laborers were making twice as much for 10 hours of work as they had made 50 years earlier for 12 to 14 hours. At the same time, however, they spoke strongly against mandating the payment of a "living wage," or one that provided for the basics of life, as opposed to the much lower, traditional wage determined by the market, by what they deemed to be "the laws of the universe."

Among those who celebrated the contributions of Spencer and Sumner were the robber barons. The *American Heritage Dictionary* definition of a *robber baron* is "an American industrial or financial magnate of the latter 19th century who became wealthy by unethical means, such as questionable stock market operations, or exploitation of labor, or political connections."

The U.S. economic culture, during the period 1860 to 1910, followed almost the identical cycle followed by the British economic culture during the period 1800 to 1850. Facilitated by the freedom inherent in the laissez faire approach, the strongest of the strong rose quickly to the top to dominate the marketplace and to force government to do their bidding. In the United States this ascendancy was even more pronounced and more vicious.

The robber barons, during an approximately 50-year period, changed the United States from a society of farmers and merchants to a unified industrial society. But they did so at the cost of great suffering. Their ranks included John Jacob Astor, Cornelius Vanderbilt, Jay Gould, Jim Fisk, J. P. Morgan, Philip Armour, Andrew Carnegie, James Hill, John D. Rockefeller, Collins Huntington, Leland Stanford, and James Cook. Many of these men began as immigrant children. All of them, with the exception of J.P. Morgan whose father was a banker before him, began poor. All of them were products of the strict, austere, Protestant tradition.

Most of the robber-barons-to-be left home at a young age to seek their fortune. Most tried various occupations, hoarding their pennies, finding pleasure only in work. Most of them were introverted, extremely intelligent men consumed by the challenge of making more and more money. They respected no one. Their only objective was to win, no matter what the cost to others. They were pure examples of modern-day Machiavellian humanism.

Yet, most of the robber barons, in their own way, were extremely religious. They strongly supported the Protestant teaching that one gained grace by working hard and that increased wealth was the evidence of such hard work. They believed (perhaps conveniently) that they were required by God through predetermination to do what they were busy doing. John D. Rockefeller, for example, explained his actions as follows:

> I believe the power to make money is a gift of God...to be developed and used to the best of our ability for the good of mankind. Having been endowed with the gift I possess, I believe it is my duty to make money and still more money, and to use the money I make for the good of my fellow man according to the dictates of my conscience.[1]

Obviously, Rockefeller had read John Calvin. At the same time, however, employees, for some reason, did not fit into his category of "mankind." Employees, instead, were like a herd of dairy cows, to be fed as little as possible and milked for as much as possible.

Concerning "...to use the money I make for the good of my fellow man,..." some of the robber barons, indeed, contributed handsomely. Many of our current colleges and universities, for example, especially those designed to deliver technical training, were originally funded by or received strong financial support from these men. Rensselaer Polytechnic Institute, founded in 1824, is an example. Other examples are the Massachusetts Institute of Technology founded in 1861, the Michigan Technological Institute founded in 1885, and, of course, the Carnegie Institute.

The more pragmatic purpose behind these donations to education was to help locate promising students and to give them the skills necessary to contribute to industry, thereby improving the fortunes of the barons, who wanted to use academia to enhance their own power and wealth. They also wanted leverage in the academic community in order to cut down on dissent. They discouraged the teaching of the humanities — philosophy, history, sociology — because such courses might stimulate the wrong questions and attitudes. They tried to use their power to get rid of teachers who openly questioned their activities.

John Jacob Astor, a German immigrant butcher's son, was one of the first barons. Astor learned the fur-trading business at an early age, eventually opening a series of outposts across the country to buy furs from and to sell liquor to the native Americans and frontiersmen. Astor then invested his profits mainly in New York real estate, building such an empire that his son eventually became known as "The Landlord of New York."

Cornelius Vanderbilt, an uneducated Dutch immigrant, worked as a boy on a ferry line. He built his fortune in shipping. As a businessman, even as a family man, he was extremely crude, harsh, and parsimonious. He allowed his wife, who eventually went mad, and their nine children to enjoy none of the benefits of his wealth.

Andrew Carnegie came to the United States as the child of a poor Scottish family in 1848. He began working at age 14 as a bobbin boy in a New England cloth mill, spending 12 hours a day in a dark cellar. At 15 he became a telegraph clerk, and eventually got into the railroad business, then into the steel business. Carnegie was reported to have never been satisfied with the efforts of his employees, constantly driving them. He was also reported to have been a "pirate," changing previously agreed-upon prices without a qualm whenever he thought he could get away with it. His rationalization for such actions was that he had to do so in order to remain true to the law of supply and demand, the core element of the laissez faire philosophy. Carnegie was totally against any form of government intervention. "Oh, these grand, immutable, all-wise laws of natural forces," he would lament, "how perfectly they work if only human legislators would let them alone."[2]

John D. Rockefeller was born the son of a wandering vendor of quack medicine who did little to support his family. John contributed to his siblings' survival by working on neighboring farms. He spent almost none of what he saved personally and eventually was able to loan $50 to a local farmer charging

7% interest. He was an introverted loner. Once he had grown up and was living on his own, if he went out at all, it was usually to church. Rockefeller was reported to have despised waste in any form. He apparently spent hours talking to his pillow while he lay in bed at night, compulsively seeking ways to cut costs in his growing empire of businesses.

Many of these men, including Morgan, Cooke, Huntington, Gould, Fisk, and Rockefeller, understood the value of controlling the financial books, the numbers. J. P. Morgan, of course, and Jay Gould worked their way up in the world of banking and finance. It was suspected that Gould's drive to fortune began with his growing skill at mismanaging the books of companies he had been hired to run.

It was during the Civil War that most of the robber barons received their big break. They began trafficking in the wares of conflict, often making unscrupulous deals which enriched them but which hampered the efforts of their side in the conflict. An example would be Vanderbilt renting rotten, unsafe ships for the transport of Northern troops at exorbitant rates. Another would be Philip Armour of the Chicago stockyards selling sometimes tainted pork to the military.

By 1870, the United States had become a serious competitor in the world marketplace. Carnegie had gained control of the steel industry. Rockefeller, now head of the Standard Oil Company, had developed a conspiracy, complete with a secret pledge, to take over the oil-refining business. He forced competitors to join and to play by his rules. If they refused, he drove them out of business, using any measures necessary.

By 1875, four men, the most powerful being Philip Armour, heading four companies, had monopolized the meat-packing industry and had reached an agreement to fix prices.

J. P. Morgan, the most powerful of all the barons, eventually saw the possibility of gaining control of the entire U.S. economy through the consolidation of key industries. He had taken charge of the banking industry, personally causing in 1891 a panic in the stock market that ruined thousands of investors and caused massive unemployment. When asked by a reporter during this episode, "If some statement were not due the public," he replied, "I owe the public nothing."[3]

So great was Morgan's financial power that in 1894 he actually helped keep the U.S. government from going bankrupt by loaning it $500,000,000. The following year he was asked to make another such loan for similar purposes. In both cases he charged an exorbitant rate of interest which the government was forced to pay.

Ownership of the railroads was less clearly defined; a number of the barons, including Morgan, battled it out. Railroad rates affected everyone — meat packers, oil shippers, steel shippers. When unfair rate structures began to affect the bottom line of these industries seriously, owners immediately called for government regulation, or resorted to violence. All the embellishments, all the laissez faire rhetoric went out the window.

These men generally "owned" the government during their reign. Politicians and political decisions were "bought." As railroad magnate, Collins Huntington wrote, "If you have to pay money to have the right thing done, it is only just and fair to do so."[4] Money flowed freely during elections. The concept of the "lobbyist" evolved during this period. It meant a discreet go-between.

This was Mark Twain's *Gilded Age*, when the rich were very rich and very ostentatious. Thorstein Veblen later coined the term "conspicuous consumption." In his 1934 book entitled, *The Theory of the Leisure Class: An Economic Study of Institutions,* he described the activities of those who consumed for the sole purpose of showing that they had more money than others. In accordance with the "economic man" model borrowed from Europe, they were the winners. A middle class existed and was growing, but the majority of the population still belonged to the laboring class, which enjoyed little if any opportunity to improve its fortunes.

However, those who had "won" and their apologists showed little sympathy for the laboring class. S. C. T. Dodd, for example, solicitor and a spokesman for the Standard Oil Company, said that poverty existed, "because nature or the devil has made some men weak and imbecile and others lazy and worthless, and neither man nor God can do much for one who will do nothing for himself."[5]

Labor Seeks a Voice

While laissez faire, hands-off economic policy in its purest form might have produced "the greatest good" in Thomas Jefferson's visualized agrarian society, it was obviously not capable of addressing the problems of an increasingly intense industrial era. The *scarcity mentality* still prevailed. The share of wealth siphoned off by the wealthy, contrary to Smith's prediction, was continuing to grow long after the amount necessary to satisfy reasonable needs and desires had been obtained. The relative share left to the workers continued to shrink. As Ricardo had said, they were being allowed to survive, but little more.

By 1885 labor was trying desperately to rally its forces. The robber barons, setting the tone for their associates and supporters in the business, political, academic, and religious communities, continued to show no doubt concerning the "rightness" of their ruthless pursuit of wealth. They continued to show no doubt concerning their right to get as much out of their workers for as little as possible. Finally, they showed no doubt concerning their right to crush employee attempts to improve their situation by organizing and striking.

Hoards of poor immigrants were pouring into the country. The barons strongly supported the Statue of Liberty's "Give me your tired, your poor...." But their motive was not quite as altruistic as that of the French who had given the lady to the United States as a gift. Many of the immigrants chose the challenge of the frontier, immediately moving west. But enough stayed in the Eastern cities to provide an almost endless supply of cheap labor. Workweeks of 60, 70, 80 hours were common. Laborers, including children, worked 7 days a week, often in unsafe conditions, often for as little as $1 per week. Carnegie's steel company in Pittsburgh set up a system to bring in especially poor Slavs and Italians because they were considered more docile and more willing to work extra hours without pay.

These people were generally uneducated and did not speak the English language. As a result of this inability to communicate effectively, combined with the heat, the constant noise, and the exhausting work in the steel mills, employees died daily. Carnegie's plant soon gained the nickname, "the slaughterhouse."

The barons did whatever they could to increase profits. In the coal mines, for example, they "altered" the weight of a required ton of shoveled coal from 2000 to as much as 4000 pounds. They kept their labor force as small as possible, overworking employees, then discarding them when they wore out and picking someone new from the line at the door.

Also, once again following the lead of Britain, the barons forced employees to live in housing provided by the company. Carnegie's "Painter's Row" in Pittsburgh held 500 people living in back-to-back houses with no ventilation; with cellar kitchens; with dark, overcrowded sleeping quarters; with no drinking water available indoors; and with no toilet facilities. For these accommodations workers were forced to pay exorbitant rents. In Pennsylvania mining towns the outhouses were lined up down the middle of the unpaved street so that they were the first thing you saw (and probably smelled) when you opened your front door.

The earliest strikes occurred in the textile mills of New England, the major issue being the 13-hour workday. From there, strikes spread to the mines, railroads, and steel mills, growing much more violent than those in Europe. Owners hired "toughs," frequently Pinkerton "detectives," to beat and kill strikers. The strikers fought back in the only way they could. They formed secret societies that began killing in retaliation.

One of the best known of such secret societies was the Molly Maguires, a network of Irish coal miners in the fields of eastern Pennsylvania. In 1874, the mine owners, led by Franklin Gowen, cut mine worker's pay by 20%. A 7-month strike ensued, but Gowen had stockpiled coal in advance to meet the anticipated shortages. Miners eventually had to give in and accept not only the 20% pay cut, but another 10% cut on top of that. Gowen labeled the workers who continued to protest his excesses the Molly Maguires. Members of this society were accused of stirring up discontent, setting off explosives, destroying mine property, and, eventually, of killing several mine foremen. Their leaders were caught, found guilty in a trial orchestrated by Gowen, and hanged. Such groups provided the labor movement with martyrs, but little more.

The alternative to violence, unionization, materialized more rapidly in the United States that in Europe. The first national labor organization, the National Labor Union, was organized in 1866. Its first major issue, interestingly enough, was an 8-hour workday. A law mandating the 8-hour day was passed in 1868 but could not be enforced. The National Labor Union folded in 1871 as a result of internal conflict and pressures from the outside.

The Knights of Labor (KOL) was formed in 1869, initially as a secret society, by Uriah S. Stephens. It maintained this secrecy until 1882 in order to protect members from being discriminated against. The organization strove to make every person his or her own master, to give every employee the ability to improve his or her quality of life. Its two main stated objectives were as follows:

1.   To change the existing labor relationship so that the depersonalizing and specialized aspects of mass production could be avoided; to halt or even reverse the advances of technologies which created this situation (shades of Ludditism);
2.   To attain moral betterment for employees and for society in general.[6]

By 1886, at its peak, KOL membership was approximately 700,000. Managers as well as all types of employees were invited to join the regionally defined network of "local assemblies" spanning the country. The governing body was the extremely paternalistic "General Executive Board" which made all important decisions and "instructed" the membership.

Leaders of the KOL tried to reintroduce the concept of Christian humanism to the workplace. They had four basic strategies in their drive for change. The first was political action. Representatives competed with the robber barons for the attention of government officials. The second strategy was to encourage the formation of both production and consumer cooperatives to increase workers' control over their lives and their livelihoods. The third strategy was to seek arbitration and to avoid strikes whenever possible because strikes were considered injurious to society as a whole. The fourth strategy was to educate workers and the general public concerning evils in the workplace and in society and to present the KOL ideas for creating an increasingly moral atmosphere.

The KOL called for the outlawing of convict and child labor; for equal pay to women for equal work; for the establishment of state bureaus of labor statistics; for stricter safety regulations; for compensation for those injured on the job; for weekly payment of salaries in cash; for a graduated income tax; for issuance of legal tender currency by the government directly to the people without banks acting as middlemen; for government purchase of railroads, telegraph, and telephone services.

A major target of the KOL was the railroad industry where, due to the amount of training, expertise, and teamwork necessary, replacing workers who had been fired was not so easy. In 1885 the Knights enjoyed their first taste of success. They forced Jay Gould's Missouri Pacific Railroad to negotiate contract terms. Although Gould had no intention of abiding by the language of the agreement and continued to discriminate against union members, labor had at least brought an owner to the table.

The downside of this union victory was that it helped consolidate the forces of the opposition. A "blacklist" was created. Employees were forced to take an "iron-clad oath" not to join the union. In May of 1886 a rally was held in Haymarket Square, Chicago. It was part of a nationwide strike in support of the 8-hour workday as a means of reducing unemployment. Somebody threw a bomb, killing seven policemen and wounding 60. Afterwards, the public, swayed by the robber baron–influenced media, accepted the barons' charge that the labor movement was out of control, that it was in danger of being taken over by anarchists. They rallied behind the barons' effort the crush the labor "conspiracy."

Severe measures were enforced. The Interstate Commerce Act, which disallowed "conspiracy in the restraint of trade," had originally been passed by Congress in the futile attempt to combat the excesses of the robber barons. The Act was now used to punish striking railroad workers, who by their actions (interrupting the flow of rail traffic by striking) were restricting interstate trade.

The KOL, partially because of its reluctance to act boldly to protect members in situations like the Haymarket rally, partially because of its paternalistic leadership style, partially because of the lack of government protection, began to lose its leadership role in the labor movement. In 1886 a new, more pragmatic organization called the American Federation of Labor (AFL) broke away under the leadership of Samuel Gompers. The AFL did not buy into the KOL moralizing. It believed that in order to win, labor had to play by the same rules as the owners, the same rules (or lack of rules) that the original Machiavellian humanists had played by. This was perhaps the true beginning of the adversarial relationship which continues to exist today between organized labor and management in the United States.

Unlike Stephens, Samuel Gompers was an advocate of free enterprise and technological advancement. Rather than changing the existing system, he wanted to support and to enhance it, but to do so for the purpose of improving the lives of workers rather than solely the lives of owners. Two major strategies were brought into play. The first was the strike. The AFL introduced the "sit-down" strike, workers standing or sitting idle at their workstations instead of leaving the factory so that replacements, strikebreakers, could not be brought in. The second major strategy was, instead of lobbying, to use the votes of workers as a way to influence politicians.

Rather than trying to bring all employees together under one banner, one philosophy, to be shepherded by leaders, the AFL allowed the various unions to maintain their own identity. Its role was not so much to guide and instruct these unions as it was to coordinate and support their activities, and to help them support each other's activities. The AFL focused on making direct, economic gains for the workers at the local level. It wanted to take as much profit away from the owners as possible and to give it to the workers. The AFL was not interested in changing or reforming society as a whole. Its main target was the barons, and it believed that while the barons were too strong to attack on a societal level, individual factories might prove more vulnerable.

One of the best-known confrontations between the barons and labor, which broke the power of unions in the steel industry for at least a decade, occurred at the Homestead Steel Works in 1892. The works was owned, again, by Andrew Carnegie. Although the factory was extremely profitable, in order to make it more so, Carnegie brought in Henry Frick who had run the coke industry and was a known enemy of the union movement. Before offering a new contract, Frick fortified the mill and hired several hundred Pinkerton guards to defend it. When they arrived by barge to take up their positions, the workers were waiting, complete with two cannons. A fierce battle ensued, resulting in numerous deaths, torture, a 5-month occupation of the mill by the workers, and the eventual intervention of the national guard. The workers were forced to accept the new contract. Frick and Carnegie became heroes among the barons and their supporters for their stand against anarchy.

Again in 1892 at the Bunker Hill and Sullivan Company mines in Idaho, workers went on strike protesting hours and wages. Strikebreakers were brought in and the battle was joined, the strikers trying, at one point, to blow up a mine with 750 pounds of black powder. The explosion killed and injured 20, causing the Idaho attorney general to state, "The mob must be crushed with overwhelming force."[7]

Public sentiment did not begin to shift toward labor until the Latimer massacre of 1897 in Pennsylvania. This massacre occurred when a group of several hundred miners began marching from mine to mine encouraging workers to strike in order to protest a wage reduction, an increase in the workload, unsafe work conditions, and to demand their rights as citizens. On the given day, close to 400 were on the march, many accompanied by wives and children. They carried no weapons, only an American flag.

At Latimer, the sheriff and 87 deputies, all junior executives of the mining company, blocked their path. A scuffle followed. The flag was grabbed away. Then someone yelled "Fire!" and the deputies began emptying their weapons into the crowd. In the end, 38 people were wounded, most shot in the back as they tried to flee, and 25 died. The sheriff and deputies were tried for murder. None was found guilty. The incident, however, received a great deal of publicity, and the nation reacted angrily.

Another incident that triggered the shift occurred in Lawrence, Massachusetts in 1912 during a textile workers strike. As the situation grew increasingly tense, the strikers had begun sending their children to other cities to protect them. The mill owners, afraid that this would arouse sympathy for the workers, had the police stop 40 children from boarding a train to Philadelphia. Instead, the children were to be taken to the municiple home for neglected children. The parents resisted, heads were broken, and 50 arrests were made.

By the early 1900s it had become quite obvious that neither Adam Smith's "invisible hand" nor Hamilton's trickle-down effect were working in the United States. The robber barons has begun consolidating industries into trusts and monopolies in an effort to avoid competition and to gain complete control of the pricing structure. By doing this, they totally neutralized the laws of supply and demand that they had once so strongly defended. The U.S. population had grown tremendously, along with the number of attendant social problems. Industry was now the major source of revenue rather than agriculture. Whereas in 1860 approximately 15% of the total population lived in cities, by 1900 that percentage had grown to nearly 40%. These people were tiring of a seemingly endless parade of depressions and severe recessions.

The robber barons shortsightedness contributed to most of the economic downturns. Depressions and recessions were frequently the result of their financial manipulations. The barons continued to reinvest in production in order to increase their wealth. At the same time, they continued to pay their employees as little as they could get away with, thus making it impossible for employees to purchase the things manufactured. In this instance, the law of supply and demand, once again, set in. When no one bought the steadily increasing numbers of products being shipped out to markets, the barons began losing money. In order to cut their losses plants were shut down, labor was laid off. But because they had lost their salary, the workers could afford still fewer products, so that the situation worsened.

. Government began moving to counter this situation. In 1890 the Sherman Anti-Trust Act was passed regulating the barons ability to consolidate companies. By the turn of the century, banks, insurance companies, and utilities were regulated or were on the way to being regulated. By 1900 most states were also regulating wages and the number of hour worked. Many states had reached the 8-hour workday with at least 1 day a week off to rest. Women were no longer allowed to work in mines. Children under 14 years of age were no longer allowed to work in factories. Company stores were no longer legal. Neither was discrimination against union members. By 1900 almost all states had boards of health and compulsory education. While in 1878 fewer than 800 public schools had existed in the United States, by 1900 there were more than 6000.[8]

Christian Humanism Makes a Comeback

Laissez faire was now being vigorously attacked on all fronts. The attack actually began in Germany during the 1870s when a group of economists started arguing that ethics could not be left out of economic formulations, that the "economic man" concept was false, that social welfare had to be a factor.

As we remember, the early empiricists during the Protestant Reformation period had said that values, because they were not quantifiable, could not be included in the search for truths upon which to build reality. The "new school economists" disagreed. They borrowed a quantitative tool, statistics, from the world of empiricism, of scientific exactness, to use in their effort to prove that it was absolutely necessary to take values and social considerations into account when making economic decisions.

This new (or perhaps a better word would be "rediscovered") school of thought was brought to the United States by a group of young economists who had traveled to Germany to study. When they returned they helped form what was labeled a "Christian school of political economy" which focused on the belief that man and his development rather than the accumulation of ever-increasing amounts of wealth should be the driving force behind economic pursuits on the national as well as the personal level.[9]

The new school advocated cooperation and teamwork, as had Robert Owen in England. It did not believe that a competitive, every-man-for-himself atmosphere in the workplace was the most productive. It used scientific research to prove its point. New school economists said that laissez faire economics might be an appropriate tool for breaking free of the domination of state regulation, but that as societies matured this approach had proved itself increasingly to be an impediment to development, rather than the key to liberation. They argued that in a relatively progressed society appropriate government intervention actually *increased* rather than *decreased* the degree of individual freedom enjoyed.

As a result of their beliefs and findings, the new school economists called for natural resource planning. They called for the government to take over certain industries vital to societal development including the post office, telephone service, electricity, and water service. They also, of course, supported the labor movement.

Francis Amasa Walker, a professor at Yale during the 1870s and 1880s, was considered to be the John Stuart Mill of the United States. He supported the laissez faire philosophy in general, but also saw a need for government regulation. He said that if competition were perfect, if it were truly ruled by the law of supply and demand, government intervention would not be necessary. But, he continued, as events had proved, such "perfect" competition did not exist. Those who gained power were frequently all too quick to use that power to pervert the contest and to prevent competitors from enjoying equal opportunity.

At this point, it might be of value for us to take the time necessary to define the concept of *competition*. In order to have true competition several things are necessary. One is a set of rules agreed on by all contestants. Another is a referee acceptable to all contestants responsible for enforcing the rules, be that referee Adam Smith's "invisible hand" or a government. A competition has two levels. On the first, on the field of play, we have a win–lose situation. Teams or individuals compete and try to beat each other. On the second level, however, we have a win–win situation. Everyone wins. In a sport, team members, although they might have lost on the field, benefit in the long run though physical, mental, emotional development. They benefit from the prestige of being members of the team and from interacting with the other players.

In an economic "competition," players on the first level, while "winning," while increasing their own wealth, do so in a way that benefits society (society being the second level). Such economic competitions, however, turn into *conflict* when the rules are ignored or are changed to benefit only some of the contestants, when there is no referee, or when the referee has been "bought" by some of the players and makes decisions to benefit only them. Conflict is a straight win–lose situation that too frequently turns into a lose–lose situation. Conflict is almost always detrimental to society.

Largely because the scarcity mentality remains dominant in our culture, conflict is what has evolved whenever laissez faire has been adopted as an economic philosophy. Eventually, populations realize that something more forceful than an invisible hand is needed to help define the rules and to referee the game. The church has long since lost most of its clout. The only other reasonable candidate in modern times is government.

By the turn of the century, then, the "welfare state" concept was rapidly gaining ground in the United States. The robber barons were growing old. Their reign, that of unbridled, unregulated laissez faire self-interest, had, once again, proved itself too simplistic an approach, too insensitive to shape an increasingly complex society. The president who did the most to help develop the welfare state concept was Theodore Roosevelt. When McKinley was assassinated in 1901, Roosevelt, a reformer who had been made vice president in order to neutralize him, took over. By 1902 he had begun to attack the great trusts in an attempt to prove that government was capable of regulating big business.

During the same year approximately 150,000 miners struck for an increase in their barely subsistence level wage. The industry appealed to J. P. Morgan, still king of the barons, to settle the dispute. Morgan refused to intervene until the miners went back to work which, of course, would have spelled their defeat. As national coal supplies dwindled, President Roosevelt took this opportunity to step in and force the two sides to arbitrate. Over the protest of Morgan and the barons he appointed a commission to investigate mine conditions as a part of the negotiations. The commission reported to the nation that conditions were unsafe, unsanitary, and, in general, appalling. The miners were awarded a raise in pay. A government bureau was set up to oversee the mining industry.

Roosevelt believed neither in "unrestricted individualism nor in socialism." He saw the welfare state as "a corrective to socialism, an antidote to anarchy." He believed that big business and free enterprise, with its efficiencies, was good for the national interest so long as government effectively monitored and regulated the process. He said:

> A blind and ignorant resistance to every effort for the reform of abuses
> and for a readjustment of society to modern industrial conditions rep-
> resents not true conservatism, but an incitement to the wildest radical-
> ism, for wise radicalism and wise conservatism go hand in hand, one
> bent on progress, the other bent on seeing that no change is made unless
> in the right direction.[10]

To combat depression, Roosevelt introduced public works projects. And in 1912 he called for a "living wage," for every employee, saying to those who protested, "The man who holds every human right to be secondary to his own profit must now give way to the advocate of human welfare which rightly maintains that every man holds his property subject to the general right of the community to regulate its use to whatever degree the public welfare may require."[11]

Thus, as in England, following the excesses bred by laissez faire, the pendulum of economic philosophy was now swinging sharply in the opposite direction, toward socialism. The United States was beginning its struggle to discover the best way to develop and release the positive, constructive potential of all its citizens.

The Third Alternative

One of the more interesting characters of this period was Andrew Carnegie, who, while a robber baron of the first order, also considered himself a

Renaissance Man and a thinker. He spoke frequently of leaving industry to follow other, more enlightening pursuits.

In 1889 Carnegie published his *Gospel of Wealth*, which introduced to the world his interpretation of the concept of Christian humanism. He equated wealth with intelligence, saying that the citizens who had accumulated the most wealth were obviously the ones best suited to deal effectively with social issues. He agreed with the new school economists that the pursuit of economic self-interest was not the solution to all problems. He believed that people also had to accept social responsibility consciously. He argued that while the laissez faire philosophy was the best guide for the generation of wealth, in terms of its distribution the fortunate themselves, without the intervention of government, should contribute all "surplus revenues" directly to projects that would benefit society as a whole — schools, parks, libraries, hospitals, etc.

What Carnegie preached obviously flew in the face of what he practiced. The man, however, must be credited with the realization that the current social decay had to be dealt with, lest it destroy the world in which he had been so successful. He had also realized that government was growing stronger, that government would soon take the lead in dealing with this decay if someone else did not step up.

Other businessmen who saw the benefit of such thinking were quick to help develop the concept of "welfare capitalism." Following Robert Owen's earlier example, they created insurance funds, libraries for workers, music halls. They build decent housing for their employees and, in some instances, instituted a form of profit sharing. All such efforts, however, were localized, each industrialist doing his own thing at his own work sites. And all such efforts were extremely limited when compared with the enormity of the problems being attacked. Despite all the positive publicity this "good will" received, therefore, it was a case of much too little coming much too late.

In terms of our exploration of socioeconomic theory, the main importance of Carnegie's contribution, the main reason we have mentioned it was that, coupled with Roosevelt's contribution, it allows us to define clearly the three alternative approaches to economic development. These approaches are — every man for himself (laissez faire/Machiavellian humanism); government control (socialism/Christian humanism); and individual moneymakers accepting social responsibility (laissez faire/Christian humanism). All three have inherent strengths and inherent weaknesses in terms of individual and societal progress. The challenge from this point in history on to the present, then, has been to find the best combination of the three.

Topics for Discussion

1. What factors were key in the early economic evolution of the United States?
2. What kind of personality do you think it took to become a successful robber baron?
3. Why did the American Federation of Labor survive while the Knights of Labor failed?
4. How do the obstacles faced by the labor movement today differ from those originally faced?
5. What were the original attempts by government to get the economy under control, how well did these attempts succeed?
6. What factors enabled President Theodore Roosevelt to successfully introduce his "welfare state" concept?

Notes

1. Matthew Josephson, *The Robber Barons 1861–1901*, New York: Harcourt, Brace, 1934, p. 325.
2. Sidney Fine, *Laissez Faire and the General Welfare State*, Ann Arbor, University of Michigan Press, 1966, p. 103.
3. Josephson, *op. cit.*, p. 441.
4. *Ibid.*, p. 354.
5. Fine, *op. cit.*, p. 98.
6. William Holley and Kenneth Jennings, *The Labor Relations Process*, New York: Dryden Press, 1997, p. 38.
7. *Ibid.*, p. 38.
8. Fine, *op. cit.*, p. 359.
9. *Ibid.*, p. 201.
10. *Ibid.*, p. 382.
11. *Ibid.*, p. 389.

7

The Late Industrial Revolution: Efficiency vs. Effectiveness

After Reading This Chapter You Should Know

1. How President Franklin D. Roosevelt helped improve the situation of workers.
2. How the labor movement grew, prospered, split, caused problems for itself.
3. When and why "management" itself became an area of study as a result of Joseph Wharton's ideas.
4. What "scientific management" is and how it revolutionized efforts to increase productivity.
5. Why Frederick Taylor eventually became disillusioned with owners and grew sympathetic to the union movement.
6. How the concept of "growth" affected management theory.
7. How Henri Fayol and Max Weber dealt with the problem of integrating organizations as a whole.
8. Who the early leaders in the human relations school were and what they taught.
9. How Mayo's and Roethlisberger's work at the Hawthorne, Michigan plant gave the Human Relations School legitimacy.
10. What Oliver Sheldon's contributions were in efforts to humanize the workplace.

Real Reform

As elections became more democratic, politicians in both Europe and the United States began focusing on social welfare reform. They wished to win favor with the economically lower-class population of voters, which was now expanding rapidly. During the late 1800s and early 1900s British parliament passed a wide range of work-related acts. One was a National Insurance Act, the first effort to provide universal medical insurance. A second included legislation to protect at least some workers against unemployment. A third, passed in 1908, created the original old age pension. Britain was also the first country to collect income taxes, at least part of which were used to help build a national education system.

So, once again, Britain led the way, this time toward reform. The United States continued to lag but, also, continued to catch up. Labor remained on shaky ground in the United States during the late 1800s and early 1900s. The right of workers to organize and the right to collective bargaining had not yet been recognized by the government. The court system continued to side with management. When a strike was called, any judge could issue an injunction forcing employees back to work, making the activity illegal and opening the way for police or troops to be sent in.

It was not until the crisis of World War I that representatives of labor were asked to sit down with those of government and management and to take part in planning efforts. Reform in the United States was also encouraged by the 1929 stock market collapse and the ensuing economic depression. President Franklin D. Roosevelt in 1933 introduced the "New Deal." Like his predecessor, Theodore Roosevelt, he started public works projects to provide jobs. He also championed the creation of a "welfare system," which would distribute government funds to the needy in an effort to feed money into the economy and to restart it in a way that benefited the needy.

In 1935 President Roosevelt shepherded the Social Security Act through Congress. Again like his distant cousin, Theodore, he stressed the right to financial security and to economic opportunity. He said that every individual should have the right to work, to a decent salary, to a decent home, to health care, to a good education, and to protection during old age. The Fair Labor Standards Act of 1938 set a minimum wage. It also put a limit on the number of hours people could be forced to work daily.

By the 1930s the union movement in the United States was rapidly gaining ground. A tremendous boost was given in 1932 with passage of the Morris–LaGuardia Act by Congress. This act officially recognized the right of labor to organize. It also disallowed the issuance of injunctions by judges unless specific circumstances could be proved. Then, in 1935, the Wagner Act was passed creating the National Labor Relations Board, a high-level administrative agency responsible for protecting the legal rights of labor. The act said that collective bargaining was in the best interest of the general public. It said that owners did not have the right to obstruct unionization efforts if correct procedures were followed.

The face of the union movement was also changing. At the end of World War I over 3,000,000 employees were members of a union; by the end of World War II over 9,000,000 belonged. A rate of growth like this, however, especially in such a varied and volatile population, never occurs without trauma. Corruption seeped in. Political extremists including communists tried to use the union movement as a springboard to power. Organized crime infiltrated some unions, including the Teamsters and the Longshoremen. Union leaders resorted increasingly to violence to force nonunion workers to join.

At the start of World War II union leadership pledged not to call any strikes. As the war progressed and the cost of living increased, however, unions did decide to strike, at times putting the war effort in jeopardy. One example is the Teamsters strike led by Jimmy Hoffa that idled thousands of trucks. Once again, unions began to lose the support of the public. Also, the movement had internal problems that were becoming increasingly serious. Due to mechanical advances following World War I a growing number of workers did not have to learn any technical skills at all. Their job was simply to push a button or pull a lever or screw a bolt onto a nut. The AFL (American Federation of Labor) refused to recruit these people.

As a result, in 1938 the CIO (Congress of Industrial Organizations) broke off under the leadership of John L. Lewis to represent unskilled labor, battling the AFL, sometimes with fists and clubs, for membership. The CIO pushed three central issues — job security, wages, workplace safety — and quickly grew to be the largest organizer of unions in the country.

Size as the Issue

Businesses during the Medieval period were organized with one level of management, the owner, and usually two or three levels of craftsmen. Because most businesses were so small, owners worked closely with the employees. Everyone was involved in every step of the input, throughput, output continuum with the exception, in most cases, of bookkeeping.

With the advent of cottage industries and the dispersion of the workforce, distance was created between the controlling merchant and employee levels. Responsibilities were more sharply divided. The merchants now took total charge of the acquisition and distribution of raw materials and of selling the finished products. Workers were responsible solely for production.

With the rise of manufactories and the rapid growth in size of the workforce, this trend toward the dispersion of responsibility continued. Large companies soon employed hundreds. The main challenge was now to make growing numbers of workers productive, and to integrate their efforts. The management structure of choice remained, not surprisingly, the hierarchy. But how could the steadily increasing number of levels and departments best be integrated? What skills should the managers at different levels possess? How should authority and responsibility best be allocated? How could employees best be motivated? These questions grew increasingly important.

In response to this challenge, a man named Joseph Wharton gave the University of Pennsylvania $100,000 in the year 1881 to create a "school of finance and economics." The purpose of this project was to make available to young men the skills necessary to manage large firms. While other business leaders had financed programs aimed at producing students capable of dealing with technical problems, Wharton's focus was on the financial management and the "social," or people, management aspects of business.

Joseph Wharton was, himself, an extremely successful businessman. He started as a apprentice bookkeeper with a countinghouse in the dry goods industry. Eventually, however, he shifted to metallurgy, making his fortune mainly in the lead, zinc, nickel, iron, and steel industries. The mineral-rich Lehigh Valley north of Philadelphia was the site of most of his economic activities.

Wharton eventually became a director of the Saucon Iron Company, later renamed the Bethlehem Iron Company, later renamed Bethlehem Steel, and triggered much of its growth during his period of leadership. He encouraged innovation and brought in military contracts. It was the growing pains of Bethlehem Steel that alerted him to the need to train future business leaders in the art and science of management.

At that time "commercial colleges" already existed. They offered a 3-month course in business arithmetic, elementary bookkeeping, and penmanship. Wharton did not consider this training sufficient. He believed that these schools produced, at best, "clerks" instead of the well-educated, well-rounded leaders necessary. Wharton thought that an "intellectual hiatus [existed] in the business life of the nation," that the economy was being run by a group of relatively uneducated, narrow-minded men.[1] While he was by no means a liberal himself, joining the robber barons to fight fiercely for the right to limit competition by fixing prices and controlling markets, fighting fiercely for protectionist tariffs, Wharton had enough vision to understand that as organizations expanded management systems would become increasing critical to productivity.

Because of his suspicions concerning the narrow-mindedness of current business leaders, Wharton also believed that a good liberal arts foundation that focused on the social sciences was critical to achievement of the required business-education breadth. Thus, instead of creating his own school, he contributed his start-up money to one of the leading liberal arts colleges of the time, the University of Pennsylvania.

Wharton had at least some roots in the Christian humanism camp. He insisted that students in the new program be lectured on "the immorality and practical inexpediency of seeking to acquire wealth by winning it from another rather than by earning it through some sort of service to one's fellow men."[2] Professor Robert Thompson, the first dean of the new program, carried this theme further by teaching that "grave injuries have been inflicted on the laboring classes by the conflict between labor and capital" and that in order to restore harmony between the two sides "profits should be shared." Thompson, however, did not go so far as to advocate the creation of cooperatives. Strong leadership was necessary to the success of modern companies, and cooperatives, in his mind, did not foster strong leadership.

The Birth of Management Science

Joseph Wharton also facilitated a second, major contribution to management theory by bringing one of the world's first management consultants, Frederick Taylor, to Bethlehem Steel. Taylor, a mechanical engineer, made his contribution during the latter part of the 1800s and early part of the 1900s. As with Adam Smith and Robert Owen he shaped one of the pieces key to modern-day management theory.

Taylor believed the two primary problem of production to be (1) the lack of standardization in all areas and (2) poor management practices. He worked to standardize and improve tools. He worked to standardize and improve technical systems. He worked to standardize and improve the relationship between workers, managers, and machines. His efforts in this latter area centered on the development and introduction of "scientific management," an attempt to apply scientific principles along with scientific rigor to the solution of management problems.

Taylor's overall philosophy concerning work could be summed up as follows:

1. "Break the work process into the smallest possible components;
2. Fit jobs into structures that clearly emphasize the duties and boundaries of each job rather than its part in the total process;
3. Whenever possible use individual or small group monetary incentives, gearing pay to output;
4. Subtract skill and responsibility from the job and make them functions of management."[3]

His basic strategy concerning responsibility was to centralize control. He developed the concept of the "planning room" where each day's production and all related activities were mapped out in detail.

Frederick Taylor was obviously an engineer. He was also a true individualist. Like Joseph Wharton, he was born into the Philadelphia Quaker "aristocracy." The fact that he was extremely intelligent became apparent during his early education. It also became apparent that he had a great deal of energy, loved to work, and was obsessed with detail.

Taylor was accepted into Harvard Law School. At that point, however, he decided to follow his own instincts. In 1874 he turned down Harvard and, instead, took a job as an apprentice pattern maker and machinist. He immediately observed and commented on the fact that the apprenticeship system, while teaching necessary skills, did not meet the *physical security* needs of most new workers because apprentices, during their first 3 to 5 years, received almost no salary.

When his apprenticeship ended, Taylor could find no work in his trade. As a result, he took a job as a common laborer. He became a lathe operator at the Midvale Steel Works. The Works then employed approximately 400, making it a large company for that era. It was after Taylor's promotion to the position of "gang boss" at Midvale that his real efforts and struggles began. As a lathe operator he had been part of an employee system called *soldiering*. In order to ensure that everyone had enough work, that no one got laid off, and that owners did not raise the piecework requirement for the same hourly wage, employees had agreed to underproduce, turning out, by Taylor's calculations, approximately one third of what was possible.

As a gang boss, Taylor fought for 3 years to stop this practice and to increase productivity. He eventually won, but only after instituting extreme, authoritarian, sometimes harsh measures. When a machine "broke down," for example, Taylor held the operator responsible, fining the person, sometimes heavily. When fines didn't work, he fired people.

It was during this battle against soldiering that Taylor realized how few standards existed, in terms of technology as well as management procedures. Concerning technology, the tools workers used, since their early development, had been highly personalized. They had been among the owner's most valued possessions, an extension of the owner, shaped to do the job as defined by the owner and to meet the owner's aesthetic tastes. Early machines, then, were understandably viewed in the same light, operators personalizing them, modifying them as they saw fit with little concern for the effects of these modifications on product specifications.

Concerning management procedures, production levels had been set haphazardly. There was no standard for a day's work based on well-kept records or scientific research. Also, lines of authority and areas of responsibility in terms of decision making had not been clearly defined.

It was at Midvale that Taylor introduced the "time study," one of the key techniques of scientific management. The time study involved a precise analysis of how long it took to complete a task. Steps in this analysis included:

1. Divide the work of a man performing any job into simple elementary movements.
2. Pick out any useless movements and discard them.
3. Study, one after another, just how each of several skilled workmen makes each elementary movement, and with the aid of a stopwatch select the quickest and best method of making each elementary movement known in the trade.
4. Describe, record and index each elementary movement with its proper time so that it can be quickly found.
5. Study and record percentages that have to be added to the actual working time of a good workman to cover unavoidable delays, interruptions, and minor accidents, etc.
6. Study and record the percentage that must be added to cover the newness of a good workman to a job, the first few times he does the job.
7. Study and record the percentage of time that must be allowed for rest, and the intervals at which rest must be taken, in order to offset physical fatigue.

8. Add together into various groups such combinations of elementary movements as are frequently used in the same sequence in the trade, and record and index these groups so that they can be readily found.
9. From these several records, it is comparatively easy to select the proper series of motions which should be used by a workman in making any particular article, and by summing the times of these movements, and adding proper percentage allowances, to find the proper time for doing almost any class of work.
10. The analysis of a piece of work into its elements almost always reveals the fact that many of the conditions surrounding and accompanying the work are defective; for instance, that improper tools are used, and that the machines used in connection with it need perfecting, that the sanitary conditions are bad, etc. And knowledge so obtained leads frequently to constructive work of a high order, to the standardization of tools and conditions, to the invention of superior methods and machines.[4]

What Taylor was suggesting seems relatively simplistic and obvious to us today, but during his time it was revolutionary, especially concerning the degree of exact, recorded detail required. And that was not all. Taylor added a second, equally radical dimension to his model that was even more daring, given the climate of the day in management circles.

After the bitterness of his Midvale experience, he had decided that in order to put an end to soldiering, in order to get workers to accept scientific management and to follow his procedures willingly rather than solely out of fear of punishment, management needed to introduce an incentive tied to productivity. Taylor did not initially harbor much respect for the laboring class. He said that laborers had a "natural instinct" to take it easy whenever possible. But he saw the illogicality of expecting laborers to work harder and more efficiently to improve the fortunes of owners while, at the same time, gaining no improvement in their own fortunes.

The result of this realization was Taylor's "task and bonus" concept. Workers were to receive each day from the previously mentioned management "planning center" written instructions describing what was to be accomplished, the time that was to be spent accomplishing it, and the step-by-step procedures to be followed. If they completed their task successfully within the allotted period of time, they would receive a bonus, sometimes as much as 30 to 100% above the going rate.

A second reward, if they were fast enough, was a shorter working day. If they took longer than the allocated time to finish the required work, no bonus would be received. If they took less than the allocated time, the bonus would be received and they could go home early.

All Those Opposed, Raise Their Hands

The logic underlying Taylor's "improvements" was radical enough to stimulate immediate resistance. On the one side, workers and their union representatives were displeased for several reasons. The first was that by increasing operational efficiencies Taylor was taking away jobs. At one point, during his consulting assignment with Bethlehem Steel Company, Taylor estimated that he could cut the workforce by three quarters. At another, based on his research, the number of employees shoveling coal was reduced from 600 to 140 while the average daily worker output tripled.[5] Also, the yard work staff was reduced from 400 to 150.[6]

A second reason for worker and union resistance was the further depersonalization of work that occurred when scientific management was implemented. Taylor was a "mechanist." He believed that the more closely workers resembled "well oiled machine parts" the better. He called for "cooperation" between labor and management, but cooperation to him was workers showing "unquestioning obedience" to managers. Taylor's own words were, "When he tells you to walk, you walk. When he tells you to sit down and rest, you sit down...and what's more, no back talk."[7]

Samuel Gompers, then president of the AFL, perhaps best presented the union's view of Taylor's approach to work when he said:

> So there you are wage-workers in general, mere machines — considered industrially, of course. Hence, why should you not be standardized and your motion-power brought up to the highest possible perfection in all respects, including speeds? Not only your length, breadth, and thickness as a machine, but your grade of hardness, malleability, tractability, and general serviceability, can be ascertained, registered, and then employed as desired. Science would thus get the most out of you before you are sent to the junkpile.[8]

Taylor, with his standardization and simplification of tasks, was also making the apprenticeship program unnecessary. Employees in this system needed little training and could start earning a full wage almost immediately. But, despite the obvious benefit of this change, unions balked. Apprenticeship was a key phase in the union culture, a "rite of passage," so to speak, and was difficult to give up. Union-backed bills were introduced in Congress during the early 1900s to outlaw the use of stopwatches, as well as the use of Taylor's bonus system on government contract jobs.

Taylor, in turn, considered unions in his ideal world to be an inefficient vehicle for improving the lives of workers. He saw union regulation as being detrimental to efforts to increase productivity. He understood the original need for unions. He said that so long as ownership continued its exploitive practices unions would serve a worthwhile purpose. But Taylor also believed that once scientific management was accepted in the workplace the confrontational attitude of unions toward management would be antithetical to the harmonious labor–management relationship necessary to improving conditions. By continuing to restrict productivity and to oppose management, unions would be hurting rather than helping the working person.

As Taylor matured, however, his opinion changed. Taylor began to understand that most business owners had little real interest in his proposed changes. (Do not forget that this was the era of Social Darwinism, William Graham Sumner being one of the most influential U.S. figures in the world of management philosophy.) The unions were at least willing to listen to what he said. Eventually, they even began to accept it. In 1920 Samuel Gompers, who had earlier been so opposed to the "mechanization" of work and of workers wrote:

> The trade union movement welcomes every thought and plan, every device and readjustment that will make expended effort more valuable to humanity....To the idealism and aggressiveness of the labor movement, the technical skill and the inventive genius of the engineer are fitting and needed complements.[9]

Taylor's desire to help the working man increased as time passed. In 1916 he himself wrote:

> [My work] is done entirely with the idea of getting better wages for the workmen — of developing the workmen coming under our system so as to make then all higher class men — to better educate them — to help them to live better lives, a worthy object for a man to devote his life to. It would seem to me a farce to devote one's whole life and money merely to secure an increase in dividends for a whole lot of manufacturing companies.[10]

His problems with the other side, the owners, arose partially from statements like this and partially from his increasingly belligerent attitude toward the smug resistance of the owners. Taylor was straightforward, honest, and honorable. He had little tolerance for what he saw as the short-sighted greed of these men, for their unwillingness to admit that a way more effective than bullying might exist to improve productivity. At one point, in extreme frustration, he wrote:

> Personally, my experience had been so unsatisfactory with financiers that I never want to work for any of them....As a rule, they are looking merely for a turnover. It is all a question of making money quickly, and whether the company is built up so as to be the finest of its kind and permanently successful is a matter of complete indifference to almost all of them.[11]

Lower-level managers, of course, were also very much threatened by this "intellectual" trying to tell them how to do their job, and balked at implementing his system. As part of his paradigm, Taylor had given them four specific responsibilities rather than the loosely defined ones enjoyed to this point. The first responsibility was to keep the records and gather the data necessary to the scientific redesign and improvement of the work overseen. The second responsibility was to select and train workers, developing their potential. The third was to ensure that workers followed the principles of scientific management. The fourth was to facilitate the efforts of workers by providing detailed schedules and the proper equipment. For the most part, managers refused to cooperate, unless forced to do so.

The attacks continued from all sides, wearing Taylor down until he eventually lamented, "I have found that any improvement of any kind is not only opposed, but is aggressively and bitterly opposed by the majority of men, and that the reformer must usually thread a thorny path."[12]

The Results of Taylor's Efforts

Academia was the first sector to acknowledge the value of Frederick Taylor's contribution. The University of Pennsylvania (with the encouragement of Joseph Wharton, of course), Dartmouth College, and Harvard, during his lifetime, incorporated scientific management into the curriculum of their business education tracts.

As his work progressed, Taylor also cultivated a number of disciples, some of whom became well known for their own contributions. One was Henry Gantt who developed the original "task work with bonus" pay system. He was also credited with "humanizing" Taylor's piece-rate system by introducing a guaranteed base salary to underpin the bonus. In his own work Gantt focused on developing the same type of standards for managerial work that Taylor had developed for hourly employees. As part of his project Gantt devised production charts and cost-monitoring systems that are still in use today. Gantt was the Taylor disciple who initially pushed to make social reform a major objective of the "engineering" school's work.

Perhaps the best known of these followers, however, was Frank Gilbreth who focused on the *motion* part of time–motion studies. He introduced the motion-picture camera as a tool for investigating and streamlining work activities. Using this tool, he and his wife, Lillian, cataloged 17 individual hand motions used in manual labor, identifying the most appropriate combinations for a variety of jobs. Perhaps his most famous effort was to reduce the number of motions necessary in the laying of bricks from 18 to 5, thus almost tripling the number of bricks that could be laid in an hour.

There was also a growing group of "efficiency experts" who claimed allegiance to Taylor but who, instead, catered to the desires of the owners and executives, doing exactly what Taylor refused to do, delivering "comfortable" pieces of the scientific management model instead of the whole. The arguments of these men, who advocated what became known as the "engineering approach" to management were, and still are, supported by the belief, which was emphasized during the Protestant Reformation, that work was a period of *sacrifice* during which employees were able to earn the money necessary to pursue pleasure and developmental activities during their nonworking hours. As Mitchell Fein, a leading consulting engineer and modern-day member of this group said as late as 1975, "Most workers do not come to work for fulfillment from work itself. They come to work to eat, to exchange their time, effort, and skills for what they can buy outside the workplace. ... They want to satisfy their material aspirations."[13]

Most executives during this period still practiced the Machiavellian humanism philosophy of management, the monopolistic philosophy, still followed the lead of the Social Darwinists, and would have agreed. Being of the "economic man" school, they were not interested in Taylor's social agenda. What they *did* appreciate was the efficiency-increasing techniques offered by scientific management. These techniques shrank costs and increased profits. But the part about sharing the new revenues generated, that part made no sense to them at all, and they ignored it.

As a result, employees were forced to continue working the same long hours. At the same time, productivity demands were raised because the new scientific techniques allowed workers to produce more. However, no increase in pay related to the increase in productivity was given.

It was the same, early Industrial Revolution story, the same old scarcity mentality thought pattern — get as much as you can for as little as possible. And if workers balked, well then, they could be replaced by others who had just been laid off by other firms due to increased efficiencies. It was a "win–win" situation for owners — the profit gained from increased individual productivity coupled with the expenses cut by a shrinking workforce — and a "lose–lose" situation for workers — more work required for the same wage coupled with loss of job security.

Social Darwinists liked Taylor's scientific approach for a second reason as well. By defining work processes in empirical, scientific, and, therefore, necessarily quantitative terms, it allowed efficiencies to be identified in an increasingly rigorous manner. But more important, it allowed owners and executives to turn workers into numbers, thus eradicating their human characteristics entirely. It was much easier to erase a faceless number than to lay off human beings with needs and emotions, with children to feed, a good work record, with fears about being unable to find another job. The quantitative approach allowed those with power to build a secure wall of digits between themselves and the lives they were affecting.

Finally, "scientific management," by focusing attention on the numbers in an acceptable (scientific) manner, encouraged industry to think solely in terms of "growth" when defining success. Growth, by definition, pertains to increase in size. Growth is all that numbers are capable of describing — growth in the bottom-line figure, growth in the number of machines in operation, growth in the number of widgets produced, growth in the number of facilities owned, growth in the Gross Domestic Product.

This emphasis on growth introduced another even more subtle, but again critical change in management philosophy. Up until this point in history, based on the previously discussed Newtonian belief that the universe was a machine created to do God's work, organizations were also viewed as machines, but machines created to serve the purposes of the owner. Machines, as we know, do not possess *values* (in the human sense of the concept). Therefore, they cannot define their own *purpose*. (Inherent values are necessary to the definition of purpose.) Rather, machines are given their purpose by their designers. And, obviously, moving down one level, the parts of machines do not have a purpose of their own either, other than that designed into them by the engineer.

Taylor, again, was a "mechanist" at heart. But by introducing techniques that allowed the *growth* of profits to occur through the redesign of work processes rather than solely through longer hours at less pay, he sowed the seeds which produced a critical shift in our management paradigm. While owners still wanted their companies and workforce to function "like well oiled machines," another, ultimately more important dimension had been added. They now wanted their organizations and the size of their workforce, as a result of functioning like well-oiled machines, to *grow.*

But machines cannot *grow.* They can be added onto; new pieces can be attached; but in themselves they do not have the ability to grow. Only living things can grow. Therefore, if growth had now become the major objective, it was no longer possible to think of companies solely as *machines* designed to serve the purposes of their owners. Living things, because they are alive, have a purpose of their own. Organizations, therefore, because they were now being defined as capable of growth, as being alive, had to be allowed to have a purpose of their own. The parts of the organization now had to be designed so that the organization as a whole could grow of its own accord. Serving the purpose of the owner was still important, but the needs and desires of the living, "purposeful" organizations now had to be taken into account as well.

This discovery led immediately to another problem. If organizations were now thought of as *purposeful,* then, as with any other living organism, as with a human being, for example, the activities of their often unruly, uncooperative parts had to be integrated. The brain handled this job of *integration* for humans, following a set of clearly defined and precise procedures. In organizations, the executive corps was created to fill the role of the brain. What was lacking at that point was the set of clearly defined and precise procedures to guide the activities of the parts.

Other Major Conceptual Contributors

In order to satisfy this need, several theorists soon stepped forward. One was Henri Fayol, another engineer, this time French, who offered a set of 14 management principles which fit neatly with Taylor's concept of scientific management. While Taylor and his disciples had identified the specific steps necessary to *complete individual tasks,* Fayol, and then Max Weber, identified the procedures necessary to *run entire organizations.* One could say that they, in effect, had applied scientific management to organizations as a whole.

Fayol's principles addressed the necessary division of labor, the necessary centralization of authority, the need for a well-defined chain of command, the tenor of labor–management relations, remuneration, discipline, and the need for clearly defined levels of managerial authority. While Fayol's principles encouraged the respectful treatment of employees, they more strongly emphasized the need for managers to be in charge, to give the orders, and to be obeyed, because managers were the ones who best understood the "purpose" of the organization.

Max Weber, a German sociologist and historian who did his work during approximately the same period as Taylor and Fayol, was another outstanding theorist in the quest for order in the managerial ranks, in the quest for procedures. Weber helped clarify the need to move from the mechanistic to the *organismic* perspective. He said that employees tended to display more loyalty to their owners (I am part of my owner's machine) or their immediate supervisor (I am part of my boss's machine) than to the organization as a whole (I am part of a purposeful organization. My responsibility is to dedicate my energies to the achievement of the overall purpose of the organization, rather than simply to that of my supervisor or the company owner).

Due chiefly to this lack of the necessary breadth of perspective, according to Weber, resources were *not* being used in the most efficient manner to achieve organization goals. Weber called for managers to be trained to remove themselves as the focus of employee attentions and to function in an "impersonal and rational manner." He called for a Tayloristic breakdown and simplification of tasks. He called for a strict, pyramidal hierarchy of authority. He called for a comprehensive set of rules and procedures similar to Fayol's that governed every aspect of every employee's job.

Thus, with Weber's more comprehensive perspective was born the concept of *bureaucracy* which centered on the depersonalization of the management function. At the same time that Taylor was depersonalizing the workplace at the laborer level, Weber was doing the same at the management level.

The Social Darwinists, and monopolists, of course, were extremely pleased with Weber's work (except for the part about the purpose of the organization being more critical than that of the owner, but, then, nobody is perfect). The bureaucratic, impersonalized approach to organization gave them even more control, and control was considered the key to winning.

It is interesting to note, briefly, at this point, how thought in other fields of social endeavor is influenced by and often mimics that generated in the economic arena. In the field of psychology, for example, during this same period, an American named John Watson is credited with having helped develop the "behavioral" approach, which is empirical, objective, and science based. He was reacting to "psychoanalysis," a more rationalistic, subjective, intuitive, introspective approach to understanding human psychology that had been fathered earlier by Sigmund Freud.

Watson insisted that psychological research, in order to be effective, needed to become more rigorous. He used the results of rigorous laboratory experiments to formulate his "stimulus–response" theory which said that emotional responses resulted from measurable physical changes in muscles and glands. He and others in the field, including Tolman, Hull, and B. F. Skinner, worked to prove that emotional reactions were learned through conditioning at a young age and could be changed through reconditioning.

Behavioralism, in turn, affected child-rearing theory. Parents were taught that in order to raise the most successful children, described as "well-oiled little machines," they should not confuse them with unplanned and excessive attention. Rather, they should condition the children to an exact schedule, carefully defining the amount of time spent together, carefully planning activities to be introduced during that time so that the right stimuli would be presented and eventually absorbed into the subject's psyche.

This child-rearing philosophy, which became extremely popular, could be viewed as the application of scientific management to the art of parenting. It could also be viewed as an attempt to prepare children to function in businesses managed "mechanistically," businesses where efficiency was the sole focus, and where attempts were made to manipulate employees with rewards.

Birth of the Human Relations School

There were, however, other sectors of society that did not buy into this new, hybrid *mechanistic/organismic* view of the workplace, this new emphasis on total managerial control, this ongoing attempt to dehumanize labor.

The most important of these was the "human relations" school of management theory. Human relations advocates believed that the key to increased productivity and profits was the realization that workers were not machine parts at all. Neither were they nonpurposeful parts of an organism/organization focused solely on growth. They were, instead, very much alive themselves, with very real purposes of their own besides growth, with very real needs and desires of their own. If management attempted to identify and to satisfy these needs and desires, the workers would, in return, strive harder to meet the objectives of the organization and to increase productivity. Tools and techniques were only as effective as the workers using them. The primary focus must be on understanding and motivating the worker as a human being.

This school of thought was obviously an outgrowth of *new school economics*. It introduced concepts based on the economic philosophy of men like Francis Walker, then converted these concepts into workplace applications. In the United States, Mary Follett and Elton Mayo were early movement leaders. Eric Trist, Douglas McGregor, Frederick Herzberg along with many others followed.

Mary Follett was trained in political science and economics but eventually became interested in the problems of business administration. A growing number of businessmen in England and the United States wanted to move beyond the economic man model, beyond the view that the generation of ever-increasing amounts of profits was the sole purpose of business, to move beyond the limited perspective of scientific management to something broader and more humanistic. Other industrial leaders were simply trying to find an alternative to the growing appeal of unions.

Follett urged management to allow decision making to become more participative. She said that the workers responsible for carrying out orders should contribute to the shaping of those orders. She said that such change would be best facilitated by breaking down the boundaries between units, developing strong cross-unit relationships so that workers did not have to keep "running up and down the ladder of authority." She said that it was necessary for units to begin thinking more in terms of the organizational "whole," rather than simply their piece, that to do so would encourage the necessary coordination.

Follett said that the lines between workers and managers in terms of responsibilities should be blurred, rather than being made more distinct. She also said that the lines between one's work life and "normal" life should be erased. It was wrong to think that people did not have the same needs and desires in the workplace that they had outside. Life in the workplace as well as outside should be *developmental*. Executives should focus on making it so for all employees.

Follett's belief that work itself should be developmental for employees was another revolutionary breakthrough, although, as with many revolutionary breakthroughs, people at first paid little attention to it. The role of *work* in society, people's feeling toward it has been slow to change. The ancient Greeks had actually considered work a "curse" to be avoided if at all possible; they had said that it was a "revenge" forced upon them by gods who did not like mankind. To the ancient Hebrews it had been "an expiation through which men atoned for the sins of their ancestors." The early Christians had seen work as painful and humiliating, as a "scourge for the pride of the flesh."

And the leaders of the Protestant Reformation, of course, had made hard work, no matter how unpleasant, a requirement for salvation.[14]

Work had traditionally been defined as sacrifice, either forced or necessary, as a negative experience. Very rarely before this point had anyone said that it should be developmental in nature, that employees should benefit directly from it in terms of the development of their individual potential.

The Need for Proof

Christian humanism was obviously making a comeback. What was missing was scientific proof that the human relations approach worked. It would obviously be much harder to produce such proof because the focus was now on motivating humans as living, emotional beings, rather than as machine parts or as brain-controlled parts of an organism. The number of potential variables that had to be taken into account in the research had increased dramatically, the task of isolating them had become much more difficult. For example, did Joe the machine operator produce more today because he was being treated better by his supervisor, or because his wife had kissed him good-by in the morning? Did he produce less today because his boss yelled at him, or because he had a bad hangover?

The first recognized effort to produce such proof was mounted by Elton Mayo and Fritz Roethlisberger of Harvard University. The project began as an attempt to measure the effects of increased lighting on the productivity of workers in the Western Electric Company Hawthorne Plant near Chicago. When Mayo and Roethlisberger took the project over in 1927 they added the length and frequency of rest pauses, the inclusion or exclusion of a lunch break, the length of the workday and week to the list of variables to be taken under observation.

Five women employees who spent their day testing parts were isolated with an observer in a workroom. There were no supervisors. The observer assumed that role. For the first several months conditions were kept the same. Nevertheless, productivity improved. When positive changes in working conditions were gradually introduced, productivity improved again, but much more so than expected. Then, when the positive changes were taken away, productivity fell off, but not to the extent expected.

The data were difficult to interpret. It was realized that other, unidentified variables, perhaps more important than those being tested for, were at play. The researchers found, eventually, that the most important of these unidentified variables was the nature of supervision. Previously, the women had been under strict supervision. They had been given a set series of procedures to follow. The supervisor had made sure that they followed them. Now, in the test room, with the experimenters running the show, the atmosphere had become more relaxed and participative. The workers were allowed to talk freely. When decisions were made, their input was solicited. They were given the opportunity to develop interpersonal relationships and to bond into a team. Finally, they were obviously receiving more personalized attention from management.

During a follow-up phase of the Hawthorne Plant research project a group of 14 men working together under normal supervision was studied for 7 months. The scientists functioned simply as observers. The objective was to define the culture of this group and the effects of that culture on productivity. The key discovery was that there was "more social organization in the factory than meets the eye." A self-imposed, strict code of behavior existed among the workers which strongly resisted rigid, nonparticipative supervision.

As at the Midvale Steel Works, laborers at the Hawthorne Plant had agreed to underproduce purposely in order to ensure job security. But more importantly, they had done so in order to demonstrate that they still had control over their lives. The research done here showed that "social considerations outweighed the economic and logical" and that "the chief function of the informal groupings which organized themselves on the working line was resistance to change or to any threat of change in their established routines of work or in their personal interrelationships."[15]

This part of the study showed the limitations of Frederick Taylor's research, and why the improvements he introduced were so strongly resisted by the workforce. Taylor's improvements forced the workers to accommodate to rapid changes which they had not initiated (or had any say in). By so doing, these improvements "robbed the workers of the very things that gave meaning and significance to their work — their established routine, their personal relations with fellow workers, even the remnants of their tradition of craftsmanship. All of these were [now] at the mercy of the consultant. Workers were now not allowed either to retain either their former traditions and routines or to evolve new ones of any probable duration."[16]

As a result of their findings Mayo and Roethlisberger argued that management, if it desired to win the cooperation of labor in achieving organization goals, must attempt to understand and work with the "non-rational" nature of the informal employee culture, rather than designing work simply according to the formal dictates of the organization.

Supporters of scientific management, of the economic man theory, of Social Darwinism, of course, leapt to the attack, and with some justification. A major point of dispute was the researchers' claim that monetary incentives played a minor role in performance improvement. According to critics, the data showed this claim to be inaccurate. Monetary incentives had proved, as always, to be a driving force. Mayo's interpretation had been influenced by his own, personal bias.

Another, more emotional, less rational objection was that the researchers' findings could not be accurate because, in calling for collaboration they contradicted reality, they contradicted the fact that "accommodated conflict" was inevitable between management and labor due to the "scarcity mentality," due to the limited nature of the profits which had to be split up and because, by definition, the roles of workers and managers precluded cooperation.

A third criticism, which inadvertently helped open the door to a giant step forward in management and organization theory, was a criticism that Mary Follett and Max Weber helped lay the groundwork for in their writings and speeches. The criticism was that Mayo and Roethlisberger had focused totally on the individual and his or her relationship to the small group, ignoring the individual's relationship to the organization as a whole. At some point, this latter relationship also needed to be taken into account.

Despite these criticisms, the main conclusion derived from the Hawthorne study, that relationships between workers and supervisors were more important than wages and physical working conditions in terms of performance, was hailed as "The Great Illumination" by human relations advocates. It provided impetus for a new approach to formal management education, for major changes in supervisory training, and for the development of employee-counseling services. Finally, it helped set the stage for the quality-of working-life movement which will be discussed in the next section.

Trying to Tie It All Together

One more person we need to mention who made a major contribution during this period was Oliver Sheldon, an Englishman who, like Robert Owen, spent his adult life in industry. Based on his experiences he realized that neither the engineering approach nor the human resources approach held all the answers, that the need existed to meld the best of both into a comprehensive whole.

Sheldon also strongly espoused the belief that the primary responsibility of management was "service to the community" and that the workers, as part of this community, were more important than the machines. The workforce had begun "awakening," at this point in history from the lethargy induced by nearly a century of exploitation. Europe had just passed through the severe trauma of World War I during which the old order had been shattered, creating cracks of opportunity for cultural change. The workers, sensing their chance, had begun demanding greater opportunity for self-development. They had begun demanding more leisure time during which to pursue it.

Sheldon pieced together a Christian humanist–oriented, developmental management philosophy that included the following.

1. Industry existed to provide the commodities and services necessary for the good life of the community in the volume required.
2. Industrial management must be governed by principles based on the concept of service to the community.
3. Management, while keeping industry on an economic basis, must achieve the communal objectives for which it exists through the development of efficiency in both the human and material elements of the factory.
4. This efficiency is developed by management through the use of science in management and the development of the human resources of industry.
5. Efficiency is dependent upon a structure of organization based on a detailed analysis of the work to be done and the facilities needed to do it.
6. The activities of management are divided into four functions: first, those concerned with the inception of manufacture as design and equipment; second, the actual operation of manufacture; third, those functions which facilitate the manufacture which are transport, planning, comparison, and labor; fourth, those functions necessary to the distribution of the product as sales, planning, and execution.
7. The use of scientific methods for the economical utilization of the people and the things of the factory involves the following: first, the use of research and measurement in the activities which management undertakes or controls; second, the preparation and use of definitions for the makeup of each item of work; third, the determination of references and working standard for the justifiable and precise determination of desirable achievement; fourth, the institution of these standards to ensure the most economical methods of production and management.
8. The policy of responsibility to the community demands certain practices in regard to the human element of production. Associations of workers must be recognized as long as they are not detri-

mental to society and their self-development toward the goal of service to the community should be facilitated. An effort should be made toward the promotion of individual and corporate effectiveness of effort through leadership and equitable discipline. In relation to the worker as an individual, the following rules should be followed. First, all the workers should share in deciding the conditions of work. Second, the workers should receive a standard of living in keeping with the civilized community. Third, the worker should have adequate leisure time for self-development. Fourth, the worker should be secure from involuntary unemployment. Fifth, the worker should share in industrial prosperity according to his or her contribution. Sixth, a strict spirit of equity should be found in all relations between labor and management.[17]

In sum, Sheldon's contribution reintroduced the belief, which had been losing ground since the Medieval period, that the major responsibility of business was to the community. He also produced an overall philosophy of management that gave management a distinct identity, one that remains applicable in modern times. Finally, and most important from our perspective, Sheldon realized the need to somehow wed the feuding camps of scientific management and human relations. He knew that neither could stand by itself, that they were two sides to the same coin, that both held ingredients critical to success. The question was, however, when the combatants stood at completely opposite ends of the spectrum and seemed quite unwilling to budge, "How do we encourage such a union, or reunion?"

At this point, a theoretical breakthrough was obviously necessary.

One other comment should be made before we move on. This again concerns the "spill-over" of management philosophy into other social sciences. Earlier, we discussed the psychological school of "behaviorism," its relationship to scientific management, and its effects on child raising. In 1945 a doctor named Benjamin Spock published a modest book, *Baby and Child Care*, on the same subject that became an instant success and is still extremely popular. Spock said, basically, that instead of depending on scientific research, instead of trying to condition our children to be "perfect" through reinforcement and rigid schedules, we should follow our instincts, react naturally to what we see happening, treat the children the way we would wish to be treated ourselves.

This was pretty much what Follett, Sheldon, and others in the human relations school of management had been saying. Application of these principles in the home, however, was much easier than implementation in the workplace. Advocates of the human relations philosophy in the workplace obviously had some very serious obstacles to overcome, obstacles parents did not have to deal with. These included the lingering scarcity mentality, the competitive environment still found and encouraged in management circles, the ingrained antagonism between labor and management, the efficiency-at-all-costs mind-set that still appealed to many.

A start back toward Christian humanism in the workplace had been made, but success, if it was possible, remained a long way off.

Topics for Discussion

1. What measures did President Franklin Roosevelt take to improve the situation of the worker and how was he able to implement them?
2. Why did the labor movement frequently become its own worst enemy?
3. What prompted Joseph Wharton to start an academic program that focused on the improvement of management skills?
4. How did Frederick Taylor propose to improve productivity?
5. Why did both management and labor have trouble accepting the changes Taylor suggested?
6. Why were Fayol's and Weber's contributions important?
7. What were the contributions of the early leaders of the human Relations School?
8. Are student's companies run mechanistically or organismically?
9. To what degree have Sheldon's ideas been realized in the modern workplace and society?

Notes

1. Steven Sass, *The Pragmatic Imagination: A History of the Wharton School,* New York: Philadelphia: The University of Pennsylvania Press, 1982, pp. 19–20.
2. *Ibid.,* p. 38.
3. *Ibid.,* p. 36.
4. American Society of Mechanical Engineers Paper, "The Present State of the Art of Industrial Management," 1912 (Taylor Collection).
5. Pamela Lewis, Stephen Goodman, and Patricia Fandt, *Management: Challenges in the 21st Century,* New York: West Publishing, 1995, p. 44.
6. Sass, *op. cit.,* p. 18.
7. Sudhir Kakar, *Frederick Taylor: A Study in Personality and Innovation,* Cambridge, MA: The MIT Press, 1970, pp. 145.

8. *Ibid.*, p. 183.

9. H. B. Drury, *Scientific Management: A History and Criticism*, New York: Columbia University Press, 1922, p. 29.

10. Taylor to Porteenar, June 10, 1916 (Taylor Collection).

11. Frank B. Copley, *Frederick W. Taylor, Father of Scientific Management*, Vol. 1, New York: Harper and Bros., 1923, p. 338.

12. Kakar, *op. cit.*, p. 182.

13. David Whitsett and Lyle Yorks, *From Management Theory to Business Sense*, New York: AMACOM, 1983, p. 62.

14. Kakar, *op. cit.*, p. 76.

15. Luther Gulick and L. Urwick, *Papers on the Science of Administration*, New York: Institute of Public Administration, 1937, p. 155.

16. *Ibid.*, p. 156.

17. Claude S. George, *The History of Management Thought*, Englewood Cliffs, NJ: Prentice-Hall, 1968, pp. 125–127.

8 Bringing the Industrial Revolution Era into Perspective

After Reading This Chapter You Should Know

1. Why Adam Smith, Robert Owen, and Frederick Taylor together can be considered the most important shapers of the early workplace.
2. Why idealism can sometimes lead to bad results.
3. How and why the various camps — Machiavellian humanism, Christian humanism, mechanism, human relations — divided.
4. What "adolescent arrest" is and its workplace relevance.
5. To what psychologists attribute the Machiavellian humanist mind-set.

The Alternatives Jell

The early Industrial Revolution, although it lasted only approximately 50 years in both Western Europe and the United States, was a period of rapid and frequently traumatic change which affected every segment of society. It made obvious the waning power of the church to enforce traditional values once people had tasted the opportunities and benefits wealth allowed. It forced government to redefine its role, to shift its allegiance from owners to workers and from increasing the opportunity of the few to protection of the many. It forced the evolution of public education as a means of providing employees with the necessary skills.

The early Industrial Revolution was, at the same time, one of the most glorious periods in the history of Western civilization and one of the darkest. It unleashed a stream of creative energy that has swelled rapidly and without pause ever since. It also, however, in many instances condoned, even encouraged a type of exploitation more savage, more degrading than slavery. Because slaves were usually purchased, the owner had at least an investment to protect. Industrialists during the early Industrial Revolution were saddled with no such concern. Workers could be used in that way which best maximized profits and, when worn out, could then be discarded and replaced at no additional expense.

This attitude, generally accepted in the business sector, was encouraged by a galaxy of popular rationalizations, many of them distortions of the contributions of people whose aim had initially been to improve the lot of both the individual and society. Those rationalizations included the Protestant work ethic, Calvin's theory of predetermination, Adam Smith's theory of laissez faire economics, Malthus's theory of population expansion, utilitarianism, the concept of economic man, Spencer and Sumner's concept of Social Darwinism, and, finally, Frederick Taylor's scientific management. The rationalizations had been piling up for at least 400 years, and, when interpreted correctly, had allowed, frequently even encouraged owners not to factor the welfare of workers into their quest for ever-increasing personal gain.

While the thinking of a great number of participants helped shape the early Industrial Revolution, the contributions of three men — Adam Smith, Robert Owen, Frederick Taylor — stand out in terms of our discussion. Adam Smith gave us rules of the game for economic development which, with varying degrees of modification, have withstood the test of time and are currently being followed by every industrialized nation in the world. Robert Owen defined and demonstrated the approach to management that most effectively utilized employee potential. Very little that is happening in modern-day organizations in terms of innovative management, in terms of the "humanization" of the workplace does not find at least some roots in Owen's textile mill at Lanark, in his concept of cooperatives, or in his writings. Frederick Taylor made science the friend of productivity by demonstrating how scientific method could be used to measure and increase the efficiency of both machinery and the individual laborer and, therefore, how it could be used to improve the bottom line.

Economic theory, management theory, and production theory are the three cornerstones upon which the modern business world has been built.

At least two of these, however, have been used for purposes other than those intended by their originators. While Adam Smith saw the laissez faire approach to economics as a means of benefiting society by unleashing individual potential, others saw it simply as license to focus entirely on self-interest, as license to get away with anything they could. While Frederick Taylor saw scientific management as a vehicle for increasing productivity so that workers as well as owners could benefit, many owners saw it simply as a way of getting more work and squeezing more profit out of labor.

The problem was that although these three men were obviously brilliant, although they obviously made valuable contributions, all three suffered from the same weakness. That is, they were all idealistic. They did not take the frailties of the human condition into account when developing their models. The logic of their arguments was so obvious, so positive, so compelling to their own minds, that they could not help but assume that this logic would be inescapable to others. Each one of these men believed that people would be willing to share, that they would see the advantages of sharing. Owen even proved the advantages of sharing with his cooperative concept. But the cooperatives were isolated experiments. Most did not last very long.

So, although a great deal of good has come from the contributions of especially Smith and Taylor, a great deal of harm has also resulted. These men obviously did not understand the staying power of the scarcity mentality. They thought that it and the attitudes it produces could be overwhelmed and dissipated by the generation of increased wealth alone. In thinking this, although well ahead of their time, they played right into the hands of the Machiavellian humanists. This might actually have been unavoidable. Members of the human species have traditionally shown an uncanny knack for turning change, no matter what its original intent, to their own advantage.

Of course, there was a reaction. Christian humanism had been on the defensive for most of the early Industrial Revolution. But once the shortcomings of the Machiavellian humanism approach became unavoidably obvious, Christian humanists launched an aggressive assault on the "convenient" logic upon which most current management theory was based. Union organizers took the lead. These people were not intellectuals or people interested in economic philosophy. Rather, they were men who had spent their lives dealing directly with and feeling the pain of exploitation. It was obvious to them from personal experience that what was going on in the workplace was not fair, and they wanted to change it as rapidly as possible using whatever means necessary.

Academics were next to join the ranks of reformers, attacking the logic of men like Spencer, Taylor, Fayol, Weber, supporting their attack first with theory, then with research. The new school economists, as well as Mary Follett, Oliver Sheldon, Francis Walker of Yale, Elton Mayo and Fritz Roethlisberger of Harvard, now called the human relations school, led the charge. Their approach was different from that of the union leaders. Rather than a direct confrontation, rather than head-butting, the academicians said that their purpose was to improve overall productivity so that *everyone* would benefit. In order for this approach to work, however, they said that management had to start treating employees more reasonably, as human beings rather than as machine parts.

So now, actually, two battles were raging. The first involved the conflict between the Machiavellian humanists and the Christian humanists. It had to do with ultimate societal values and reached back at least to the Renaissance. The second, newer struggle, which Frederick Taylor more than anyone else was responsible for kicking off, was between the "efficiency-at-all-costs" mechanists and the "employees-come-first" human relations types. This struggle had to do more with management philosophy and concerned the best way to increase company profitability.

Alliances were rapidly formed between the various camps. The Machiavellian humanists were quick to adopt the mechanistic viewpoint as complementary to their own. The Christian humanists automatically sponsored and supported efforts of the human relations school. But while the Machiavellian humanists had little use for the concepts and findings of the human relations school, the Christian humanists understood the value of the quantitative tools developed by the mechanists, incorporating them into their models as well. They incorporated them, however, mainly as a *support* to the achievement of employee objectives, both work-related and personal, rather than as the dominant player in the workplace.

The Fundamental Argument Revisited

Which brings us back to the fundamental argument of this book, the ongoing argument between the Machiavellian humanists and the Christian humanists, although a lot of the former have probably never heard of Machiavelli and a lot of the latter are not Christians. Throughout this book we have tracked the effects of these two groupings on the workplace. The two personality types have exist together, have worked together, but have been at odds in terms of their objectives and values.

Machiavellian humanists are, by definition, more self-centered. Their objective is to improve their own situation, no matter what the cost to others. This does not necessarily mean that they will try to destroy the careers of co-workers or to destroy the companies for which they work. Often Machiavellian humanists realize that they benefit most by cooperating with others. It does mean, however, that when an opportunity arises to improve their own situation at the expense of others or at the expense of the company, they do so without hesitation.

Christian humanists, on the other hand, are more inclined to take into account the effects of their actions on the whole. In religious terms, they are more inclined to follow the Golden Rule, They are more willing to sacrifice a degree of personal gain so that everyone might benefit. They realize that by helping others to develop individual potential and the ability to contribute, they are helping themselves as well.

History has shown that organizations run by Christian humanists benefit society more, at least in the long run. Yet, the Machiavellian humanist presence in the business world has remained strong. Actually, it has remained strong in almost every sector of society, although in the business sector the results of this mind-set are usually more obvious.

Where do these people come from, the Machiavellian humanists? What makes them different from the majority of us? To what can their success be attributed? Are they born with these tendencies? Is it in their genes? Sigmund Freud said that as infants we are interested only in immediate self-gratification. We take what we want, not caring about the effects of our actions on others. As we mature, however, we begin to change, begin to worry about the opinions and needs of those with whom we interact. As a result, we become more considerate and begin to share. This new attitude helps us function more effectively, first as a member of our family and then as a member of society.

Is this original, focused need for self-gratification generally stronger in some people than in others, so strong that they never successfully learn to control and moderate it? Or is the difference we see solely the result of environmental stimuli, of childhood experience, of the way parents treat, or mistreat, us, of emotional or physical trauma so severe that we spend the rest of our lives obsessively pursuing the gratification of certain basic, unmet needs? The robber barons, for example, with the exception of J. P. Morgan, were all born poor. Did the deprivations suffered from poverty twist their individual psyche so much that even when they had become the wealthiest and most powerful men in their country, they were not satisfied with the piles of gold they sat upon but blindly kept battling for more?

The counterargument, of course, is that plenty of people who have been born poor, when they have gained the opportunity to develop their potential, have done so in ways that showed them to be Christian humanists. Therefore, we must assume that while poverty might contribute to such behavior, it is probably not the determining factor. Probably the determining factor is a combination of things, genetic as well as environmental, which has not yet been spelled out, or which cannot be spelled out due to the incalculable number of individual variables involved.

What we can suggest at this point, however, is that adolescence is the first developmental period during which such tendencies are allowed to surface. It is during adolescence that the Machiavellian humanist first gains license to feed his or her untamed need for gratification openly, to grab from others what is desirable, to "win" by "beating" those who are seen as standing in the way.

In the animal world, of which humans are part, adolescence is a time of testing, of discovering one's strengths, one's place in the "pack." This is done through competition with peers. Young males tend to be more aggressive, at least physically. Young rams butt heads. Young male monkeys, bears, tigers, humans wrestle, strut, flex, compete for the attention of females. The objective is to win, to defeat the opponent physically, intellectually, emotionally. Human society understands the value of, the need for such behavior as part of the maturation process. It sets up activities such as organized sports and spelling bees to encourage it.

But human society also understands that healthy individuals must eventually move beyond this testing period, this intensely competitive stage. Normal people, as they continue to mature, eventually develop enough of an acceptable self-image, become comfortable enough in a chosen social role that they no longer feel the need to butt heads. They then begin to focus more on improving themselves, rather than on beating their peers. They begin to look inward, instead of outward at everyone else. An analogy might be a footrace. While the adolescent contestants are constantly looking around to see who is behind them, who they have to catch, the more mature contestants are staring straight ahead, toward the finish tape, concentrating on doing their own personal best.

The psychologist, E. H. Erickson, describes the transition we are talking about as follows. "In this final stage, the healthy individual achieves a sense of himself as a whole person. He has a perspective on the life cycle and its meaning; he understands something of the significance of being a human being amongst other human beings."[1]

The quest for this "arriving" has been one of the major themes throughout the history of literature. W. Somerset Maugham's *The Razor's Edge*, Lawrence Durrell's *Alexandria Quartet*, Leo Tolstoy's *War and Peace*, T. H. White's *The Once and Future King*, J. D. Salinger's *The Catcher in the Rye*, and Robin McKinley's *The Hero and the Crown* are but a few examples among thousands of books that have focused on it.

The problem occurs when people are unable to make this transition, when they get stuck in adolescence because they cannot get beyond the battle for self-gratification, because they cannot develop an acceptable self-image, because, due to their lingering self-centeredness, they cannot develop an acceptable role in society. As a result such people spend the rest of their careers locked into an adolescent mind-set, butting heads and competing, frustrated by their inability to progress. As a result, such individuals spend the rest of their lives taking their frustration out on others.

Another well-known psychologist, Abraham Maslow, who was mentioned previously in Chapter 4, sets a related frame of reference for defining this problem with his "Hierarchy of Human Needs." According to Maslow, as we have said, our most basic needs are physiological, those necessary to *physical survival*. These needs include food, water, air, shelter. Then, on the second, also basic, level of the hierarchy are what Maslow calls *safety needs*, those necessary to our emotional survival. These include the need for "emotional security, stability, dependency, protection, freedom from fear, from anxiety and chaos." But at the same time they include the need for an acceptable and sheltering degree of "structure, order, limits, strength in the protector."[2]

On the third level of the hierarchy, moving upward from this foundation and progressing chronologically in terms of human development, is the need for *love and belongingness*. This stage involves efforts to become an integral part of both the family and the peer group. This level moves us into adolescence.

It is here, at the adolescent level, that we also begin our struggle to gain *esteem*, Maslow's fourth level. Maslow describes this struggle as follows:. "All people in our society [with a few pathological exceptions] have a need for a stable, firmly based, usually high evaluation of themselves, for self-respect, for self-esteem, and for the esteem of others." This level relates to the height of adolescence when competition is at its fiercest. Maslow continues, "Satisfaction of the self-esteem need leads to feelings of self-confidence, self-worth, strength, capability and adequacy, of being useful and necessary in the world. But thwarting of these needs produces feelings of inferiority, of weakness, and of helplessness. These feelings, in turn, give rise to either basic discouragement or else compensatory or neurotic behavior."[3]

If our self-esteem needs are satisfied, we can then move on to Maslow's fifth and final level, *self-actualization*. This level concerns the realization of one's potential. It is here that we begin to turn inward, that we begin to concentrate more on the enhancement of our strengths, on the improvement of our weaknesses, on the enrichment of our lives, and, as part of that, on the enrichment of other people's lives.

However, and this is key, we can reach the level of self-actualization only if all other needs have been met. They are foundational. None can be skipped over or dealt with in a partial fashion. Until they are solidly in place, we cannot move upward. And if they are eventually pulled out from under us, if, for example, we lose our job and are suddenly in danger of starving, we revert to a previous level, perhaps all the way back to the physiological level, and stay there until the involved needs are once again satisfied.

Coming Up Short

One might assume that Christian humanists have succeeded in reaching Maslow's level of *self-actualization* or are well on their way and are confident of reaching it. Machiavellian humanists, on the other hand, are stuck at the *love and belongingness* or, more likely, at the *self-esteem* level with little hope of progressing. They strike out in their frustration. They demand that they be the center of attention, that people bow down to them so they can at least pretend to be fulfilled. When things go wrong, they look for scapegoats because they are too scared to face the truth, which is that they are incapable, for some reason, of filling their current needs and making it to the last, most desirable level of the hierarchy.

While it is right to feel sorry for the Machiavellian humanists, the amount of damage they do in the workplace and in society in general has been well documented in this book and in many others. Thus, we had Andrew Carnegie who was never satisfied with anyone's performance, no matter how successfully they completed a task, who had to keep driving workers in order to demonstrate his "success." Thus we had John Jacob Astor, who respected no one, who allowed no one else to enjoy his success, not even his own family. Thus we have J. P. Morgan and his "I owe the public nothing" statement.

Thus, historically, we have had a long line of owners and CEOs whose only objective has been to make as much money as possible and to pay workers as little as possible, no matter how wealthy they have become, no matter how much suffering they have caused. Thus, we have had another long line of apologists who have spent their time fawning over such men and their "strength," rationalizing and applauded their behavior.

The business sector is where these incomplete people fit the best. It is here that the head-butting, the always competitive mind-set is most acceptable. When I say "competitive" in this context, I am not talking about competition between companies. That kind of competition is necessary to the free-enterprise system if it is to remain healthy. The kind of competition I'm talking about is that which rages between employees within individual companies, especially between managers. The kind of competition I am talking about is in-house competition which, according to modern-day guru Peter Drucker is usually fiercer and much less ethical than that between companies.

The Machiavellian humanist's strengths are most effective in such an environment, more so than those of the Christian humanist. When someone whose objective is to beat those he is working with goes up against someone whose objective is to help co-workers, the outcome is usually easy to predict. The helper shares resources. The fighter hoards them, takes whatever is offered — information, energy, expertise — while giving as little as possible. The helper pitches in whenever co-workers are having problems. The fighter steps back and tries to figure out how best to benefit from the situation. The helper tries to make co-workers look good. The fighter, when the opportunity arises, tries to make them look bad. The helper focuses on his or her job. The fighter focuses on understanding and manipulating the political system of the organization.

Such behaviors have been encouraged by a reward system that has traditionally pitted people against each other by reinforcing the scarcity mentality. Such behaviors have been encouraged by Machiavellian humanists who have fought their way to the top, then surrounded themselves with others of their kind, needing the reinforcement of like-thinkers, of direct reports and board members just as incomplete and desperate as themselves who reinforce the illusion of success.

Such bosses are good at maintaining this illusion, this image. As M. Scott Peck, author of *People of the Lie* says, "We see the smile that hides the hatred, the smooth and oily manner that masks the fury, the velvet glove that covers the fist. Because they are such experts at disguise, it is seldom easy to pinpoint the maliciousness."[4] Later he continues, "They are men and women of obviously strong will, determined to have their own way. There is a remarkable power in the manner in which they attempt to control others."[5] And still later, "They may willingly, even eagerly undergo great hardship (working extra hours, giving up family life for the benefit of the company) in their search for status. It is only one particular kind of pain that they cannot tolerate, the pain of their own conscience, the pain of the realization of their own...imperfection."[6]

How, then, do we deal with this situation? It is a bit frightening to think about how many of our companies, how much of our economic history, how much of our business philosophy have been and still are being shaped by people who are quite possibly suffering from *adolescent arrest*. It is equally frightening to realize that these people are deemed by psychologists to be the most difficult to reach and to help because of their fears, because of their elaborate defense mechanisms, because of their "success."

There are much more important questions, however. How do we create a situation where the leaders we need, the leaders who are most fully developed as individuals, the leaders who have progressed beyond the head-butting stage are encouraged? How do we develop a situation where "complete" leaders are encouraged in their climb to positions of power so that they can help guide both their organization culture and society in general in the right direction? What kind of promotion and reward systems can we develop to encourage such a scenario without killing the incentive upon which free enterprise depends?

Such promotion and reward systems do, indeed, already exist. We shall meet them in the next section as we move on to the modern-day workplace, on to its issues and innovations.

Topics for Discussion

1. How do the contributions of Smith, Owen, and Taylor fit together, or do they?
2. How did the objectives of the early human relations school reformers fit with those of union leaders?
3. Why did the Machiavellian humanists find the mechanistic viewpoint so attractive?
4. Discuss your ideas on the reasons Machiavellian humanists are the way they are.
5. Discuss your ideas on the reasons Christian humanists are the way they are.
6. Discuss the personality characteristics that differentiate mechanists from human relations types.

Notes

1. Edgar Vinacke, *Foundations of Psychology*, New York: American Book Co., 1968, p. 389.
2. Abraham Maslow, *Motivation and Personality*, 2nd ed., New York: Harper and Row, 1970, p. 39.
3. *Ibid.*, p. 45.
4. Scott Peck, *People of the Lie*, New York: Simon & Schuster, 1983, p. 76.
5. *Ibid.*, p. 78.
6. *Ibid.*, p. 77.

THE POST-INDUSTRIAL REVOLUTION ERA

The post-industrial revolution era began in the mid-1900s and will continue on into the future. It has been a period of fierce confrontation and of necessary coming together. It has been a period spent exploring alternatives in terms of the role technology should play and in terms of the most appropriate management systems for global organizations, which include sometimes hundreds of thousand of employees. But most importantly, — has been a time spent exploring alternatives in terms of which social values will best get us where we want to go.

The post-industrial revolution era is a story of U.S. industrialists who were brave enough and farsighted enough to dare to be different — among them, Henry Ford, Chester Barnard, Lyman Ketchum, Aaron Feuerstein, Ralph Stayer — people whose companies have enjoyed tremendous success because they thought and acted as Christian humanists, but whose message has been largely ignored due to the continuing pervasiveness of Machiavellian humanism and the scarcity mentality. It is the story of the ongoing battle between the *engineering* (treat employees as numbers, always go for the greatest efficiency) school of thought and the *human relations* (employees are our most important asset) school. It was the story of a new battle between those who wished to *empower* workers and those who continue to favor the traditional *autocratic*, top-down form of decision making.

The Post-Industrial Revolution is the story of attempts to wed these two schools, to create a new *systemic* management paradigm that will allow us to flourish in the new world of work we are entering. It is the story of the philosophical and scientific advances which have made the systems approach to management possible, of the work of the *pragmatists*, E. A. Singer in particular, in their attempts to join the worlds of rationalism and empiricism successfully. It is the story of Ludwig Von Bertalanffy's revelation which has forever altered the perspective of science and has made the systems approach to organization design possible. It is the story of the trinity of modern day theorists — Drucker, Ackoff, Deming — who like their predecessors — Smith, Owen, Taylor — have defined modern-day economic theory, management theory, and production theory for us. They, like their predecessors, have given us not only theory, but also the practical workplace tools necessary to progress in the right direction.

Finally, and as we have said, most importantly, the Post-Industrial Revolution era is the story of the quest for foundational social values upon which everything else rests. It is the story of continuing progress in Western European nations, progress built on a social philosophy, a value system "contributed" originally by the ancient Greeks, a philosophy against which all improvements are ultimately measured. It is the story of the United States, a relatively young country that has not yet had time to develop core social values and, as a result, has confused its *economic model* with the concept of *social philosophy*. It is the story of the resultant U.S. frustration, of its labored movement toward the same social philosophy that is driving progress in Europe, and of the tools, techniques, and concepts being developed to help ensure success in this quest.

9 The Gathering Forces of Change

After Reading This Chapter You Should Know

1. What Henry Ford's contributions to production and management theory were.
2. How both the quantitative and nonquantitative approaches to increased productivity became more sophisticated.
3. How the concept of "Sociotechnical Theory" tried to wed the quantitative and nonquantitative camps.
4. How the concept of "autonomous work groups" evolved.
5. How "dynamic conservativism" was identified as the major obstruction to organization change.
6. How the "labor–management council" concept evolved.
7. How the contributions of Chris Argyris, Frederick Herzberg, Douglas McGregor, and Rensis Likert fit.
8. Why the eventual failure of the Topeka, Kansas Gaines Pet Food plant effort to increase productivity by empowering its employees can be considered a classic case study.

Henry Ford Reshapes the Industrial World

Henry Ford, perhaps more than any other industrialist in modern history, helped sow the seeds of change in the workplace and in management theory. Ford was naïve, or perhaps we could say that he retained much longer than most the innocence of childhood. This is the innocence that allows us instinctively to understand the truth of a situation, the innocence that does not allow us to rationalize.

In his innocence, Ford did not develop the vulnerability to the "scarcity mentality" that most of us still have. Although he became one of the wealthiest men in the world, he continued to see money mainly as a tool, rather than as an end in itself. Money was required for him to do the things he wanted to do, to develop the concept of the automobile, to develop the most efficient means of production. That was the main role of money, its main purpose in Ford's mind. He lived comfortably, but not ostentatiously. He gave away huge amounts to humanitarian causes. At one point he single-handedly tried to stop World War I by bringing all the warring parties together to negotiate. This effort quite possibly provided a model for the later League of Nations and, eventually, for the United Nations. The modern-day Ford Foundation with its globe-spanning social welfare projects is still the world's most respected private philanthropic organization. Ford actually brought to life Andrew Carnegie's "third alternative," replacing the government with himself as the distributor of his wealth.

Finally, Ford proved that sharing the wealth generated by his activities with his employees on all levels benefited everyone financially. The prevailing economic philosophy of the day, reinforced by the still adamant Social Darwinists, the second-generation robber barons, and the always present Machiavellian humanists, was to keep workers at the survival level. Ford, in his naïveté, was not convinced. He believed and eventually proved that the increased productivity generated by the equitable sharing of profits more than offset the increased cost involved.

Henry Ford was born on a farm in Michigan in 1863. As a child he was fascinated by technology and took on the responsibility of tending the farm machinery. His personal objective was to improve this machinery rather than to simply maintain it, to increase its capability to reduce the tedium and rigor of farm work. But Henry had no desire to be a farmer. In 1879, at the age of 16, he moved to Detroit and took a job with a company that manufactured railroad cars. Eventually, he moved to Westinghouse where he serviced steam engines, then to the Edison Illuminating Company. Each year he returned to his father's farm to help with the harvest. During these stays, Ford worked in a shop he had set up in a shed to build an early, steam-driven version of the tractor.

Ford's real interest, however, was always the automobile. He spent most of his free time and most of his money, of which he had relatively little at that point, improving his prototype. While other inventors in this field were working to develop an electricity-driven vehicle, Ford believed the gasoline engine to be the key to the future. By the early 1900s investors had taken interest in his innovations. But most were eventually frustrated by Ford's refusal to begin production until he was totally satisfied with the model he was working on. Finally, in 1903, the Ford Motor Company was incorporated and production of the Model A Ford began.

In 1908 the Model T appeared. By that time Ford had shifted his focus to the improvement of production systems. He was interested in finding the quickest, cheapest way to produce cars. In earlier factories, the skeleton of the automobile had rested in one place. Different teams of workers had gone to it in sequence to add different parts. Ford introduced the moving assembly line, allowing the car to move to the workers. He continued to perfect his innovation until a completed car rolled off the line every 24 seconds. He had a simple philosophy in terms of product development, "Decide on your product design, freeze it, and, from then on, spend all your time, effort, and money on making the machinery to produce it, concentrating so completely on production that, as the volume goes up, it is certain to get cheaper per unit produced."[1]

In 1910 Ford opened the largest automobile assembly plant in the world. He saw immediately that management systems as well as technical systems had to be improved if he were to achieve the desired results. Employee turnover was a major problem. One issue was that foremen enjoyed total power over workers and decided their pay scale. The abuses that occurred as a result of this arrangement were magnified by the prevailing piece-rate system. Ford replaced this piece-rate system with a fixed wage and took the power to fire workers away from foremen.

The biggest change, however, the one that made Ford an instant international hero, came in 1914. During the previous year, 1913, he had often said that the abolition of poverty was the only worthwhile end for business. Then, in 1914 he, literally, "put his money where his mouth was." At that point, despite the strong misgivings of members of his corporate board of directors, he more than doubled the minimum wage of employees, raising it from $2.34 for 9 hours work to $5.00 for an 8-hour day. His reasoning went as follows:

> Our workers are not sharing in our good fortune. There are thousands out there in the shop who are not living as they should. Their homes are crowded and uncomfortable. They fill up their homes with roomers and boarders in order to help swell their income. It's all wrong — all wrong. It's especially bad for the children. By underpaying men we are bringing on a generation of children undernourished and underdeveloped morally as well as physically.[2]

Also, from a more pragmatic viewpoint, Ford realized that the key to success was not low wages and long hours. Rather, as Frederick Taylor had previously said, it was just the opposite — high wages and reasonable hours so that workers could afford to buy the things they produced and would have the time to do so, thus greatly expanding the market.

Public reaction to his decision, as would be expected, was very strong. The *New York Globe* newspaper said that Ford was creating a system that "had all the advantages and none of the disadvantages of socialism."[3] Prevailing economic theory had been turned on its head. Those opposed, however, mostly industrialists, accused Ford of undermining the capitalistic system, of planting the seeds of social revolution, of giving inherently lazy workers the means to spend only half the required number of hours on the job and the rest drinking, fornicating, and getting into trouble. The *Wall Street Journal*, traditionally a bastion of conservativism, called his decision "blatant immorality — a misapplication of Biblical principles in a field where they do not belong."[4]

Ford did not stop there. Like Owen, he realized that the problem was also cultural and got involved in an extensive community improvement effort. He used the $5 a day as a prod, saying that only those who led good, thrifty, healthy lives would be allowed to earn it. He hired a core of social workers to teach hygiene, to teach employees how to shop efficiently, how to open saving accounts, how to purchase houses. He eventually sponsored a company-owned commissary where employees could buy food and goods at as much as 90% below the prices charged in other stores. He opened a hospital that had fixed rates for all treatments. The prices in the hospital were, again, 50% below the norm.

Ford's labor policy was considered the most progressive in the world. The rest of the business community, however, despite the enormous profits resulting from these changes, treated Ford's approach mainly as an unhealthy aberration rather than as a step forward. Ford was going against tradition, against what they were comfortable with, and they could not tolerate it. Again, like Robert Owen in England, Ford was attacked from all sides. The wealthy disliked him because he was questioning their constant quest for more. The entrenched disliked him because he was forcing change. The poor were angry simply because he had so much more money than they and demanded that he share ever-increasing amounts of it. The situation of change agents such as Henry Ford, Frederick Taylor, Robert Owen was perhaps best described by our friend Machiavelli in *The Prince* when he said:

There is nothing more difficult to plan, more doubtful of success, nor more dangerous to manage than the creation of a new system, for the initiator has the enmity of all who would profit by the preservation of the old institutions and merely lukewarm defenders in those who should gain by the new one.[5]

As Ford grew older, his idealism, or perhaps simply his resolve began to fade. He had always been firmly in control of his creations. Now, because of the size of his empire, he was forced to turn increasing amounts of control over to other people who began backing away from his innovations, quite possibly with Ford's blessing. Employees were driven increasingly to improve productivity. The code of conduct became increasingly stricter. Talking with other workers while on the job was eventually prohibited. Foremen were once again given the authority to fire at will, as were the new "inspectors" who now roamed the assembly line. Employees were forced to spy on one another. Thugs were hired to deal with "problem" situations.

Ford saw unionization as another assault on his faltering control and opposed it vehemently. In 1937, union officials and representatives were severely beaten by company guards while trying, legally, to pass out handbills discussing the Wagner Act at his plant in Dearborn, Michigan. Ford fought the National Labor Relations Board and its mandates. Rumor is that he allowed his plants to be unionized only after his wife threatened to leave him if he refused to do so.

Perhaps the major difference between Robert Owen, who could have served as Ford's role model, and Ford was that, after developing his workplace paradigm and showing that his approach improved productivity, Owen eventually climbed out of the trenches. He left the business world behind, and became a guru, spreading the gospel, enjoying the admiration of disciples. Ford, however, stayed with his company, battling to the end, unable to let go.

Still, Henry Ford's contributions were great. As a result of them he joined the elite group of those who, throughout modern history, have carried production theory to a new level. Adam Smith understood that the efficiencies created by the division of labor would increase productivity. Robert Owen introduced the idea of focusing on the needs of the workers as well as those of the machines as a way to increase productivity. Frederick Taylor used scientific research to refine each segment of Smith's division of labor, then added a monetary incentive system to meet the needs of the workers. Finally, Henry Ford brought all of the above together on such a grand scale that his model could not be ignored. Also, as we have said, Ford made real Andrew Carnegie's "third alternative." He built a private empire capable of generating great wealth, then took personal charge of distributing that wealth to benefit society.

One last point should be made. Although Ford was bitterly opposed to unions, although he believed they deserved no voice in decisions made by his company, he unwittingly strengthened their hand. He provided an irrefutable example of what was possible when companies began respecting employees, began meeting and exceeding their basic financial needs. Ford gave the human relations school and the unions the proof they had been waiting for. Now the school and the unions had serious ammunition with which to continue their struggle against the modern-day Machiavellian humanists.

The Quantitative vs. Nonquantitative Struggle Intensifies

During the mid-1900s the struggle between the quantitative (numbers or efficiency-oriented) and the nonquantitative (emotions or psychology-oriented) camps intensified. The two camps were then headed in opposite directions, each pretty much ignoring the other except to throw barbs. The quantitative camp, of course, was an outgrowth of the work of Frederick Taylor and his associates. The level of sophistication in the approach of this camp had increased rapidly. One of the key characteristics of the mechanistic approach to problem solving, for example, was that now teams of specialists — perhaps a mathematician, a physicist, an engineer, and a statistician — worked together on problems to derive the best-thought-out, most efficient solutions.

During World War II quantitative techniques were used successfully to solve problems in almost every area. For example, the British military, battling German bombers, desperately sought a way to integrate their radar findings effectively with the movements of their vastly outnumbered squadrons of Hurricane fighter planes. The solution was discovered through mathematical modeling. This relatively new academic discipline, generally called "operations research," gained a great deal of respect and a growing number of followers.

After the war, use of operations research techniques spread rapidly to government and industry. The first academic course in the field was offered by Massachusetts Institute of Technology in 1948. The first full degree program was begun by Russell Ackoff and C. West Churchman along with their associates at Case Western Institute of Technology in 1951. The techniques that were developed and used to solve a wide range of industrial problems included decision theory, game theory, information theory, inventory theory, linear programming, probability theory, queuing theory, replacement theory, sampling theory, simulation theory, statistical decision theory, and symbolic logic.

The nonquantitative camp was also busy. By the middle of the 1900s a number of institutions had been developed to study social issues in management and to measure their influence on productivity. One was the Institute for Social Research founded in 1947. Staff conducted a wide range of experiments and surveys that showed the adverse effects of pressure, of *punitive* vs. *helpful* supervision. The Institute of Social Research also developed reams of data supporting the hypothesis that workers are more productive when supervisors solicit, listen to, and act on their ideas, and when supervisors encourage workers to interact with and to help each other.

Another institution active in this field was the Tavistock Institute of Industrial Relations in London, England. During World War II researchers there were impressed by the flexible integration of soldiers and tanks demonstrated by German Panzer divisions in their efforts to reach targets. After the war the Tavistock Institute tried to apply the management-related insights gained from this research to industry. At that point, the "technological imperative" (the belief that workers should be programmed to serve the machines) along with the concepts of the division of labor and of bureaucratization still held sway. Based on a growing amount of data gathered from research projects the Tavistock Institute staff, led by Eric Trist, developed "a new paradigm of work," the concept of sociotechnical systems, that contradicted the technological imperative.

This concept included the following principles.

1. The system of tasks rather than the single tasks into which that system can be decomposed, to be performed by a work group, a system which includes a set of related and interdependent activities, must now become the focus of the group as a whole.
2. Correspondingly, the work group, rather than the individual job-holder, responsible for this system of tasks must now become central.
3. In this model, internal regulation of group activities by members themselves is more important than external regulation by supervisors.

4. The design is based on redundancy of functions rather than redundancy of parts. The group members learn more than one necessary skill so that responsibilities are interchangeable. In this way group members can support and fill in for each other, as an alternative to training an outside backup person.
5. More responsibility is given group members in deciding how to do the work involved.
6. Workers are treated as complementary (equal, co-supporting) to technology, rather than extensions of it.
7. The model increases variety for both the individual and the organization. That is, it allows both the individual and the organization more flexibility in defining the most effective way to complete the system of tasks involved.[6]

This was probably the first serious attempt to wed the "mechanistic" and "human relations" schools of thought. Another result of this research was the evolution of the autonomous work group concept as the most appropriate vehicle for the realization of sociotechnical principles in the workplace.

In 1949 Eric Trist was asked to undertake a government-sponsored study in the coal mines of Great Britain. The problem Trist was asked to address was that the supply of coal had not kept up with demand in the reviving industrial sector following World War II. Men were deserting the mines for more attractive jobs in factories. Morale was low; absenteeism averaged 20%. Relations with the unions were bad.

Trist was asked to compare mines showing low productivity and morale with those showing high productivity and morale. In the former, he found the traditional division of labor, the traditional management system. In the latter, however, specifically in one mine in southern Yorkshire, he found something entirely new. The shift workers in this mine were managing themselves with minimum supervision. They changed jobs and moved from shift to shift when they desired, they decided on a daily basis who would do what task, and they trained each other, scheduled themselves, and covered for each other for illness and vacations.

This discovery was important because it signaled a reversal in management trends. Previously, based on the engineering mentality, organizations and processes, as we have said, were designed entirely around the needs of technology. The cost of this arrangement to people, the sacrifices people had to make in terms of their own needs, were supposedly compensated for first by pay (Henry Ford's major tactic), then by improved human relations (Follett, Sheldon, Mayo, etc.). In such instances, workers were having *good* things done for them to compensate for the *bad* things done to them.

The arrangement found in the mines, however, was entirely different. This was the first time that, instead of being manipulated by managers, instead of having things done *for* them or done *to* them, the workers themselves were being given control over the involved decisions. They were being given control so that their concerns and needs would be factored into the redesign of their immediate work process *up-front* and *by themselves*. It was the first time that workers were truly being *empowered*.

Actually, I should say that it was "the first time in modern history," rather than "the first time" that workers were truly being empowered. As we remember, during the Medieval, Renaissance, and Reformations periods and on into the Enlightenment, workers were in charge of production. This was because they individually crafted or manufactured complete pieces. It was with the advent of Adam Smith's division of labor and mass production that control began slipping away. Now control was returning, but with one critical difference. It was no longer possible for employees to complete finished pieces individually. Products had become too complex. No one possessed all the necessary skills. Also, time-saving, electricity-driven machines had become a critical factor and had to be incorporated into the effort.

What we had now, therefore, instead of the individual effort, was a group of workers and machines generating the finished product. With the introduction of the autonomous work group concept that group now became a "team," and the gap between the distant workplace past and the future was bridged. In this new situation, with these new principles of self-management, the team members worked so closely together and were so focused that they could actually be defined as an "individual." They were addressing the tasks confronting them as a *systemic unit* rather than as an *aggregate*.

The Beginnings of Cultural Change

The autonomous work group concept was, indeed, new. It was also a threat to the status quo. What Donald Schon in his 1971 book *Loss of the Stable State* labeled *dynamic conservativism* set in. Entrenched management began striving actively to stop change. We saw an earlier example of dynamic conservativism during the Medieval and Renaissance periods when the Catholic Church struggled vainly to stop change, to preserve tradition, and to maintain its power. We encountered it during the Enlightenment and early Industrial

Revolution in England when the landed gentry battled the industrialists over control of government policy.

In reaction to this modern-day effort to change the workplace culture, to empower lower-level employees, both sides, management and labor, balked. The National Coal Board of England eventually shut down the research being done in the coal mines and discouraged the spread of the autonomous work group concept. The board's announced objective, at that point, was to accelerate the *mechanization* of mining operations. Board members said that in order to do so management control had to be intensified rather than dispersed. Giving the workers more power would be counterproductive.

Union leaders, at the same time, saw this approach as a threat because it encouraged workers to teach their skills to others on the crew. Union leaders suspected that the approach might be a management plot that would eventually lead to a decrease in the number of job categories. The classification of jobs, keeping workers from crossing over in terms of responsibilities, was a traditional union method of ensuring job security. "If no one else can do my job, then I'm safe." Also, when the workers did cross over, when they began sharing responsibilities, pay scales became muddled. Pay was one of the major issues addressed during contract negotiations. The power of union leadership as negotiators for the workers would be diluted if everyone agreed to earn the same amount. Also, the autonomous work group concept encouraged workers to begin speaking for themselves. The jobs of union leaders might become less secure if workers began doing this.

Several other efforts to give employees control of their work and their work environment were mounted during the 1950s and 1960s. All met with initial success. Almost all, however, eventually foundered, victims to various forms of dynamic conservativism. Halfway around the world, in India, one of the contributors to sociotechnical theory, A. K. Rice, introduced the concept of autonomous work groups at the Calica Textile Mills in Ahmedhisad. The workers organized themselves into teams with the blessing of management, improving productivity and morale. The approach did not spread to other mills, however, because other owners "did not want to share power."[7] Eventually, managers at the Calica Mills also reverted to the old ways.

The Standard Motor Company in Coventry, England developed autonomous, cross-functional work "gangs." In all, 12,000 workers assisted by only 70 foremen controlled the shop floor and operations. They negotiated wages and bonuses and handled promotions themselves. The company increased its share of the market faster than competitors, automated more rapidly, and paid higher wages while producing lower-cost parts. When the company was taken over by British Leland, however, the traditional management style was rein-stituted. The new parent company was uncomfortable with the innovation.[8]

While attempts truly to empower workers were being made by a small number of companies in several countries including the United States, the practice became most common and was accepted as an integral part of the work culture only in Scandinavia.

By the early 1960s Norwegian industry had begun lagging behind its global competitors. At the same time, trade unions were demanding more employee say in the decision-making process. With help from Eric Trist and Fred Emery of the Tavistock Institute, an autonomous work group model was developed and tried in the pulp-and-paper industry and in the metal-working industries of Norway. Although the effort succeeded, again it did not spread, except to Sweden, which eventually "borrowed" the model. In Sweden, by 1973, "between 500 and 1,000 work improvement projects of various kinds, small and large, had been developed in a wide range of industries."[9]

Perhaps the best known of the autonomous work group efforts was mounted at the Volvo Corporation. Here teams of 7 to 10 workers were formed. Team members were trained to handle all the involved tasks. They decided each day who would do which job. They were responsible for order-ing materials, for hiring new team members. They made the decisions in their area of control and helped integrate their area with others in the plant. Managers, in this scenario, were troubleshooters. They were on call to the teams when problems arose. They also helped with the integration process.

One must believe that the success of such efforts in Scandinavia is due at least in part to culture. Scandinavian populations are largely homogeneous and, therefore, share the same cultural values. Possibly because of the relative harshness of their climate, they also understand better the importance of cooperation. The countries are highly socialistic. Swedes take for granted that they will pay approximately 50% of their salaries in taxes. At the same time, their government provides a wide range of free services including education at all levels, job training, health care, and childcare.

The Swedish government is obliged by law to provide employment for all citizens. It organizes tax-supported public works projects when the private and public sectors are not generating enough jobs. The espoused objective of the government is to ensure that its people enjoy a reasonable quality of life, that all citizens enjoy the opportunity to develop their individual potential.

In such a situation as this, where the basics as well as a decent lifestyle are guaranteed, the need for conflict and even competition is reduced. Also,

Scandinavians, with the assistance of government, have formed a large number of cooperatives on both the production and consumption sides. The employee/owners of these ventures are obviously more interested in long-term security than in short-term profit, again lessening the possibility of workplace conflict and of a win–lose mentality. Finally, as a result of their cultural values, the power shared between management and the representatives of labor is much better balanced in Scandinavian countries, the interaction less antagonistic.

Another vehicle developed for encouraging employee empowerment that emerged during this period was the "worker's council," currently called the "labor–management committee." These councils first appeared in several Eastern European countries during the 1920s. Workers councils are groups including representatives of upper-level management and of the involved unions that meet periodically, usually monthly. During these meetings management presents the plans of the organization. The union side brings up labor issues. The purpose of such groups is to improve communication and to deal with employee problems before they get too serious, before costly arbitration becomes necessary. Several Western European countries now require by law that larger companies establish labor–management committees.

Meanwhile, Back in the United States

Most of the work in management theory going on in the United States at this point was centered on discovering how to motivate individual employees, rather than on discovering how to motivate *teams* of employees. Chris Argyris, a Professor of Industrial Relations at Yale University focused on defending the individual worker's integrity. Reacting to the continuing workplace pressure to conform, he tried to show through his research that allowing employees to grow and to maintain self-esteem benefited the company as well as the individual. Argyris made the point that employees behave the way they are treated. It they are treated like children or adolescents, they behave like children or adolescents. If they are treated like responsible adults, they behave like responsible adults.

Frederick Herzberg, another academician, worked to define factors that made employees feel good or bad about their jobs. He interviewed thousands of employees, then divided the responses gained from these interviews into categories. The first category of responses included factors identified as creators of *job satisfaction*. These factors included achievement, recognition, the work itself, being given responsibility, the chance for advancement, and the chance for job-related growth. The most obvious common characteristic of factors in this division was their *intrinsic* nature. By intrinsic, we mean that they generated positive emotions within individuals themselves by giving each individual a feeling of control over his or her environment. The second category of responses included factors identified as creators of *job dissatisfaction*. These factors included company policy and administration, technical supervision, salary, relationships with supervisors, and working conditions. The most obvious common characteristic of these factors was their *extrinsic* nature. By extrinsic, we mean that they involved mainly things *done to* the employee, things over which the employee had little or no control.[10]

Douglas McGregor, a psychologist who had worked in industry as both a manager and a consultant, focused on managerial attitudes. He eventually formulated his well-known Theory X and Theory Y which contrast the two polar sets of assumptions upon which different types of managers base their interactions with subordinates.

Theory X assumed that:

> Workers inherently dislike work and, whenever possible attempt to avoid it.
> Since workers dislike work, they must be coerced, controlled, or threatened with punishment to achieve desired goals.
> Employees will shirk responsibilities and seek formal direction whenever possible.
> Most workers place security above all other factors associated with work and will display little ambition.

Theory Y assumed that:

> Employees can view work as being as natural as rest or play.
> A person who is committed to the objectives of work will exercise self-direction and self-control. The average person can learn to accept, even to seek responsibility.
> Creativity, the ability to make good decisions, is widely dispersed throughout the population and not necessarily the sole province of managers.[11]

While McGregor's findings were not as well documented by research as Herzberg's, he provided a clear, easily grasped frame of reference that again supported Maslow's previously mentioned hierarchy of needs and, therefore, was eagerly accepted and presented by the human relations school.

Rensis Likert, who worked with the University of Michigan Research Center, was one of the first in the United States to focus on the improvement of organization design, on the improvement of organization-wide systems rather than on the improvement of the individual situation. Based on his research, Likert identified four requirements that all employees needed to have satisfied:

1. Ego — Involving one's sense of self-importance and respect. Am I able to gain approval and acceptance?
2. Security — Do I have to worry about losing my job?
3. Curiosity/Creativity — Will I be able to develop my potential on the job?
4. Economic — While helping the company meet its economic objectives, will I be able to meet my own?[12]

Likert said that the best way to satisfy these requirements was through the use of work groups and through the use of the "link-pin" concept. In the traditional "man-to-man" organization design based on a strict management hierarchy, units on the same level were not linked together. Unit supervisors reported only to their bosses and competed for both attention and resources. Likert suggested that managers of units on the same level in the same department or division should become a group in themselves, that they should function like link-pins tying the organization together.

Likert also suggested that the link-pin groups should make decisions through consensus. Their objective should be to benefit the company as a whole, rather than simply to benefit their individual units. He said that when one link in an organization chain was weak, all those links attached to it suffered, but that when managers worked as an integrated group, these weaknesses could be dealt with better. Likert's link-pin theory, in effect, introduced Trist's team approach on an organization-wide, integrated level. It changed the manager's major role from that of an overseer to that of integrator.

Slowly but Surely

The tools, techniques, and concepts required to help society change over to a more Christian humanism approach in terms of management systems were being developed. Enough case studies of the successful implementation of the new empowering management model based on sociotechnical theory existed to prove its superiority. Yet, in the United States, as in most of Europe, very little change was actually occurring. Most organizations were not interested.

When an innovative company did mount such an effort, no matter how successful the effort was initially, it eventually foundered.

The attempt to institute the principles of sociotechnical theory at the Topeka, Kansas plant of Gaines Pet Food is perhaps the best-documented instance of an early effort in the United States that succeeded, only to be undermined by the forces of dynamic conservativism. It illustrates the mood in management circles at that point, the ongoing conflict between those entrenched in the traditional, top-down approach to management and those advocating a more participative style.

Topeka was a new operation organized by plant manager, Lyman Ketchum, with the help of a consultant, Michael Walton. Their focus was on tapping employee potential. Their approach was based on five assumptions:

1. People have ego needs. They want self-esteem, a sense of accomplishment, autonomy, a chance to increase knowledge and skills, to receive information about their performance. People invest more in situations that allow them to meet these needs.
2. An individual needs to see himself or herself as a significant part of the whole, whether in his position in a human group or in her interaction with technology.
3. People have "social" needs. They enjoy team membership and teamwork. At the same time they enjoy friendly rivalry.
4. People want to be able to identify with products they produce and firms that employ them, and people care about the quality of things and institutions with which they can identify.
5. People have security needs. They want reasonable income and employment security, and assurance against arbitration and unfair treatment. They also want to be assured of 'due process.'[13]

Ketchum and Walton decided that the best vehicle for achievement of this objective was the *self-directed work team*. One team was put in charge of production, another of the warehouse, and a third of administration. The teams were responsible for setting work standards, for designing their work, and for work-related problem solving. The screening process for new hirees was long and detailed. The pay scale was above average in order to attract top employees. Four basic pay levels were in place. No limit was set on the number of employees who could reach the top level. Initially, at least, team members decided who should be promoted to the next pay level. Further pay increases could be achieved by learning something new.

Team leaders (managers) were picked based on their willingness and ability to be "*people managers* rather than *super-operators*." According to

Walton, "The more team members can do on their own, the better." [14] Team leaders were to function mainly as facilitators. Their major responsibilities were to manage group dynamics, to facilitate problem solving, and to develop the potential of their reports.

Characteristics designed into the system included:

1. The workforce and management structure were kept lean.
2. Daily self-measurement techniques were developed so that employees could keep themselves informed about cost, yield, and spoilage.
3. A style of management was adopted which encouraged people to participate.
4. The information system was designed to encourage decentralized decision making.
5. Employees were treated maturely.
6. There were few symbols left in the place that differentiated between hierarchical levels, or between office and plant workers.
7. Broader educational and personal involvement opportunities were offered.
8. Manpower assignments were flexible.
9. Innovation by individual employees was encouraged.
10. Target-setting by teams was encouraged. [15]

In terms of bottom-line results, the experiment was unquestionably successful. It was inevitable, however, due to the newness of the approach, that some internal problems should arise. One such problem concerned the responsibility of the team leader, which had been loosely defined. Different employees expected different degrees of guidance. Older employees, for example, were used to having managers make the decisions. Younger ones were more likely to enjoy the freedom they had been given to make their own. Another issue was co-worker input on raises. In order to avoid hard feelings, very few applications were turned down. Decisions were not always based on productivity. Eventually, these decisions were taken over by the team leaders.

The major problems, however, came from the parent company, General Foods. Eventually, after the approach had proved itself, Ketchum took a corporate staff position in order to help spread the model to other facilities. Because of the highly competitive atmosphere at the corporate headquarters, however, rather than listening to Ketchum, other managers tried to minimize his success, to "cut him down to size." He had attracted too much attention. He had been promoted too rapidly. He had not paid his dues, fought his way up through the ranks. He was also a threat to the status quo and, possibly, to their job security. The more authority delegated to workers and work groups, the less work there was for managers and corporate staff functions. Ketchum's replacement at Topeka was also a problem. The replacement immediately began trying to regain control over the operation. He demanded, for one thing, that greater amounts of data be generated and funneled to him so that he could take the lead in decision making. This meant that his management core also had to assume more control. Much of the authority that had been given to the work teams was, therefore, stripped away.

The managers of corporate staff functions — finance, engineering, personnel, training — were a third problem. They had also been threatened by the changes introduced at Topeka. The autonomous work teams had taken over many of their traditional responsibilities — making pay decisions, handling design problems, selecting new team members, identifying training needs. Corporate staff functions had been held at bay as long as Ketchum remained head of the Topeka operation. As soon as he left, however, they joined the attack, demanding more involvement in plant decisions concerning their areas of expertise.

Productivity began to drop. Ketchum soon left the company. Most of the managers who had worked with him at the Topeka plant also left. This was one of the growing number of instances where parts of corporations have adopted the human relations approach and implemented sociotechnical theory. They have shown its effectiveness in terms of both the bottom line and employee morale, but then have had efforts smothered by a culture unwilling, probably unable to change. They have then had their efforts smothered by our old friend, dynamic conservativism.

In summation, during this period in the history of management theory a growing number of skirmishes were being won by the Christian humanists. But the opposition remained much stronger, firmly entrenched behind the mechanistic production model and the autocratic management model. The situation was basically a stalemate. Obviously, another major breakthrough, another paradigm shift was necessary. This shift needed to begin at the roots of our reality, in the realm of philosophy where empiricism with its strictly quantitative perspective continued to hold sway. It needed then to help create and to define better the types of change models that Eric Trist and Fred Emery and their associates at the Tavistock Institute were working on, that the Institute for Social Research was working on, that Chris Argyris, Frederick Herzberg, Douglas McGregor, Rensis Likert, Lyman Katchum, and Micheal Walton were working on. A whole new and truly comprehensive school of thought was beginning to grow.

Thus, the stage was set for the advent and the acceptance of the *systems approach* to organization design and management.

Topics for Discussion

1. Why were Henry Ford's ideas unacceptable to other corporate leaders as well as to labor leaders?
2. What is the value of operations research tools and techniques in the workplace?
3. Can students give examples of the application of "sociotechnical theory" found in their own work place?
4. How do modern-day "self-directed work groups" differ from the early autonomous work groups?
5. Can students give examples of the effects of "dynamic conservativism" found in their own companies?
6. Why are "labor–management councils" not popular in the United States?
7. How do the contributions of Chris Argyris, Frederick Herzberg, Douglas McGregor, and Rensis Likert compare?
8. How could the Topeka, Kansas Gaines Pet Food Company project have been saved?

Notes

1. Sidney Olson, *Young Henry Ford*, Detroit: Wayne State University Press, 1963, p. 186.
2. Carol Gelderman, *Henry Ford: The Wayward Capitalist*, New York: Dial Press, 1981, p. 52.
3. *Ibid.*, p. 53.
4. *Ibid.*, p. 54.
5. Niccolò Machiavelli, *The Prince*, New York: Mentor Books, 1952, p. 87.
6. Eric Trist, *The Evolution of Socio-Technical Systems: A Conceptual Framework and an Action Research Program*, Toronto, Ontario: Quality of Work Life Center, 1980, p. 12.
7. *Ibid.*, p. 18.
8. *Ibid.*, p. 17.
9. *Ibid.*, p. 26.
10. Steven Robbins, *Essentials of Organization Behavior*, 5th ed., Upper Saddle River, NJ: Prentice-Hall, 1997, pp. 49–50.
11. *Ibid.*, pp. 50–51.

12. Rensis Likert, *New Patterns of Management*, New York: McGraw-Hill, 1961, p. 104.
13. Lyman Ketchum, "A Case Study of Diffusion," in *The Quality of Work Life*, Vol. 2, New York: The Free Press, 1975, p. 142.
14. David Whitsett and Lyle Yorks, "From Management Theory to Business Sense," in *The Myths and Realities of People at Work*, New York: AMACOM, 1983, p. 195
15. Ketchum, *op. cit.*, p. 142.

10 The Post-Industrial Revolution Era: Tying It All Together

After Reading This Chapter You Should Know

1. How pragmatism finally combined the strengths of rationalism and empiricism.
2. How the statement, "A whole is more than the sum or its parts," changed the world of science.
3. How Peter Drucker provided the necessary overview for the future of work and created the concept of "knowledge workers."
4. How management by objectives (MBO) was originally offered as a means of integrating workplace activities.
5. What W. Edwards Deming's efforts to define the most productive combination of technology and employee expertise produced.
6. How Deming brought the concept of quality improvement to the forefront.
7. How E. A. Singer, Russell Ackoff, and C. West Churchman helped develop the foundational ingredients necessary to the effective introduction of the "systems approach" to the world of management.
8. How Ackoff reintroduced the "ultimate idealized truth" that provided the necessary foundation for organizational and societal change.

Singer Lays the Groundwork

As we entered the mid-1900s we found ourselves still mired between competing factions. Three major arguments currently raged. The first was between the *mechanistic* or *engineering* school of thought and the *human relations* school. Each of the two sides had something of value to offer. The challenge at this point, therefore, was to find a beneficial and acceptable *synthesis*. The second argument was between those for employee empowerment and those against it. And, of course, the *Machiavellian humanists* and the *Christian humanists* continued to fight it out, their battle flavored by the scarcity mentality and by the resultant conflict ethic that too frequently dominated the workplace.

Once again, the effort to achieve an effective synthesis, one that would incorporate the strengths of and, at the same time, weed out the deleterious aspects of these diverse mind-sets, found its roots in the fields of philosophy and science. In the world of philosophy, a new major school of thought, *pragmatism*, had evolved. The schism between *rationalism*, with its requirement for at least one "ultimate" truth upon which to build reality and the rebellious *empiricists* with their more usable belief that the truths we base our development on should be the product of experience and reflection, had persisted, literally, for centuries.

Immanuel Kant, an Enlightenment philosopher, had tried to unite the two schools in his 1781 book entitled, *Critique of Pure Reason*. His foundational thesis had been that while both *rational intuition* and *empirical observations* were *necessary* to the development of knowledge and understanding, neither, by itself, was *sufficient*. Rationalism and empiricism were, in fact, two sides of the same coin.

During the 1800s, however, despite Kant's achievements, the split resurfaced, never having been truly mended. Descendants of the original rationalists now taught the "Speculative Method," arguing that "at least some truths are to be discovered by thought, speculation, insight, intuition, faith or some other method independent of controlled observation."[1] Descendants of the empiricists taught the "Positivist Method," arguing that "all truths are either analytical [dependent for their truth on logic or language] or else must be verifiable directly or indirectly by empirical observation."[2]

In the mid-1800s a second attempt at a synthesis between rationalism and empiricism occurred. This attempt was called, as we have said, pragmatism. Early proponents of this new school of thought included Charles Peirce, William James, F. Schiller, and, of course, John Dewey. These men said that instead of building *from* ultimate truths, we should be building *toward* them, or at least toward important ones. They said that the best "pattern of inquiry" for such an effort was the one which "leads us to the most significant truths most frequently." The concept of truth, in this instance, was defined as that which works best in practice, in solving problems. The pragmatists said that the effectiveness of such an inquiry must be defined in terms of the purpose of the inquiry.

But, in response to this last claim, the question of "whose purpose should we focus on?" arose. Should it be the purpose of the individual? Should it be the purpose of society as a whole? Or, perhaps, there are purposes even more important than those of either the individual or society that should be focused on instead.

The advocate of this last option most important to our history is E. A. Singer, Jr. who made his contribution during the 1920s and 1930s while teaching at the University of Pennsylvania. Singer helped develop a philosophical school of thought called "Non-Relativistic Pragmatism" which says that, while we cannot derive absolute truths through reflection or from our investigation of reality using scientific inquiry, such truths do, indeed, exist. Their form is that of "ideals." He continued, saying that such ideals are, by definition, unattainable. However, because do they exist, or can at least be defined, they allow us to understand what the answers in our search for absolutes "ought to be." Equally as important, because ideals, due to their nature, reach beyond the constraints of scientific rigor, we are allowed, once again, in our quest for absolutes on which to base our reality, to include human values in the equation. The objective of our inquiry, then, when our perspective is that of a nonrelativistic pragmatist, is to come as close as possible to "value-full" ideals/absolutes and to move, at the same time, away from "value-free" ideals/absolutes.

Singer also pointed out that due to this new approach, this new breadth of perspective, it was no longer possible for the branches of science to remain separate in their search for solutions to problems. In order to come up with that answer which most closely approximates the ideal, we must now take into consideration the viewpoint of all sciences. The moment we start excluding branches in our inquiry, our eventual answer will begin losing richness and, therefore, will begin receding from the sought-for ideal.

The walls between the different sciences had to come tumbling down. The walls between the sciences and the "arts" had to come tumbling down. No scientist could now proceed without taking into account the effects of his or her work on other realms. For example, a new, faster, more efficient computer technology (electronics, physics, maybe even chemistry) might strain the nervous system of users (physiology) or might displace jobs (economics, psychology, sociology). Another example is the recent advances made in the field of genetic cloning (biology, chemistry, botany) which raise serious moral or values issues that need to be addressed by philosophers and ethicists. Such advances also, of course, raised important social issues.

Von Bertalanffy Broadens the Perspective of Science

At the same time that the pragmatists were putting their synthetic model together, a related, revolutionary event was occurring in the field of science. Ludwig von Bertralanffy was laying the groundwork for what was to be known as "general systems theory." von Bertalanffy began as a biologist. In his quest for an acceptable foundation upon which to build his studies he developed concepts which eventually found applications in all sciences — physical, social, behavioral, pure, and applied.

What he said contradicted the traditional approach, *analysis*, upon which scientific research had been based since the advent of empiricism. What he said introduced *synthesis* as an equal partner. Like nonrelativistic pragmatism, von Bertalanffy's new approach facilitated the break down of the boundaries between the various fields of science. Like nonrelativistic pragmatism it encouraged the reintroduction of human values.

Analysis had traditionally been the major tool of science. In order to understand thoroughly a phenomenon in nature, a machine, an argument, analysis was used to break it down into its smallest, indivisible parts. The next step was to learn the characteristics of those parts. Once all the parts were understood, the whole was presumed understood because the parts made up the whole. The sum of the characteristics of the parts then represented the characteristics of the whole.

Von Bertalanffy disagreed. He said that even though the characteristics discovered through analysis were important, "*A whole is more than the sum of its parts.*" He said that the interactions between parts were just as critical as the parts themselves, and that the interactions of the whole with the environment of which it was a part was also critical. These previously ignored interactions gave the *whole* characteristics which none of the *parts*, individually, possessed.

Based on his realizations, in 1928, several years after gaining his doctorate from the University of Vienna, von Bertalanffy published a book entitled *Modern Theories of Development* that helped trigger a revolution in the world of science. In it he said that while analysis remained important in our quest for "truths" upon which to build our reality, upon which to base individual and societal development, synthesis was equally as important.

His pronouncements broadened our perspective considerably. Because analysis moved "inward," the different branches of science had tended to become increasingly focused and isolated from each other. The systems approach encouraged science to move "outward" as well, to study interactions, thus fostering an interdisciplinary approach. In the early days of science, theory developed in one field had generally been dealt with as unrelated to other fields. Engineering theory, for example, as we have seen in the workplace, had little use for psychological theory. Rather, engineers simply expected everyone else to play by their rules.

Von Bertalanffy's systems approach now provided a meta-theory that incorporated all others, one complete with fundamental laws and principles relevant to all sciences, one which, by moving outward as well as inward, provided a thoroughly acceptable rationale for the incorporation of human values into scientific work. Values might not always affect the individual parts of a system, especially when that system does not possess a human component, especially, for example, when that system is a machine. But values certainly affect the interactions of that system with the external environment of which it is a part, the external environment that now has to be taken into account.

This breakthrough and the obvious relaxation of scientific rigor which accompanied it (remember that values cannot be quantified) encouraged scientists to become involved in workplace issues and other social problems without feeling the need to first transform the area of study into a laboratory. A new research methodology was defined, one which sacrificed some of the rigor of analysis for the richness of synthesis. The new methodology was called "participant–observer."

Basically, when using participant–observer methodology, researchers, did not take control and reorganize an operation to fit the requirements of rigor. Rather, they simply joined in and took notes so as not to disturb the natural flow of things, the natural interactions, the involved value system. In this way the researcher gained a more accurate (especially in terms of the intangibles) picture. A previously mentioned and famous example of participant-observer research, one which produced valuable results, was the employee motivation studies done by Mayo and Roethlisberger at the Western Electric plant in Chicago.

The systems perspective spread rapidly to other fields of scientific endeavor. Rapaport and Rosen took the lead in mathematics, Boulding in economics, Zerbst in physiology, Livesey and Clark in education, Grey and

Rizzo in psychology, Pattee in biology, and Thayer in the field of communications theory. The systems approach eventually reached the world of management theory under the guidance of scholars like Thorsrud, Trist, Churchman, Emery, Beer, Schon, and Ackoff.

As has happened historically, leadership toward "new world management" was also provided by a very small group of enlightened CEOs. Chester Barnard, President of New Jersey Bell Telephone, was perhaps the most notable of these. In his 1938 book entitled *The Function of the Executive*, Barnard defined organizations as "cooperative systems" and defined a cooperative system as a "complex of physical, biological, personal, and social components" which cooperate to achieve a definite end. He said that "willingness to serve," a "common purpose," and "communication" are the interdependent factors holding all organizations together.[3]

But the three thinkers who have done the most to shape modern-day management theory are Peter Drucker, Russell Ackoff, and W. Edwards Deming. Many others have made extremely valuable contributions, but this threesome has provided a comprehensive framework. Their contributions complement each other the same way those of their theoretical ancestors — Adam Smith, Robert Owen, Frederick Taylor — did. Peter Drucker, like Smith, has provided an overview of the world of work, its historic roots, its current trends and their meaning in terms of society, and its future requirements if we are to thrive. W. Edwards Deming, although his work is well grounded in theory and although the social implications of what he did were of major concern to him, made his greatest contribution, like his predecessor Frederick Taylor, on the shop floor where he dealt with the individual details of increasing productivity.

Russell Ackoff, like Owen, is the middleman. He is the most systemic of the three, joining the macro- and the microworlds, linking the necessary philosophical foundation with the nuts and bolts of change. He defined the necessary parts, then attempted to meld them into a comprehensive whole, showing how to turn management theory into productive practice. Ackoff has moved from a *rationalistic* definition of what is most important in life and how work should facilitate its achievement to the *pragmatic* redesign of the key organization processes necessary to accomplish this end.

Drucker Provides the Overview

But let us start with Peter Drucker, best known as an astute commentator on the realities of economic life and as a man with great skill at telling us what to expect as the pace of change in all sectors of our lives continues to accelerate. Drucker was born and raised in Austria. After receiving his LL.D. from the University of Frankfort, one of his first jobs was as a newspaper writer and editor. His first book, which was on political theory, got him into trouble with the Nazi regime and was eventually banned. The author moved first to England, and then, in 1937, to the United States as a correspondent for a group of British newspapers.

In the United States Drucker eventually taught, spending 20 years at New York University, then ending up at Claremont Graduate School in California. He began consulting in 1943. His first client was General Motors. He never stopped writing, producing hundreds of articles and a number of books, most of which are still popular. One of his most important works was *The End of Economic Man*. In it he argued that the world's economic systems — capitalism, socialism, communism — were all based on the assumption which first appeared during the early Industrial Revolution in England that human beings are driven mainly by their economic interests (the economic man concept). Drucker argued that this assumption was no longer valid, if, in fact, it had ever been valid. He said that with these three economic systems in place, people were not gaining the freedom they craved, were not gaining the equality they deserved. He said that people had become frustrated with this lack of progress, and, using war as their vehicle, had begun destroying the traditional order so that something new might emerge, so that an order no longer totally dependent on economic considerations might be built.

Drucker saw an industrial society as the end product of World War II. He believed that in order for it to survive, this new society would have to give its citizens *social status* (an acceptable identity) and *social function* (a meaningful role in making society work). He believed that unless *legitimate decision-making power* (democracy) was also gained, the required improvements would not occur. He believed that if the new society failed to provide these three things, individual citizens would again begin to feel disenfranchised and, eventually, would again turn against their leaders, so that the cycle of destruction would repeat itself.

Drucker saw the *corporation* as that institutional model which offered the most hope in terms of shaping and supporting the desired social paradigm. Corporations provided both social status and social function. He also thought that corporations were best at getting things done. In terms of corporate management, he believed that, "there never has been a more efficient, a more honest, a more capable and conscientious group of rulers than the professional managers of the great American corporations today."[4]

There were, however, problems with using corporations as a model for governance and as a model for the best way of distributing society's wealth.

One problem was Drucker's defined need to give citizens *legitimate decision making power* (democracy). Corporations do not do this. Corporations were not truly controlled by the stockholders who owned them; they were not truly controlled by the employees whose fate they decided. Most important decisions in corporations were made by the board of directors which, in turn, was frequently dominated by the CEO. What we had, therefore, was a dictatorship, or, at best, a form of fascism in the corporate domain, rather than a democracy.

A second problem was that, with the growing emphasis of the corporation on efficiency, we were moving back toward the economic man model that Drucker said we were trying to get away from. Employees were growing increasingly subservient to technology. Their only reward was the paycheck coupled with increased physical security. According to Drucker's beliefs, this was not enough and would lead to another upheaval.

Drucker did not know how to deal with these problems. One possible solution he offered was that the workforce should become a *self-governing community*, a democratic community. How such a transition should occur, however, what the nature of the necessary transition vehicle should be, he did not know. Social status and social function were also not assured. In his book *Concept of the Corporation*, Drucker said that corporations, by nature, should be self-renewing organizations, but that they are too frequently threatened in their progress by ossifying bureaucracies that turn employees into faceless, powerless cogs. He said that in order to help ensure social status and social function for employees, these bureaucratic, top-down tendencies had to be fought. Workers had to be encouraged to understand their individual importance, how they contributed to the whole. Employees had to be encouraged to suggest improvements. Also, their wages needed to be tied in some way to their productivity.

On the societal level, Drucker said that full employment was critical. How to achieve it, however, was again a question he did not try to answer. Neither did Drucker presume to know how to bring about the necessary change in cultural attitude, the necessary change in the current workplace paradigm. Drucker ended up, like Adam Smith, depending on the inherent goodness and rationality of man. He said that people themselves would have to take responsibility for making sure that the desired change went in the right direction.

Drucker, however, was not just a dreamer. He knew that increased productivity was the first necessity, the cornerstone to all developmental progress. He offered the concept of management by objective (MBO) as a means of getting managers especially to define their activities in terms of producing the desired bottom-line results, rather than simply in terms of running things. MBO involved all bosses sitting down with their direct reports one at a time and helping to define the report's objectives for the next year. Drucker's ideal organization was bound together by an integrated network of such objectives upon which all activities were based. All employees had to be involved in the definition of their own objectives and had to know how their objectives fit into the whole, thus giving every employee social status, social function, and control.

Peter Drucker, to this day, has stuck with his belief that the business sector provides the best models for social development and for the necessary cultural integration. Although it is trying hard, government is not capable of tying the world together. The sector that is making the most progress in this respect is industry. One example is the European Common Market, which began strictly as a vehicle for economic unification but is now becoming a vehicle for cultural integration as well. NAPTA in North, Central, and South America and the series of economic partnerships developing between the Asian countries are other examples.

Drucker has also talked at length about the fact that the most basic and important economic resource is no longer money or labor or power or natural resources. Rather, it is *knowledge*, which is information that takes values into account. He says that as technology takes over more and more lower-level jobs the workforce will have two segments. One will be the knowledge workers who are highly educated. The second will be the service workers who have less education and who will support the knowledge workers.

Drucker says that as more and more companies become knowledge based, the need for employees to be able to, to be allowed to control their own activities will grow. Everyone will become a "boss" of sorts due to constantly increasing levels of expertise. He says that as companies make increasingly effective use of knowledge to create change they will become the major destabilizers of society and, therefore, will have to take more responsibility for dealing with the instability they have helped create. He says that as "bosses," all employees will need to shoulder part of this responsibility.

Peter Drucker is obviously a Christian humanist in spirit. He is also, however, a pragmatist, understanding the need for the efficient development of resources. Drucker is one of the first modern-day management theorists to focus on generating the necessary, integrated overview of the role of the economic sector in society, that overview into which all the other pieces have to fit. He points out in his book, *The Age of Discontinuity*, that due to the increasing speed with which quantum leaps are being made in technology and in the physical and behavioral sciences, our chances of predicting future consequences of the changes fostered by these leaps are decreasing. The most viable alternative left us at this point, therefore, is to try to understand these changes within "their historical perspective and to develop the disciplines (systems thought), the techniques — and above all, the social philosophy — necessary to not merely cope with the resultant changes, but to build from them a better society for everyone."[5]

Deming Organizes the Workplace

W. Edwards Deming began at the other end of the spectrum. Whereas Drucker focuses on the macroview, Deming focused on the microview. Deming started where Frederick Taylor left off. He took Taylor's scientific management, his basically engineering school approach to increasing productivity, and improved on it greatly. He then combined these improvements with insights developed by members of the human relations school to come up with a comprehensive model for organization change that enjoyed the strengths of both. Deming, through his work, was instrumental in bringing *sociotechnical* theory, or the part of systems theory, which deals with defining the best combination of workers and technology and with defining the best way to satisfy the needs of both, to life.

Deming graduated from Yale in 1928 with a doctoral degree in mathematical physics. During his Ph.D. studies, he worked at the previously mentioned Western Electric Hawthorne Plant in Chicago. While there, he met Walter Shewhart, the acknowledged father of statistical quality control who influenced his work and contribution greatly. Deming took a job at the U.S. Department of Agriculture after leaving Yale. His research on statistical sampling led to acceptance of the concept by the Census Bureau, and then, eventually, by the governmental and business sectors of society in general.

While with the Census Bureau, Deming also worked to perfect methods of statistical quality control that would provide a means of improving the reliability of the information produced. In 1946 he began teaching at New York University and consulting on the side. One of his major clients soon became the nation of Japan, which at that point was struggling to recover economically from World War II. As a result of his work and of the successes he helped generate in Japan during the following 10 years, his theories and the tools he had developed became increasingly popular in his home country.

Deming's focus was on improving the quality of products and services as a means of improving the bottom line. He said that improving the bottom line would be a natural result of improving quality, but that without improving quality, the bottom line, at least in the long run, would not improve. Most executives in their struggle to keep stock prices up and to keep owners happy focused on improving profit margins by continually cutting costs no matter what happened to sales. Deming proved, once again, that when companies focused on improving quality instead and did what was necessary to improve quality, they cut costs and at the same time guaranteed increased sales. By focusing on quality, companies generated both loyal customers and loyal employees. As a result of the activities of these two key groups, profits went up and costs went down, with everyone happy, everyone a winner.

Deming believed that employees had to take personal responsibility for improving the quality of their product and that the best incentive, the best way to get them to do so was to show them respect. Providing job security was the number one priority in terms of this necessary display of respect. A second priority was a reasonable compensation system. Deming pointed out that in Japan, when productivity began to drop, or when customers were lost, the managers took responsibility, took the first pay cuts. In the United States, however, when things went bad, the workers were traditionally blamed and were the first ones punished with pay cuts. At the same time upper-level managers in the United States frequently continued to award themselves raises and bonuses. This practice, in his opinion, did not demonstrate the desired degree of respect.

Deming believed that good management systems and practices were also key to getting workers to take responsibility for improving quality. He believed that:

> Management is people. Most managers in the western world, however, see management as rules, regulations, organization methods and motivation techniques. But in [my] view, all of the management structure should be directed toward one aim, allowing the individual to perform his or her job to the utmost while experiencing joy in his or her work in a manner consistent with the aims of the organization. It is the leader's job to foster joy in work, harmony, and teamwork.[6]

It was management's obligation to encourage cooperation on all levels — between individual workers, between departments, between individual managers, between managers and workers, between the company and its customers, between the company and its suppliers. Deming encouraged cooperation even, at times, between the company and its competitors. He said that anything in the work environment that sparked competition should be eliminated. This included production quotas, performance evaluations, and even Peter Drucker's MBO. Unfortunately, as with so many of the business-related concepts we have studied, MBO has too frequently been perverted and used as a threat to hang over the employee's head to force increases in productivity, increases that are not accompanied by a related increase in reward.

Deming believed that when things go wrong, looking around for someone to blame is usually a waste of time. He said that 85% of what goes wrong in organizations results actually from systemic problems; that only 15% can honestly be laid at the feet of the individual.[7] Employees should focus of finding solutions, rather than on affixing blame. But to find those solutions, employees needed the appropriate training along with the right tools. One such tool is the "Plan–Do–Check–Act" cycle. The steps in this cycle include:

1. Plan and design a change that will improve.
2. Try it on a small scale at first.
3. Observe the results of the change.
4. Then either improve on the initial improvement or, if the desired results have been achieved, standardize it.[8]

In order to facilitate these steps, Deming provided seven types of charts (mostly statistics based) useful to the necessary description and understanding of key manufacturing processes and to the measurement of what the processes produced. These diagrams and charts included the *cause-and-effect* or *fishbone* diagram which depicts the causes of problems and categorizes them; *flow charts* which show the steps in a process; *pareto charts* which collect data and rank causes; *run charts* which plot the results of a process over time; *histograms* which measure how frequently something happens; *scatter diagrams* which show the relationship between two variables; *control charts* which tell what variations occur within a system and whether they are acceptable according to set standards or not.[9]

Finally, to provide the necessary overview in terms of management practices, Deming offered his now-famous "Fourteen Points":

1. Create consistency of purpose toward improvement of product and service.
2. Adopt a new philosophy which is based on a positive approach.
3. Cease dependence on mass inspections to achieve quality. Build quality into the product in the first place.
4. End the practice of awarding business based on the price tag alone.

5. Improve constantly and forever the system of production and service.
6. Institute training.
7. Institute leadership.
8. Drive out fear. People should be unafraid to question.
9. Break down barriers between departments.
10. Eliminate slogans, exhortations, and targets for the workforce.
11. Eliminate quotas and management by objectives (MBO).
12. Remove barriers to pride in workmanship.
13. Institute a vigorous program of education and self-education.
14. Take the action necessary to accomplish the transformation.[10]

Deming was obviously also a Christian humanist searching for the best mix of technology and employee expertise. He tried to find that combination of training and empowerment which maximized productivity while, at the same time, meeting the workplace needs of the employees involved.

Ackoff Creates a Systemic Whole

Russell Ackoff is another in the long line of Philadelphians who have made major contributions to management theory. In many ways he has tied the work of Drucker and Deming together, creating the necessary "whole." Ackoff has discovered, or rediscovered, the necessary "philosophical viewpoint" or philosophical foundation for societal development that Drucker has been searching for. He has then set about developing the tools and techniques of change necessary to its realization. Dr. Ackoff's initial professional degree was in architecture. He then earned his Ph.D. in the philosophy of science at the University of Pennsylvania under the tutelage of Professor E. A. Singer, Jr., focusing on the need for an "interconnection between scientific inquiry and functional, goal-seeking and purposeful [human, value driven] behavior."[11]

Ackoff and his fellow classmate, C. West Churchman, stayed at the university and set up an Institute of Experimental Method in 1946 to encourage interdisciplinary research. The rationale behind this effort according to Ackoff was that it:

> ...was already clear that the problems most pressing mankind could no longer be fruitfully treated by specialists. A synthesis of scientific disciplines was inevitable. The effort to create scientific generalists was doomed to failure because it acquired breadth at the cost of depth. Research by interdisciplinary teams was the only feasible alternative.[12]

The two men shifted from there into the leadership of the operations research movement, trying to maintain their interdisciplinary approach. But operations research, like every other science at that point, as it developed and defined itself, became increasingly narrow and analytical. By so doing the new science proved itself incapable of dealing with the broad, fundamental issues of corporate and social policy, with the issue of values.

Ackoff and Churchman refused to compromise, raising the ire of purists and of the departments whose turf they were intruding upon. They left the University of Pennsylvania in the late 1940s, carrying their work to two other institutions where they stayed for more than a decade before Ackoff returned to The Wharton School in 1973 to try again. With the help of Eric Trist from the Tavistock Institute he founded the Social Science Systems Ph.D. program (nicknamed S3) which taught the systems approach to management. The objective of the program was to develop an approach to dealing with problems at all organization levels and, eventually, with problems at all levels of society. Ackoff, his associates, and students worked with national governments, regional governments, cities, and neighborhoods, as well as with corporations, school systems, health care systems, and other nonprofit and not-for-profit organizations.

This versatility was made possible by the philosophical foundation of the program, *pragmatic rationalism*, taken from Singer's work. All students began their studies by reviewing the major philosophical schools of thought. They then focused on Aristotle's theory of human development which Ackoff believed provided the "ultimate idealized truth." This is the truth foundational to pragmatic rationalism and to societal development on any level, be it in the workplace or the neighborhood. This is the ultimate idealized truth foundational to the effective design and improvement of all corporate and community systems.

This was the same theory of human development used by leading thinkers of the Renaissance as the wellspring first for Machiavellian humanism, then for Christian humanism. This is the comprehensive piece that has been missing in our modern-day attempts to make sense of the changes that have occurred since the Church lost control of the economic world at the end of the Medieval period. The lack of this piece can be related to most of the historical aberrations that we have discussed — misinterpretation and misuse of the works of Martin Luther, Adam Smith, and Frederick Taylor, the Social Darwinism movement, the emphasis on efficiencies and growth at all costs found during the Industrial Revolution, the struggle against employee empowerment.

During these centuries, society has lacked the necessary long-term perspective to frame its efforts. People have, as a result, simply progressed from one event to the next, living each moment for itself with nothing to guide us but our instincts.

Perhaps we chose to do so purposely as a result of the still firmly entrenched scarcity mentality. Perhaps we did so in our lingering fear of church domination. Perhaps we did so because the limited perspective of the rationale we chose to adopt during this period, empiricism, served our purpose. What happened as a result of our "wanderings," however, is that we gradually forgot the purpose of "work" as well as, on a grander scale, the purpose of life in general.

Henry Ford addresses this issue in his 1922 autobiography, *My Life And Work.* He says:

> We have already done too much toward banishing the pleasant things from life by thinking that there is some opposition between *living* and *providing the means of living.* We waste so much time and energy [in this latter activity] that we have little left to expend enjoying ourselves. Power and machinery, money and goods, are useful only as they set us free to live. [They are not an end in themselves;] they are only means to an end.[13]

This is what Aristotle's theory of human and societal development offers, the necessary systemic overview in terms of a social philosophy, the necessary means for getting us back on track, and the necessary underlying reason for everything we do. It is also a reason that makes sense in that it provides the desired balance and can be applied successfully to any era, past, present, or future. At the same time, what Aristotle gave us was also practical, guiding us in our everyday efforts to deal effectively with the here and now, with the nuts and bolts of our immediate situation.

Aristotle and his students basically said that the purpose of life is *to develop and enjoy our positive human potential to the fullest possible extent.* The role of work in such a scenario was, and still is, to help generate the resources necessary to such development and enjoyment. The Greeks named four such critical resources generated either directly or indirectly through some type of work (work being defined as the expenditure of energy to achieve a desired outcome).

The first resource or "pursuit" as the Greeks actually labeled it, is "plenty." This has to do with pursuit of the wealth necessary to development, on an individual and on a societal level. We require enough wealth to afford the things necessary to survive, enough wealth to meet our basic *needs* including food, shelter, security. In order to achieve the physical security mentioned in Chapter 4, we also need enough wealth to meet our reasonable *desires* (things that are important, but are not requisite to survival). It is hard to think about developing our potential when we are forced to work constantly in order to simply survive. Wealth is the most important input. Without it, the others cannot be generated.

The second resource necessary to development is what Aristotle labels "truth." This has to do with pursuit of the key ingredients of education — data, information, knowledge, wisdom. It has to do with the obligation of society to put vehicles into place which encourage and allow the individual and the general public to gain access to data, information, knowledge, and wisdom and, at the same time, to learn how to learn.

The third resource necessary to development is "good." This concerns the formation of a "government," of a means of regulating and integrating "society" on every level including the workplace level. It concerns the pursuit of a system of governance that encourages citizens or workers to develop and enjoy their potential. An enlightened *autocracy* might be capable of doing so. Overall, however, the autocratic approach has produced the worst results historically.

Several alternative forms of government allow specific segments of society the power to ensure their rights in terms of developing individual potential. These include the *plutocracy* (rule by the wealthy) and *fascism* (rule by extremely conservative business and governmental leaders). The form of government, however, that most effectively encourages the pursuit of "good" by the largest percentage of people if they are willing to participate is a *democracy.*

The fourth resource is "beauty." This pursuit has mainly to do with the environment. It is extremely difficult to develop one's potential when one is trying to do so in a situation that is noisy, dirty, too cold, too hot. Where the air is polluted, where our surroundings are bleak and unattractive, where those we must interact with are nasty, it is difficult to perform. Research indicates that environmental conditions affect creativity, and they affect even our ability to think clearly. In order to encourage development, an environment must be both soothing and stimulating. This is not impossible. This is not an either/or situation, as we might think. Beauty, and perhaps only beauty can combine and simultaneously possess these two characteristics. Take, for example, a magnificent sunset, one that inspires awe, feelings of fullness, the excitement of having tapped into the power of the universe while, at the same time producing a feeling of deep inner peace. In the modern-day workplace, because of our obsession with efficiency, the pursuit of "beauty" has traditionally been a low priority.

One additional idealized input might be added to the list in order to address our current situation. That input is "time." We might have enough wealth. We might, at the same time, be well educated and well governed. Our environment might be both stimulating and peaceful. But if we do not have the time to take advantage of our situation, to utilize these inputs, their value is wasted. Time is especially relevant as a necessary input in the United States and in parts of Asia. While many Europeans enjoy 6 weeks of vacation, most employees in the United States are allowed only 2. While the work week in Europe is gradually growing shorter (closer to 30 hours than 40), allowing more time for developmental activities, the work week is growing steadily longer in the United States (closer to 60 hours than 50). And the situation, in terms of free time, is frequently even worse in Asia.

It is the role of society to facilitate individual development and enjoyment of positive human potential to the fullest possible extent. It is our responsibility as citizens, in turn, to support society's efforts. Five key resources are necessary — plenty, truth, good, beauty, time. Ackoff revived the development ethic as a philosophical foundation for the systems school of thought and as a springboard for the reorientation of society. What he did, in effect, along with Peter Drucker and W. Edwards Deming, was to set the stage for a paradigm shift, for a major shift in the way society thinks. Ackoff, Drucker, and Deming then began to develop the tools necessary to facilitate this shift. While Ackoff has helped shape many such tools on both the quantitative and nonquantitative sides, the two most important in terms of our discussion are probably his *interactive planning model* (sometimes called "proactive") and his concept of the *circular organization* or the *democratic hierarchy.* Both will be discussed in detail in Chapter 11.

What we need to say here is that both of these tools engender an atmosphere that encourages Christian humanism. They both effectively combine the strengths of technology with those of the workforce. They both encourage the development of employee potential as well as that of the organization as a whole through the generation and equitable distribution of the necessary resources. In other words, they both are the kind of tools necessary for making the development ethic a reality, for finally giving Christian humanism the advantage.

Topics for Discussion

1. How did nonrelativistic pragmatism bring about the eventual synthesis of rationalism and empiricism?
2. Why did von Bertalanffy's revelations concerning "systems" allow "participant–observer" research methodology to evolve?
3. What was the major change that Peter Drucker saw necessarily occurring in the nature of the workplace?
4. What were the three things that Drucker thought society needed to provide its workers with, and how did he propose for society to do so?
5. With what tools and techniques did W. Edwards Deming arm employees so that they could take responsibility for improved product quality?
6. Why was Deming against the use of management by objective?
7. What was the "ultimate truth" that Russell Ackoff offered as the philosophical foundation for positive change in the work culture?
8. How do Drucker, Deming, and Ackoff complement each other in terms of their contributions?

Notes

1. C. West Churchman and Russell Ackoff, *Methods of Inquiry: An Introduction to Philosophy and Scientific Method*, St. Louis: Educational Publishing Co., 1950, p. 117.
2. *Ibid.*, p. 117.
3. Chester I. Barnard, *The Function of the Executive*, Cambridge, MA: Harvard University Press, 1938, p. 65.
4. John J. Tarrant, *Drucker: The Man Who Invented the Corporate Society*, Boston: Cahners Books, 1976, p. 28.
5. *Ibid.*, p. 239.
6. Rafael Aguayo, *Dr. Deming: The American Who Taught the Japanese about Quality*, New York: Carol Publishing Group, 1990, p. 181.
7. Mary Walton, *Deming: Management at Work*, New York: Perigree Books, 1990, p. 20.
8. *Ibid.*, pp. 21–22.
9. *Ibid.*, p. 24.
10. Aguayo, *op. cit.*, p. 124.
11. Churchman and Ackoff, *op. cit.*, p. 326.
12. *Ibid.*, p. 326.
13. Henry Ford, *My Life and Work*, Salem, NH: Aayer Company Publishers, 1922, pp. 1–2.

The Post-Industrial
Revolution Era:
The Slowly Shifting Tide

After Reading This Chapter You Should Know

1. Why the United States began encouraging quality improvement and why the movement did not produce the desired results.
2. How the computer is changing the concept of "work."
3. The difference between "data," "information," "knowledge," and "wisdom."
4. The four types of "work" that have existed historically.
5. The evolution of the "leadership" role in the workplace.
6. The relationship between a society's socioeconomic philosophy and the management style encouraged.
7. How the interactive planning paradigm makes the best use of employee expertise.
8. How the "circular organization" concept introduces democracy in the workplace.
9. How organization processes are best improved by a systemic quality improvement effort.

The Battle Continues

Meanwhile, down in the trenches, the Christian humanists were getting their act together. They were generating increasing amounts of evidence that treating employees with respect produced the best bottom-line results, and, more important, that if the advancement of society in general was the major objective of the economic sector, employee involvement was the only acceptable alternative. The *development ethic* was beginning to make a comeback as the major motivational force of society. Despite all this, the battle between the quantitative, engineering, efficiency-oriented school and the people-oriented, human relations school continued to rage.

Nowhere was this battle portrayed more clearly than in the U.S. quality improvement scramble. This scramble began when Dr. Deming's work in Japan helped Japan begin to capture a steadily increasing slice of the world market in a growing range of product areas including cars, computers, toys. European nations, recovering from World War II were also biting into markets that the United States had "owned" since the 1940s. The issue was product quality. Because the United States had faced little or no competition during this period, it had been able to sell just about anything. The concept of "planned obsolescence" had been accepted as part of the U.S. economic philosophy. Products were designed to last a limited period of time. The logic was that such a system would increase sales, keep production levels high, and help keep people employed. Of course, their quality of life would not necessarily improve due to the fact that families were continuously having to replace broken-down cars, watches, refrigerators, shoes.

The second weakness of this argument was that recycling had not yet become a serious consideration. The United States began consuming a major share of the world's available resources, by some estimates up the 80%. The United States, during the period following World War II, was called the "throw-away" society.

Europeans and Japanese quickly honed in on the resentment generated by planned obsolescence and focused on product quality, forcing the United States to react and to start its own quality improvement movement in the 1970s and 1980s. Two camps immediately evolved mirroring the "engineering" and the "human relations" schools. The first focused on increasing efficiencies, combining jobs, improving manufacturing and service delivery systems through modeling, getting rid of excess functions and employees. This approach was "expert" driven. Consultants with quantitative backgrounds were brought in to do the necessary analysis and to develop the necessary models. Deming was a hero to this camp because of the statistical measurement tools he had developed. Most of the involved consultants, however, ignored the other 90% of his systemic model that was nonquantitative and that focused on effectively utilizing employee expertise.

The quantitative approach grew more sophisticated with the introduction by Michael Hammer in the 1990s of "reengineering," a technique that was first used, at least in modern times, by Henry Ford. Reengineering is the process of continually taking apart products and redesigning them to improve performance. Hammer applied this same approach to entire organizations. In that it addresses the organizational "whole," it is systemic. But that is where the similarity ends. Reengineering is efficiency oriented and rarely takes into account the perspective or ideas of employees except those at the highest level.

A reengineering effort starts by identifying the distinctive competencies of an organization, by defining what the organization is good at, or what it wants to be good at. The effort then identifies and evaluates the core processes which support these distinctive competencies. It defines weaknesses in them and possible improvements to them. One of the techniques used during this second phase is the identification of processes that are not really necessary, that do not "add value." Expert, cross-functional teams are then formed at the top levels of the organization to redesign the support processes with emphasis on increasing efficiency and cutting costs. Managers are a popular target of these efforts in terms of reducing costs (salaries), although all levels usually suffer cutbacks and the workload of those left grows rapidly.

Increased competitiveness and greater profitability are obviously the major objectives of reengineering, rather than *development* as we have defined it. Emphasis is solely on increasing *one* of the required inputs, *plenty*. The rest are ignored. However, reengineering remains extremely popular in the late 1900s. A recent survey found that with manufacturing firms 44% of those surveyed in the United States said that they were involved in a reengineering exercise or were thinking about starting one. With insurance companies this figure was 52% and with utilities it was 48%.[1]

The approach to quality improvement offered by the other camp, the modern-day human relations camp, was also expert driven. These consultants, however, had backgrounds in psychology, organization behavior, organization development. This group focused on making the individual employee more productive, on building teams, on improving interpersonal communications, on improving morale. Technology became secondary.

Both groups, therefore, suffered from the lack of the necessary comprehensive overview. The engineering school, following its tradition, refused to take the needs and potential of employees into account in its blind quest for greater efficiencies. The modern-day human relations champions suffered because of their focus on the "pieces" and because of their lack of an integrating mechanism that would make sense of the whole they were building. Obviously, as has been true throughout modern history at least, a systemic approach was necessary in order to integrate and take advantage of the strengths of both camps.

The Computer as the Development Ethic's Best Friend

This need for a systemic approach was intensified greatly by the appearance of a new player on the block, the computer. This new technology is in the process of changing everything from the role of work in society to how we accomplish it. To understand the significance of the computer, we have to go back again and follow another historical progression. This progression has to do with the nature of work. Three parts of the human organism — our *hands*, our *memories*, our *thinking minds* — are important to the accomplishment of work-related tasks. Initially, during the Medieval period, all three played a role. Most of the work was done by peasants in the fields and by craftsmen using their hands to both provide the necessary power and to shape the product. Techniques were learned and remembered (memory). Workers themselves were constantly trying to discover new ways to improve both products and processes (thinking minds).

This situation changed with the advent of improved technology and with the division of labor concept introduced and perfected during the Industrial Revolution. Now workers no longer provided the energy with their hands. They no longer shaped the product with their hands. At the same time, workers were also no longer responsible for improving the involved processes. Engineers took care of that. Now workers used only their memories. They memorized their tasks, which were usually extremely simple, and repeated the same movements over and over in the most efficient manner possible. Use of their thinking minds was discouraged. The fear was that they might decide to do something differently and, as a result, might decrease the efficiency of the operation.

Then, in the late 1940s, came the computer, which caused another dramatic shift. Computer-driven technology replaced hands in the fields. Computer-driven robots replaced hands in primary industry as well as in a growing number of service-related industries. Memory of the involved tasks was now also built into the computers and stored there. What was and is left for humans in the workplace, therefore, were two tasks. The first was the evaluation and the effective use of the data gathered by the computers. The second was the incorporation of individual and societal values into decisions.

This change being forced by the computer in our workplace role is rapidly turning us into a society of Peter Drucker's "knowledge workers." The effect of the computer on our work culture will be greater than that of any previous technology, including the steam engine which triggered industrialization. In the late 1800s approximately 80% of the U.S. workforce was involved in farming, working on the land to produce food. In the late 1900s this figure has shrunk to around 5%, technology, a lot of it computerized, having taken over. In the early decades of the 1900s a majority of our employees worked in primary industry, in factories. Now, that figure has shrunk to around 15%, computer-driven technology having taken over.

At this point in history, approximately 80% of our workforce holds jobs in the service sector. But again the computer is making serious inroads. The banking industry, for example, could be almost totally computerized. Computers are playing an increasingly important role in the entertainment industry, the health care industry, the education industry, the insurance industry. Some skills, of course, cannot be effectively duplicated by technology. Most of these have to do with the need for human contact, with the need for the human touch.

Another type of work that computers cannot take over, as we have said, is work which calls for "value-full" thought and decisions. Computers are incapable of incorporating human values, with all their richness, into the equation. They are incapable of addressing the "why" questions that humans must deal with in terms of both individual and societal development. Computers can assist in the necessary planning; they can provide the requisite *data*, the requisite *information*. But they are incapable of generating either the *knowledge* or the *wisdom* necessary to the "best" answer.

It is important, at this point, to understand the differences between data and information, between knowledge and wisdom.

1. *Data* — Raw facts and figures generated by some kind of analysis. For example, machine "A" produced 1067 widgets today, 67 of which were defective.
2. *Information* — Data combined in a way that makes it useful. For example, machine "A" produced the same number of widgets and half as many defects as machine "B." (Time to figure out why this happened so we can improve the productivity of machine "B").
3. *Knowledge* — Information that incorporates values. These values can be either positive or negative. Machiavelli had a lot of knowledge, as did Adam Smith's "monopolists" and the Social Darwinists. Their

knowledge, however, was used for strictly selfish gain, rather than for developmental purposes. They would have picked the approach to the machine "A" and "B" situation that produced the most profit for themselves, without considering the plight of the workers who might be laid off.

4. *Wisdom* — Knowledge that is grounded in developmental values, knowledge grounded in the belief that the purpose of work, of any human activity should be to enable participants and all affected to develop and enjoy their positive potential to the fullest possible extent. Those with wisdom in the case of machine "A" and machine "B" would have definitely taken the effects of their decisions on employees into account.

Redefining Work

Another way to discuss the impact of the computer is in terms of existing types of "work." Four types can be defined based on the amount of *control* and the amount of *opportunity* enjoyed. These are *slave, subsistence level, situation improvement,* and *developmental.* In slave work the person has no control at all and enjoys no opportunity. The slave does what he or she is told on threat of punishment or even death. The only reward is survival. No chance to improve one's situation exists. Many employees during the early Industrial Revolution, as we have said, were locked into slave-type work. They were owned, perhaps not in the legal sense, but as a result of their never decreasing debt to the "company store." For those forced to endure such a situation, neither physical security nor emotional security existed.

In subsistence-level work, employees gain a small degree of freedom and control. They can leave their jobs if they want, but only if other opportunities exist, for the degree of physical security enjoyed is minimal. They also experience a small degree of emotional security resulting from their limited ability to choose. Those subsistence-level workers, however, generally have little formal education, so that the chances for advancement, for improving their situation, for enhancing their level of both physical and emotional security are extremely limited.

Situation-improvement work is what most of us are currently involved in. We are not just meeting our survival-related needs, we can now also afford many of the things we "desire" in order to improve our quality of life. Our degree of physical security has increased tremendously as a result of our increased affluence, as a result, indirectly, of the higher level of education enjoyed by people in this group, as a result of the increasing range of opportunity available to us. True emotional security has also begun to materialize, but is still limited due to our continued emphasis on increasing our wealth (the scarcity mentality persists). Also, although our overall degree of control in life has improved greatly, our control in the workplace still remains limited. Most of us still do what we are told to do, follow the directives given us by bosses, find ourselves involved in work that is repetitious and nondevelopmental.

The ideal, then, in terms of both the degree of control enjoyed and the degree of opportunity enjoyed, is what we call developmental work. In this kind of work people define their own objectives, design their own tasks, control their own time to a large degree. Most important, people involved in developmental work have the opportunity to continue learning, to continually increase their knowledge base, to continue developing their positive potential. Workers qualified to hold developmental jobs are usually highly educated. Examples are researchers, employees of think tanks, consultants, professors, doctors, entrepreneurs. In developmental work employees enjoy both physical and emotional security, physical security because these jobs are usually among the highest paid and emotional security because the greatest degree of control is enjoyed.

Developmental work is exactly the direction in which technology, once again our best friend, is pushing us. Computer-driven technology is now capable of completing the vast majority of slave and subsistence-level jobs that are low-skilled, dull, repetitious, and, most important, nondevelopmental, and of doing them more efficiently than humans. Computers are being programmed to handle an increasing number of situation-improvement jobs. Work of the developmental type is least vulnerable to invasion by the computer. Perhaps that is the reason the entrepreneurial sector of the U.S. economy is the fastest growing. This is as it should be. This is the kind of work that humans should be doing.

The result, then, is that a majority of workers in developed cultures will be employed in the service sector. They will be doing either Drucker's knowledge work or will be supporting those doing the knowledge work. The types of jobs held will obviously be determined mainly by education level. Education, therefore, will become our largest industry, larger even than health care as the emphasis in health care swings toward prevention, toward health maintenance and away from after-the-fact treatment. Designing and implementing the changes necessary in the education sector to meet this growing demand will be one of our greatest challenges.

Because a growing percentage of jobs will be developmental in nature, and because, more than any other type of work, developmental work will provide emotional as well as physical security, the scarcity mentality will begin to fade. Humankind and technology together will have generated sufficient physical security to meet the needs and reasonable desires of the population in at least economically advanced societies. The changing nature of work and the workplace itself will encourage emotional security.

One of the most critical changes resulting from increased physical security and, at the same time, one that will enhance the degree of emotional security enjoyed, is that employees at all levels will be more willing to work in teams. They will be more willing to cooperate and to pool their expertise and talents for the sake of the whole.

As the aforementioned autonomous or self-directed work groups, workers councils, quality improvement teams, and task forces begin to play an increasingly important role in production, leadership in the workplace will also be forced to change radically. The *boss* mentality — You are here to do what I tell you. I make the decisions. I don't care what you think of me so long as you obey — will become increasingly counterproductive and, therefore, will disappear. The traditional *manager* — I want your input. I want your respect. But I still make the final decisions. You are still responsible to me — will also grow increasingly ineffective as jobs become steadily more complex.

The style of leadership that will eventually prevail will be facilitatorship. *Facilitators* are leaders who no longer considers themselves superior to the rest of the team. Facilitators believe only that they are bringing a different set of skills to the effort. "New world" workplace facilitators will focus on developing and effectively integrating the potential and activities of the other team members. This will become their major responsibility, rather than decision making. The team itself will take over the responsibility for making most decisions.

Culture as the Key

This change will come more slowly in some societies than in others as a result of the relationship that exists between socioeconomic philosophy and management style. For example, as we have said, the concept of autonomous work groups was developed in England. However, it did not flourish there. In most cases it did not even survive. England was the birthplace of laissez faire economics, and its industrial success has been built on this approach.

The economic concept of laissez faire, to this day, remains a key ingredient in British policy formulation. Laissez faire economics, due to its "every-man-for-himself" approach to the generation of wealth, reinforces the scarcity mentality. It reinforces the *conflict/competition ethic* between management and labor, between individual employees. It is, therefore, antithetical to the cooperation needed for autonomous work groups to succeed and for the facilitator style of leadership to evolve.

The Scandinavian countries, however, as we have said, adopted a more socialistic economic philosophy. The main objective has been to ensure that *every* citizen enjoys a decent quality of life. Because a respectable quality of life is ensured in Scandinavian countries and because at the same time individual initiative concerning the accumulation of excess wealth as a safeguard against economic uncertainty has been stifled to a large degree by taxes, the scarcity mentality has begun to lose its power to shape the workplace. In that everyone now depends on government to a large degree for prosperity and in that government taxes are dependent on revenues generated by the business sector, it has made increasing sense to work together to ensure those revenues. The concept of empowerment and the facilitatorship style of leadership, therefore, fit.

Eastern European communist countries, as we have said, were the first to introduce workers councils. But these countries went no further in terms of management innovation and empowerment. Communism, as we have also said, is the most extreme form of socialism. The government owns and regulates all businesses. One might suspect that with this economic philosophy in place the scarcity mentality and workplace competition would disappear completely.

But, as we know, the scarcity mentality and workplace competition did not disappear in communist societies. Even though communism has proven itself a relatively efficient vehicle for redistributing a nation's wealth in countries where that wealth had been concentrated in a tiny percentage of the population and even though communist regimes have been fairly effective at providing the basics of survival for all, communism has proven itself woefully incapable of generating the additional wealth necessary to improve the general quality of life for the general public beyond a certain level. While the Scandinavian countries have been able to generate that additional wealth and have constantly been ranked among the top nations in terms of overall quality of life, the communist countries have not. They continue to be ranked among the lowest in the industrialized sector.

As we have said, wealth is foundational to the generation of the inputs necessary to development. Until enough wealth exists on the *individual* level to ensure that each person can fulfill both his or her *basic needs* and *reasonable desires*, people will continue to do whatever they must to gain more. Communism has not allowed this fulfillment to occur. The lesser degree of socialism practiced in a number of other European nations, however, obviously has.

The self-directed work group concept is just now beginning to gain a degree of popularity in the United States. However, relatively few companies have implemented it successfully due largely to even stronger laissez faire tendencies than those found in England. Labor–management councils are also rare in the United States as a result of the traditional antagonism found between unions and management. Finally, there exists a reward system and a corporate resource allocation system that continues to encourage or even to force competition and conflict between peers, between department, between divisions. As a result, quality improvement teams are not producing the desired results, so that by the end of the 1990s the quality improvement movement has been pronounced dead by many.

The third major economic force in the world at this point, in addition Europe and the United States, is Japan, which, since the late 1940s has modeled its economic growth on the West, especially on the United States. Japan has learned from that country's mistakes as well as its successes. The progress of Japan in the world marketplace has been well documented. A major part of this progress has been attributed to teamwork (cooperation) and to the respect that binds workers and leaders together. The scarcity mentality has also inspired competition in Japan, but not between individual workers, not between labor and management, not even so much between companies generating the same product.

Rather, the focus in Japan is on competition between that country as a team and the rest of the world. The economic philosophy of Japan has been laissez faire. Those guiding the Japanese economy, however, have taken the concept to a different level. This is where tradition has played such an important role. Japanese history has been one of almost constant warfare. The key to success in battle has been considered the unquestionable loyalty (to the death) of warriors to their commanders and, in turn, the respect that commanders have shown toward their troops. Conflict within the ranks and the questioning of leadership have been unacceptable.

This tradition of loyalty has carried over into the workplace. Employees work together to "win the battle" and are loyal to their leaders and to each other, so that in-house competition is unusual. Respect is demonstrated by a traditional practice — when a leader receives a bonus, the leader shares the bonus with his or her loyal workers. Concerning the effective utilization of employee expertise and ideas, however, one has to wonder. When the Japanese leader (as facilitator?) asks for worker input concerning a project, does the leader really want it? Or is this mainly a *formality*, a *display* in a culture that historically has demanded at least the appearance of respect? And when the workers voice their total support for the approach chosen and go to work on it wholeheartedly, are they doing so because they really believe this is the best way, or because they believe it would be disrespectful to voice concerns?

So Japan's claim that it exercises a truly participative approach to organization leadership, like that found in Scandinavian countries, is questionable. Also, Japan's love affair with the laissez faire philosophy has begun taking its toll, just as it did in England and, later, in the United States. The 1990s greed-driven scandals in the Japanese banking industry and the discoveries of collusion among industrialists, bankers, and government are reminiscent of the robber baron era in the United States. The tradition of respect is being seriously challenged. The scarcity mentality is gaining a stronger foothold. Japan obviously has some thorny cultural issues to resolve.

Meeting the Planning Challenge

The historic evolution of management theory we have discussed thus far in this book has led us to the point *where the major challenge of society has become finding ways to empower employees so that they can contribute most effectively in the team setting.* Increasing numbers of companies are moving to meet this challenge by thinking systemically. When we think systemically, we talk of organizations mainly in terms of *function* (how the future of the organization and its role in society are decided), *structure* (how the organization as a whole is designed, how the parts are designed and integrated), and *key organization processes* (characteristics of the organization's approach to communication, access to information, problem solving, decision making, training, evaluation, reward).

Function, structure, and key organization processes — these are the necessary parts (on the organization level) that make up the necessary whole.

The systems school, with Ackoff in the lead, has again generated alternatives to the traditional shaping of these "parts," alternatives that do a better job of empowering employees.

Concerning function (the way in which organizations plan their future), organization planning paradigms have traditionally been either expert driven or management dominated, or both. In *expert-driven* planning, a department at the corporate level provides information or both information and recommendations to top-level executives based on the data and information generated by reference projections, environmental scanning, obstruction analysis, and other techniques. Top-level executives then use this input to define the long-range objectives of the organization and pass the objectives down, each level formulating its own "subplan" based on what it receives from above.

Management-driven planning, on the other hand, starts at the lowest levels. Individual units generate a budget along with a wish-list of desired improvements (more employees, updated technology, new desks, etc.). Management at each higher level consolidates these budgets and lists, defines its own priorities, and then passes them on upward. When the top level is reached, final decisions are made and passed back down.

"Interactive planning" has been offered by Ackoff. In order to be systemic, in order to define and integrate a comprehensive "whole" so that it becomes more than just the sum of its parts, more than just an "aggregate" lacking the characteristics critical to a core identity, planning efforts following the paradigm must have four fundamental attributes.

First, planning efforts must be truly *participative*. All employees must be involved, not only as generators and providers of data and information, but as decision makers in their own areas of expertise.

Second, planning efforts must be *organization-wide* and *integrated*. Every part of the organization, every level must be involved and must understand how what they are working on fits into the whole. If the effort is not truly participative, this second characteristic can obviously not be achieved.

Third, planning efforts must be *ongoing*. In order to be truly effective, planning cannot be done in a 2 weeks or in a 2-month-long yearly exercise. The environment and the markets being planned for change constantly. Therefore, planning has to become part of everyday organizational activities.

Fourth, the planning effort has to help give organizations the ability to *learn constantly* from their environment and to *adapt quickly* to changes occurring in that environment. The entire organization has to become an "adaptive learning system." The necessary learning cannot be left up to one department or to top-level management, not if the best results are to be achieved. Neither can the adaptation part.

The technique used by systems people in an interactive planning process is *idealized design*. Instead of identifying current problems, desired improvements, prioritizing them, then battling over resources, participants start by idealizing their own work environment. They answer the question, "Suppose when we come to work tomorrow morning we find that the company, our manufacturing process, our service delivery system, our accounting system, our management system, our filing system, our telephone system, our office building have disappeared during the night. *If* we are charged with the task of recreating everything from scratch with no constraints except that only existing technology could be used in the design and that what participants come up with has to be able to survive economically, what is the best we can do?"

People all over the organization accept this challenge for their part of the operation. They then begin integrating the designs until one comprehensive idealized design exists for the entire company, a design that everyone has contributed to and everyone agrees to. The next question addressed is, "What are the gaps that exist between where we are now and where we want to be?" The gaps identified are then prioritized based on which improvement will bring the company closest to the ideal the fastest and according to monetary constraints. Finally, work is begun on making initial improvements.

The interactive planning process, however, does not end there because, as we have said, the environment is continually changing, which forces participants (*learners*) to *adapt* their part of the idealization continually. These changes, in turn, create a ripple effect that triggers other changes in other parts of the organization, and so on.

Meeting the Organization Design Challenge

In terms of structure, Ackoff has succeeded in designing the "democratic society" that Peter Drucker wanted as a foundation for organization culture. Organizations have traditionally been autocratically run. That is, leaders at every level, in the early days *bosses*, then *managers*, have been responsible for the final decisions. Ackoff and others have wondered why, in cultures such as the United States dedicated to democracy as the best and fairest form of government, in cultures that realize, at least intuitively, that democracy best facilitates both individual and societal development, why our corporations and our other critical institutions are run *autocratically* rather then *democratically*.

The answer, of course, is that the hierarchical, top-down approach has seemed the best alternative for controlling and integrating the wide range of activities necessary to most operations. Originally, this approach made sense.

Employees, as we remember, were little more than living machine parts; they were not supposed to think. The boss was usually that person who had been working with the company the most number of years and, therefore, understood the machinery involved the best.

But as the education level of the workforce rose and as processes grew increasingly sophisticated, employees began to understand the processes better than their boss. "Leadership" itself became an *art* requiring a specific set of skills frequently unrelated to the technical ones of the employees. Therefore, the need to find effective ways to get employees involved in decision making grew. Autocratic leadership in the workplace became rapidly obsolete and needed to be replaced by a more democratic style.

Efforts have been made to move in this direction, the previously discussed autonomous work group concept being one of the more successful. But the autonomous or self-directed work group concept has not been applied organization-wide in most cases, only on the lowest levels. The hierarchy is still considered necessary above that to integrate things properly. The also previously discussed quality improvement movement has stressed increased employee involvement, but, again, has usually gone only part way. In most quality improvement efforts management assigns projects to teams. Managers usually lead the teams. Managers make the final decisions concerning solutions. It is still the traditional hierarchy, the traditional autocracy. The only change is that there is increased input from those supervised.

Ackoff's "circular organization" does, indeed, go all the way. It truly empowers employees on all levels by making the organization management system democratic. First, we need a definition. A *democracy* exists when those being led exercise control over their leaders. That is it. The basic concept of democracy is that simple. In politics we normally elect our leaders and, therefore, have the power to replace them in the next election by voting for someone else if we do not like how they perform. Holding periodic elections in the workplace, however, would be too time-consuming. It would not be cost-effective.

As an alternative, Ackoff has introduced the idea of installing "boards" at all levels. A corporate board of directors traditionally has three major responsibilities: (1) To hire and fire the CEO and to monitor that person's activities; (2) to set overall organization policy; (3) to authorize major transactions evolving usually from the long-range planning effort. Ackoff's question is, why not establish a board for every leader? On this board would sit the leader whose board it is, the leader's immediate supervisor, and all of the leader's immediate subordinates, as well as anyone else from within the organization or without, on a full- or part-time basis, whose input is considered important.

Because the leadership hierarchy is still in place, this would mean that each board, except those at the highest and lowest levels, would have input from multiple levels. Remember that the unit leaders' supervisors also sit on the boards of *their* supervisors, as do their supervisors' supervisors. The same is true in the opposite direction. The leaders we are describing sit on the boards of all those supervised, as do managers from the level below that one. They, in turn, bring input from their supervisees, on whose boards they sit, and so on. Therefore, up to seven levels can be represented, either directly or indirectly, on any board.

The responsibilities of these boards include the following:

1. Planning for the unit whose board it is. The type of planning that best fits this setup is, of course, *interactive*. The board arrangement provides a ready-made vehicle for involving employees at all levels, for ensuring that the planning process is *participative*. The network arrangement of the boards that mimics the organization design ensures that the planning process is *organization-wide and integrated*. The fact that the boards are foundational to the management system ensures that the planning process in *ongoing*. Finally, as a result of their responsibilities, the boards ensure continual *learning and adaptation* during the planning process.

2. Policy making for the unit whose board it is. Leaders still make the decisions. The boards, however, set the policy upon which those decisions are based. Also, when requested, the boards provide advice to the leader making the decision. Boards can directly implement any plan or policy that affects only their unit. When a decision affects any other unit, however, that unit must be involved in the process and must agree to the change before it is made.

3. Coordinating plans and policies of the immediate lower level.

4. Integrating plans and policies — its own and those of the immediate lower level with those made at higher levels.

5. Improving the quality of the work lives of subordinates on the board. The boards should provide the means for employees to identify necessary and desired improvements and, when reasonable, to take the lead in designing and implementing these improvements.

6. Enhancing and evaluating the performance of the leader whose board it is. This it the responsibility that introduces the concept of democracy. In a board-driven organization a new leader cannot be hired without the approval of involved board members. Also, that person

cannot keep his or her job without their ongoing approval. Boards cannot fire their leader from the company. That can be done only by a higher-level leader. Boards, however, can remove the leader from that position. In actuality, this rarely happens. The realization is that because board members have been given a major say in hiring and firing their leaders, because board members have been given "ownership" of that leader, they are obviously going to do their best to see that the person chosen succeeds.[2]

The most commonly asked question concerning the circular organization concept is, "When do leaders have time to get their work done? Most of them sit on their own board, their supervisor's board, and maybe 8 to 12 boards of subordinates. That makes up to 14 board meetings. If the boards sit at least once monthly and meetings last 2 hours, that is at least 28 hours. Multiply that by the number of managers in the organization, and you end up with a very large chunk of time.

Ackoff's answer is quite simple. The responsibilities of the boards include planning, setting policy, coordinating activities on their own level, integrating the activities of their level with those of the levels above and below, finding ways to improve the quality of the work lives of their members, and working to support and improve the performance of their leader. What else is there? What these boards are doing, in fact, is the essence of modern-day organization leadership. The boards are, in fact, taking over a large part of the leadership function.

The leader in this scenario becomes, by our definition, more of a "facilitator," than a "boss" or a "manager." Leaders work with board members to help them develop and effectively utilize their potential in the interest of the organization. Leaders oversee the implementation of board decisions between meetings, help coordinate and integrate efforts within the unit as well as between that unit and others. The board approach, in sum, helps organizations move toward the desired facilitator style of leadership by providing the necessary supports.

Meeting the Challenge in Terms of Key Organization Processes

In terms of a vehicle that allows employees to contribute effectively to the definition of key organization processes, a systemic quality improvement effort is currently the most appropriate choice, at least until organizations adopt the interactive planning model and the circular organization structure. A systemic quality improvement effort, for one thing, helps prepare organizations for Ackoff's developmental approaches to function and structure.

Although quality improvement is and has been a "buzzword" in good currency in the United States for the last decade, and in Europe and Japan for at least the last two, most organization efforts lack the characteristics necessary to make them truly systemic.

A systemic quality improvement effort is built around an organization-wide network of integrated teams responsible for identifying and implementing their own projects. These teams include either hourly workers or leaders, but not both, at least not initially, so that they can be truly participative. The teams meet on an ongoing basis.

Perhaps most important, however, systemic quality improvement efforts are built around a set of "ground rules" which mimic the requirements established to shape the behavior of Ackoff's boards. These ground rules, which everyone in the organization must agree to support, include the understanding that:

1. Teams have direct access to all company personnel to meet their informational needs.
2. All decisions are made by consensus.
3. Improvements/projects that might affect other parts of the operation must be agreed to by anyone else affected. Such "stakeholders" must also have a chance to contribute before implementation occurs.
4. Team-suggested improvements must be justified by a cost–benefit analysis when possible or by a quality of work life rationale when not.
5. Response to team questions/suggestions must be received within 1 week.[3]

W. Edwards Deming's quality improvement model, of course, either includes all of the above characteristics directly or sets the stage for their incorporation, combining them with the necessary technical tools to create a comprehensive whole.

In summary then, at present society has everything it needs to reshape organization culture, to make it *developmental* in nature, to turn *work*, as Mary Follett said, into an activity that produces more than just a salary for employees. We have the necessary philosophical underpinnings — Aristotle's development ethic — borrowed from antiquity and tailored to meet modern-day need by Ackoff. We have technology capable of "freeing" us from dehumanizing tasks. We have the systems paradigm and the organization models emerging from it that allow us to react effectively to "new world" challenges. We have a definition of leadership that enables us to move from the era of "bosses" and "managers" to that of empowering "facilitators." We have all the necessary ingredients, at least in the economically developed portions of the world.

And, indeed, the sought-for workplace and societal changes are occurring, especially in Western Europe, where our story began. The United States as a major economic power, however, is having more difficulty bringing the concepts of work and development together. Why this is so and what the United States must do to "catch up" again, at least from a developmental perspective, will be the central theme of our final chapter.

Topics for Discussion

1. Is quality improvement in your organization approached in a systemic manner?
2. Why is reengineering by itself not a long-term solution to improved productivity?
3. How has the computer affected your work life?
4. In which of the four categories would you place the kind of "work" that you do?
5. Are your leaders "bosses," "managers," or "facilitators"? Which are you as a leader?
6. What are the advantages of "idealized design" as a technique used in interactive planning?
7. Does the "circular organization" concept increase or decrease the workload of managers?

Notes

1. Stephen Robbins, *Essentials of Organization Behavior*, 5th ed., Upper Saddle River, NJ: Prentice-Hall, 1997, p. 206
2. Russell Ackoff, *The Democratic Corporation*, New York: Oxford University Press, 1994, pp. 124–133.
3. William Roth, *Quality Improvement: A Systems Perspective*, Boca Raton, FL: St. Lucie Press, 1998, pp. 49–61.

12 Bringing the Forces That Have Driven the Evolution of Management Theory into Perspective

After Reading This Chapter You Should Know

1. The development ethic, survival ethic, development ethic, work ethic, development ethic, growth ethic, development ethic progression through history and the things that have produced it.
2. Why the Enlightenment is considered the most productive period in terms of shaping the evolution of Western society.
3. The difference between "growth" and "development."
4. Why the United States is stuck in the "growth ethic mentality."
5. Forces driving the United States toward the "development ethic."
6. Constraints to U.S. socioeconomic progress that must be overcome.
7. How Europe has once again taken the lead and become the model in terms of both workplace and overall societal progress.

Filling the Gap

Historically, every great era has been built around one primary ethic, one central theme that has flavored the activities of society, that especially has shaped the involved economic activities. The primary ethic of the Hellenistic period in ancient Greece was, as we know, Aristotle's *development ethic.* The resources of society were utilized to encourage citizens to develop and enjoy their positive potential. Citizens, in turn, were expected to contribute to the development of others. This attitude, of course, was not universal. Ancient Greece, for sure, had its share of robber barons and monopolists and Social Darwinists, although they were called other things. However, the popularly accepted ethic, that ethic practiced by leaders in every field who wished to be applauded, was the development ethic.

The Roman Empire, which absorbed much of the philosophical underpinnings of ancient Greece, adding its own genius for organization and engineering, also accepted the development ethic as the most productive alternative, encouraging its practice even among the newly absorbed citizens of conquered nations. It was only during the following decline of European civilization, which began roughly around the year A.D. 500, that the development ethic lost its relevance. This period was called the Dark Ages, which was appropriate because life was pretty miserable and very short for most. As a result of constant war, famine, lack of sanitation and proper shelter, untreatable disease, and so on, the average life expectancy was around 30 years, if one survived infancy. What little wealth that existed was absorbed by the church and the nobility. Poverty was the rule. The inputs of good, truth, and beauty were far beyond the grasp of most.

The prevailing ethic at that point, therefore, was one of simple *survival.* The holistic development of potential was not even a consideration for most. The *survival ethic* shaped society during the Medieval period.

And to make matters worse, the pope persuaded several of the European kings to go to war to rescue the Holy Lands from the Muslims. Relatively few of those who set out in the invading armies returned. The venture proved a military disaster. At the same time, however, it allowed Europe to enter a new, more promising era. It opened new markets to the east, introduced new technologies, made available new sources of raw materials. It helped usher us into the Renaissance period of European history during which wealth, generated mainly through trade with new partners in different parts of the world and through the exploration and conquest of new territories, increased tremendously.

This new wealth of the Renaissance was still controlled by a relatively small percentage of the population. The fortunate ones, however, immediately began talking once again about *the development of individual potential as life's ultimate objective.* The concept of the "Renaissance Man," which arose from those conversations, has carried over into modern times. A Renaissance person is someone with good business sense, a good sense of social justice, a broad and thorough education, and someone who shows skill in at least one of the arts. It is a person who has gained access to and, in return, has provided society with plenty, good, truth, and beauty. The ruling class, at least during the Renaissance, refocused on the *development ethic* as the primary force driving society.

Still, however, Europe lacked enough plenty to pursue the *development ethic* on a society-wide level, so that the focus of the population remained on improving the economic dimension. The next era, the Protestant Reformation, which was actually as much an economic as a religious movement, gave increasing numbers of people the right and incentive to get involved in the generation of wealth. From this movement sprang the *work ethic*, which held, in effect, that if individuals were willing to *sacrifice* a majority of their daytime hours doing work which was usually not developmental in nature, they could eventually make enough money to meet their basic security needs. This achievement, in turn, would enable them to pursue developmental activities during their free hours.

The economic success of the Reformation led to the optimism of the Enlightenment. Leading thinkers of this period were so sure that we now had the wealth necessary to pursue the *development ethic* on a society-wide level that they set about redesigning key systems with this end in mind.

In terms of the quest of society for the ideal of *plenty,* two economic systems were identified during the Enlightenment, both with the same end objective — to give all individuals the chance to gain the financial resources requisite to realization and enjoyment of their potential. One was Adam Smith's *laissez faire* approach which people called free enterprise. The other was *socialism.* The means employed by these two systems — as little government regulation as possible vs. total government regulation; self-interest as the driving force vs. the good of the whole — were at opposite ends of the spectrum. But the desired end was the same.

In terms of *good,* democracy is the system that gives individuals the greatest voice in societal decisions affecting them, in decisions concerning what is acceptable and what is not. Democracy was a product not so much of the U.S. Revolutionary War effort and Constitutional Convention as it was of Enlightenment-era salon and drawing room conversations in Europe. Benjamin Franklin, Thomas Jefferson, and John Adams picked the concepts up during their diplomatic tours and carried them home to help shape a new nation.

In terms of *truth,* Pestalozzi, Comenius, Condorcet, Rousseau, Jefferson, and others designed systems for universal education, refuting the argument that learning should be only for the elite, emphasizing the fact that in a society that wishes to progress, every individual should have access to the necessary building blocks. These pioneers generated much of the philosophy that, even today, forward-thinking educators use to build their models on.

In terms of *beauty*, the arts exploded, one of the major themes being societal development. Architecture and city planning became increasingly important professions. Emphasis was on aesthetics, on designing buildings and neighborhoods that both soothed and stimulated those who lived in them and visited them.

During the Enlightenment, we worked on generating the blueprints for a development ethic–driven culture. But still, it turned out, we continued to lack the amounts of wealth necessary to realize Aristotle's dream on a society-wide level. So we focused once again on the generation of plenty and moved, with the help of a steady stream of new technology, into the Industrial Revolution, where we proceeded to generate plenty with a vengeance.

The Sticking Point

During this last transition we also adopted a new ethic, the *growth ethic* which simplified our efforts by focusing on the numbers. The main objective of the growth ethic was, quite simply, to increase the numbers, the number of widgets produced, the number of dollars earned, the number of customers seen, the number of bolts tightened. Emphasis was on *efficiency* which, by definition, must be measured quantitatively, by the numbers.

Because machines were obviously more efficient than people, logic told our industrial leaders that they should do their best to turn employees as well into machine parts. This stratagem did not work too well. Some of the differences between humans and machines could not be overcome. Eventually, however, as organizations grew, top-level management did succeed in creating the distance necessary to allow them to depersonify employees and turn them into faceless numbers, which facilitated their more efficient manipulation.

There can be no doubt about the success of the Industrial Revolution. We produced massive amounts of wealth in a relatively short period of time, enough to easily achieve our long-term objective, at least in highly industrialized nations. But the Industrial Revolution is also where the United States "lost" it. It was during this period that our perspective faltered. We were so pleased with the success the *growth ethic* brought that we began to confuse it with the *development ethic.*

We had finally generated enough *plenty* to turn that historic corner, to build a development-oriented society, the dream of the ages. Western Europe is, indeed, turning that corner. But the United States, instead of joining Europe, instead of slipping around it as well and continuing on our historic journey, has remained rooted, fixated on *growth*, and just keeps grinding away. We have begun increasingly to define development in quantitative rather than qualitative terms. The more money, the more pairs of shoes, the more cars, the more rooms we have in our house, the more "developed" we are.

Wealth has become the symbol of success. Money has ceased to be viewed mainly as a tool critical to provision of the inputs necessary to individual and societal development. Rather, it and the "impression pieces" it makes affordable gradually have become an end in themselves. They have become the definition of success, the definition of *development*.

This mentality was honestly portrayed several years ago by the well-known CEO of a U.S. automobile manufacturing corporation. He was asked during an interview why he needed a multimillion dollar salary. Being very direct, his reply was something like, "I don't. Nobody needs a multimillion dollar salary." The next question was, of course, "Well, then, why...." He thought for a moment before replying, "I'll never use it all. I give away a good deal. But it makes me feel successful to be paid that much. That's how people at my level show our success, by making more money than anyone else."

Wealth and the impression pieces it allows us to purchase have become our major status symbols. With the help of Madison Avenue we have often replaced the history-driven quest for *content* with one for *image*, or appearances, and we are suffering the consequences. We work really hard, do what we are supposed to do to succeed, gain the wealth that is supposed to bring respect, collect all the right labels... and still we do not feel right. Not really. In fact, we feel frustrated because something is missing. Despite all the hype, all the reinforcement from peers trapped in the same charade, we know, instinctively, that something very important is missing.

As a way of better understanding what is being said, let us compare the growth ethic with the development ethic.

- Growth is built on *efficiencies*. Attempts are made to reduce everything, including people, their needs, and their desires, to numbers.
- Development is built on *effectiveness*, which incorporates efficiency into something much richer and more meaningful in terms of our instinctual drive toward bettering ourselves, our society, and our world. The development ethic realizes that a lot of inputs necessary

to the realization of potential cannot be reduced to numbers. Development is, as Russell Ackoff says, "Value full rather than value free."

■ Growth, as a result of its sole focus on the generation of plenty, creates competition/conflict. There is always a limited supply of what is important that must be divided up, fought over.

■ Development, with its focus on the overall quality of life, encourages a cooperative atmosphere. The inputs other than those related directly to the accumulation of plenty are not necessarily limited in nature and, therefore, are usually best achieved through a team effort.

■ When the growth ethic prevails, success is measured mainly in terms of what you have.

■ When the development ethic prevails, success is measured mainly in terms of what you do with what you have and by what you contribute to society.

■ The growth ethic makes it necessary to keep those managed under control, to make sure they do not do too well, to keep them from threatening what one has worked and fought so hard to achieve.

■ The development ethic encourages the fostering of talents and creativity in those managed. It realizes that the richest and best-thought-out results usually come from group efforts. It realizes that the more positive potential we release in society the more we all benefit.

■ The growth ethic thrives on simplicity of task and on repetition in order to gain the greatest efficiencies. Work under it, therefore, remains largely sacrificial.

■ The development ethic thrives on challenge (from the task, not other workers). Work under it grows increasingly developmental in nature.

Searching For The Cause

So why has this happened? Why is Europe moving along while the United States is not? One of the major considerations in our discussion must be the lack of solid philosophical underpinnings in the United States. While European and Asian cultures have been struggling with the issue of core values for close to 2000 years, the United States as a nation, has been at it for a little more than 200. Also, as we remember, most of the values that have played an important role in U.S. history were imported originally from Europe, and Europe, during the start-up period of the United States, was busy discovering *empiricism* and debating its relationship to *rationalism.*

During the early days of North American colonization, Descartes was making his pronouncement in Europe that ultimate "truths" did, indeed, exist upon which we should build our reality, but that these truths were defined by the individual. This pronouncement was foundational to the religious movement that produced the new Protestant sects — the Pilgrims, Puritans, Moravians, Quakers. The people involved in this movement were discovering their own truths and emigrated to the colonies so that they could practice them without being persecuted for doing so.

Francis Bacon's resurrection of empiricism at this point, with its empowerment of people to improve their own lot instead of depending on external powers to do so was also eagerly embraced by the new U.S. culture. As we have said, the Protestant Reformation was as much an economic movement as a religious one. The Protestant forefathers of the United States carried with them the belief that they had the right, that they had the obligation, according to Luther and Calvin, to improve their lives, and that increased wealth, gained through hard work, was the key to such improvement.

This perspective was reinforced by an interesting historical coincidence. In 1776 not only was the United States born, but also the concept of laissez faire economics with the publication of Adam Smith's book, *Inquiry into the Nature and Causes of the Wealth of Nations.*

The point I am trying to make is that the United States has not had time to get beyond its original mind-set, to really question this mind-set, to delve seriously, as a nation, into the meaning of life, into what life should be about. As a result, the United States has continued to follow along behind Europe, absorbing its values and sometimes improving on them as was demonstrated by the emphatic "take over" by the United States of the Industrial Revolution and the incredible degree of success it has enjoyed.

But here, as we have said, the United States got stuck. The problem was that it confused its "economic model" with the concept of a "social philosophy." The Industrial Revolution had been driven successfully by the laissez faire economic model. In Europe, however, this laissez faire model overlay traditional core social values, overlay the development ethic. Laissez faire was used in Europe as a *means* of helping that civilization achieve an end (the increased amounts of plenty necessary to facilitate society-wide development). It was not, however, considered the ultimate *end* in itself. The same had been done earlier in Europe, as we remember, during the Protestant

Reformation with the work ethic. The increased amounts of wealth generated during that period led to the developmental advances of the Enlightenment.

The United States, has grown in population and increased in power very rapidly since its birth. The United States started as a "greenfield site" experiment involving democracy and laissez faire economic theory. The U.S. founders chose not to include in their luggage the wisdom of the ancients when they sailed over from Europe, but preferred the pronouncements of the moderns. Economic progress has been the major U.S. focus almost from the beginning. For all those reasons, the development ethic has not yet, to this day, been taken into consideration as foundational to cultural evolution. Instead, the prevailing economic model has been shaped to serve as the U.S. *social philosophy* as well, although it in no way is capable of satisfying the complex range of social needs involved.

The major reason that the pure laissez faire approach to economic growth lost its acceptance so rapidly in Western Europe was that it conflicted too greatly with the social philosophy, with the development ethic. The main reason it has survived in the United States is that, up to this point, the United States has lacked a social philosophy, has lacked the development ethic. And, thus, while Europe is moving on, the United States remains trapped in what I have labeled the "Growth Ethic Mentality," which is little more than the laissez faire approach to economic growth applied to societal evolution as well.

Is There a Way Out?

Enough said. The point should be made. So how do we get back on track? How do we move on to the development ethic now that we have the amount of *plenty* required to turn that corner and focus as a society on the realization of human potential?

Three things are driving us. The first is instinct. It is in our genes. We as a species suffer from a primal urge to improve life constantly for ourselves and for our children. As a very simple proof of this, look how far civilization has come in just 800 years. Remember the Medieval period, where life for most was a day-to-day exercise in survival; where all one aimed for was enough to eat and a safe place to hide when the armies came; where one bout of the plague alone killed a third of the total European population; where what limited education existed was a privilege enjoyed only by the elite? It is awesome. Some of us might be off track at the moment, but we will get back on. There are too many generations of ancestors peering over our shoulders for us to go astray now.

The second driving force is technology — computers, fiber optics, virtual reality, and so on and on and on. Technology has been our friend from the start. It played a major role in lifting us out of the Dark Ages. It has been responsible for most of the advances made in our quest for sufficient *plenty* since then. It is going to continue to force movement in the right direction.

One way it is currently doing this is by radically reducing the number of simplified, repetitive, deadening jobs available, those upon which our growth ethic–oriented culture was originally built. It is making human input less necessary to the generation of *plenty*. It is causing us to rethink the concepts of *work* and *training*. It is currently causing us, in effect, to redefine our work life reality.

Part of this necessary rethinking and redefinition results from the fact that technology has made traditional management systems obsolete. We are being forced to give employees increased responsibility and authority. For example, technology has already made it more cost-effective for a growing number of employees to complete at least part of their work in their homes. Communications technology companies are pushing all sorts of new gadgets to make the traditional office obsolete. How do we effectively "manage" employees working out of their homes?

The third driving force is the increasing number of examples of good leadership appearing in the United States. Aaron Feuerstein is the CEO of family-owned Malden Mills. When three manufacturing sites at the Malden complex in Lawrence, Massachusetts were destroyed by fire in December 1995, Feuerstein continued to pay the displaced employees and to provide benefits while the sites were being rebuilt. The employees, in return, dedicated themselves to bringing the business back. Within several weeks of the fire, Malden Mills was producing more yards of fabric than before.

When asked why he had made this gesture instead of just taking the insurance money and moving his operation south where labor was cheaper, Feuerstein replied, "I have a responsibility to the workers....I have an equal responsibility to the community. It would be unconscionable to put 3,000 people on the street and to deliver a death blow to the city."[1] Also, he said, "If you think that the only function of a CEO is to increase the wealth of shareholders [growth ethic], then any time he spends on scripture or Shakespeare or the arts is wasted. But if you think the CEO must balance responsibilities [development ethic], then he should be involved with ideas that connect him to the past, present, and future."[2]

Ralph Stayer is the owner and CEO of Johnsonville Sausage Company in Wisconsin. Although Stayer's business has been successful, growing at a rate of approximately 20% yearly, Stayer eventually became dissatisfied with the level of employee commitment and with the company's resultant lack of ability to adapt to a rapidly changing market environment. Eventually, he realized that the way to increase employee commitment was through empowerment. He began to couple authority with responsibility. He realized that as long as he and his managers continued to make all the decisions, the workers would continue to wait to be told what to do and would not take the initiative in terms of improving performance.

To change this attitude, Stayer removed himself almost totally from the operational decision-making process. At the same time, he converted his managers to "coaches." The employees began functioning in teams responsible for hiring and training new members as well as for decision making in their area of expertise. Pay raises resulted from learning a new skill. He gave every employee an education allowance. He developed an organization-wide bonus system based on the overall profitability of the organization.

Eventually, Stayer realized that all these changes had to fit into and support a systemic whole that encouraged the development of employee potential and made the best use of it in terms of achieving organization objectives. At one point he said that he considered it "immoral to be the leader of a business and to not allow employees to develop their talents [potential] fully."[3]

Feuerstein, Stayer, and an increasing number of industrial leaders like them, perhaps without knowing it, are moving toward the development ethic. Feuerstein did so by first ensuring that foundational *plenty* remained in place for his employees. Stayer did so by focusing on *truth*, tying it to *plenty* once *good* had been established though the introduction of self-directed work groups. Both CEOs continue to run extremely profitable businesses, thus proving, once again, the effectiveness of what we call the Christian humanist approach.

These two men, however, remain in the minority, at least in the United States, in their refusal to agree that improvement of the bottom line is the primary objective or that *growth*, no matter what the cost might be to employees and to society, is the primary goal. The "majority" is headed by the modern-day "robber barons," the hostile takeover artists who find their challenge in gaining control of companies, stripping them of their assets, or making them more profitable in the short term by downsizing, then selling them off with no concern for the employees or for the effects of the actions on society. Today's robber barons are actually more Machiavellian than their ancestors. While the original robber barons *built* the U.S. infrastructures —

the railroads, the steel industry, the oil industry, the banking industry — as part of their wheelings and dealings, the major activity of their modern counterparts seems to be *tearing things down* solely for the purpose of increasing their own personal wealth.

Once Again Following Europe's Lead?

In Western European countries, while the financial community remains important, it is not allowed to play the pivotal role that it plays in the United States. Legislation has been passed to make the financial community a partner to, rather than an exploiter of, the business sector. The banks that provide financial support form long-term relationships with the companies they support. Representatives of the banks often sit on the "supervisory boards" of the companies and participate in developing their long-range plans. Workers also sit on these boards; in Germany, by law, half of the seats, in larger firms at least, must be filled by lower-level employees.

The European approach, of course, is not perfect. Due in part to the old-boy syndrome, which is found in all industrial cultures but which is perhaps stronger in Europe than in the United States because it has been around longer, European firms frequently lack the flexibility, the initiative of U.S. firms. As a result, they are beginning to adopt, to a degree, more aggressive U.S. management techniques. These include breaking conglomerates up into independent companies; offering unit managers stock options as part of their reward to focus them on the company as a whole; encouraging shareholders to become more active.[4]

The central ingredient of relationships in the European economic community, however, continues to be *trust* based on *cooperation*, trust between the financial community and the industries it supports, trust between labor and management. Both trust and cooperation, as we know, are critical to *progress* as we have defined it. Evidence of the successful progress of Western Europe toward the development ethic is apparent in every sector. While Western Europe has fewer multimillionaires than the United States, it also has a far smaller percentage of chronically poor and a higher average standard of living. Unemployment, welfare, and job-training systems in Western Europe are much more supportive as the result of an economic philosophy that strives to combine the best of the laissez faire approach and the best of socialism. Western European countries are all democratic. Western European countries provide free education of roughly equal quality to all those qualified.

Concerning the aesthetic dimension, Western European countries no longer see nature as something to be conquered and used in any way possible to make money, no matter what the long-term consequences. Rather, they have adopted comprehensive conservation programs which protect, nurture, and carefully manage natural resources in a way that allows the public continuing, free access to them. Western European cities are generally clean, well managed, and visually pleasant, instead of being dirty, dangerous, and having to struggle constantly to survive financially. Finally, in terms of time, European workers, as we have said, control a much greater number of hours in their day, week, year, than either their U.S. or Asian counterparts.

It is obvious, at this point, that Western European nations are much farther along the road to the adoption of the *development ethic* as their primary, society-driving, philosophical foundation than the United States. The current question concerning the United States is how long it will take our nation to "outgrow" the *growth ethic* mentality and to get back on track; how long it will take our nation to realize the need for a bedrock social philosophy, as well as a supportive economic one; how long it will take the United States to discover the value of the *development ethic,* the gift of the ancients, and to make that ethic the core of its social philosophy.

Once the necessary decision is made, Christian humanism will become the predominant mind-set in the United States, as it is now becoming in Western Europe. The systems approach to organization development will be accepted as the approach necessary to our continued advancement. Leaders will become more willing to empower their employees. The engineering and human relations schools of thought will become more willing to combine their strengths under the umbrella of systems theory and the development ethic in efforts to improve continually the benefits derived from that part of our lives spent "working."

Once this decision is made, we will finally be able to turn that historic corner and will *truly* begin to realize our potential, not only as individuals, but as a nation, as a society, as a world.

Topics for Discussion

1. Why has society historically continued to revert back to the development ethic?
2. How have conceptual developments made during the Enlightenment helped shape modern society and the modern world of work?

3. Why can it be said that "growth" is part of "development," but not vice versa?
4. What do we mean when we say that the United States has confused its economic model with its social philosophy?
5. Can students name factors, in addition to those mentioned in the chapter, that are driving the United States toward the development ethic?
6. What are the steps that need to be taken in the United States to remove the "scarcity mentality?" Or should it be removed?

Notes

1. "They Call Their Boss A Hero," *Parade Magazine,* September 8, 1996, p. 5.
2. *Ibid.,* p. 5.
3. Ralph Stayer, "How I Learned to let my Workers Lead," Harvard Business Review, Nov.-Dec., 1990, p. 70.
4. Anonymous, "Le Defi Americain, Again," *The Economist,* London: July 13, 1996, p. 4.

Bibliography

Ackoff, Russell, *Redesigning the Future*, New York: John Wiley & Sons, 1974.

Ackoff, Russell, *The Democratic Corporation*, New York: Oxford University Press, 1994.

Ackoff, Russell and Emery, Fred, *On Purposeful Systems*, New York: Aldine-Atherton, 1972.

Ackoff, Russell and Garajedaghi, J., *Prologue to National Development Planning*, New York: Praeger, 1989.

Adler, Mortimer, *Aristotle for Everybody*, New York: Macmillan, 1978.

Aguayo, Raphael, Dr. Deming, *the American Who Taught the Japanese about Quality*, New York: Carol Publishing Group, 1990.

American Society of Mechanical Engineers Paper, "The Present State of the Art of Industrial Management," 1912 (Frederick Taylor Collection).

Anonymous, "Le Defi American, Again," *The Economist*, July 13, 1996, pp. 3–6.

Beard, Miriam, *A History of Business*, Vol. II, Ann Arbor: The University of Michigan Press, 1965.

Beer, Stafford, *The Brain of the Firm*, London: Penguin Press, 1972.

Bernard, Chester, *The Function of the Executive*, Cambridge, MA: Harvard University Press, 1938.

Boone, Louis and Kurtz, David, *Contemporary Business*, Philadelphia: The Dryden Press, 1997.

Brinton, Crane, Ed., *The Portable Age of Reason Reader*, New York: Viking Press, 1956.

Buck, Lawrence and Zophy, Jonathan, *The Social History of the Reformation*, Columbus, OH: Ohio State University Press, 1972.

Childs, Marquis. Sweden, *The Middle Way*, New Haven, CT: Yale University Press, 1938.

Churchman, C. West and Ackoff, Russell, *Methods of Inquiry: An Introduction to Philosophy and Scientific Method*, St. Louis: Educational Publishers, Inc., 1950.

Cobban, Alfred, Ed., *The Eighteenth Century: Europe in the Age of Enlightenment*, New York: McGraw-Hill, 1969.

Cole, Margaret, *Robert Owen of New Lanark*, New York: Oxford University Press, 1953.

Commager, Henry, *The Empire of Reason: How Europe Imagined and America Realized the Enlightenment*, Garden City, NY: Doubleday, 1977.

205

Copley, Frank, *Frederick W. Taylor, Father of Scientific Management*, Vol. 1, New York: Harper and Bros., 1932.

Dannenfeldt, Karl, *The Renaissance: Medieval or Modern?* Boston: D. C. Heath, 1959.

Davis, Louis and Sherns, Albert, Eds., *The Quality of Working Life*, Vol. 2, New York: The Free Press, 1975.

Dolan, John, *History of the Reformation*, New York: The New American Library, 1965.

Drucker, Peter, *The Age of Discontinuity*, New York: Harper and Row, 1968.

Drucker, Peter F., *Post Capitalist Society*, New York: Harper Business, 1993.

Drury, H. B., *Scientific Management: A History and Criticism*, New York: Columbia University Press, 1922.

Ferguson, Wallace, *The Renaissance*, New York: Holt, Reinhart and Winston, 1940.

Feuerstein, Aaron and Clark, Michael, "Malden Mills Weaves Success from Strong Ties to Workers and Community," *Innovative Management*, Vol. 2, No. 1, Fall 1996, pp. 4–11.

Fine, Sidney, *Laissez Faire and the General Welfare State*, Ann Arbor: University of Michigan Press, 1966.

Ford, Henry, *My Life and Work*, Salem, NH: Ayer Publishers, 1922.

Freud, Sigmund, *The Ego and the Id*, New York: W.W. Norton & Co., 1960.

Gay, Peter, Ed., *The Enlightenment: A Comprehensive Anthology*, New York: Simon and Schuster, 1973.

Gelderman, Carol, *Henry Ford: The Wayward Capitalist*, New York: The Dial Press, 1981.

George, Claude, *The History of Management Thought*, Englewood Cliffs, NJ: Prentice-Hall, 1968.

Gross, Bertram, *The Managing of Organizations*, Vol. 1, London: Collier-Macmillan Limited, 1964.

Gulick, Luther and Urwick, L., *Papers on the Science of Administration*, New York: Institute of Public Administration, 1937.

Hammond, J. and Hammond, Barbara, *The Skilled Labourer: 1760–1832*, New York: Harper Torch Books, 1970.

Herzberg, Frederick, *Work and the Nature of Man*, New York: The World Publishing Co., 1966.

Herzberg, Frederick, Mausner, Bernard, and Snyderman, Barbara, *The Motivation to Work*, New York: John Wiley & Sons, 1962.

Hobsbawm, E. J., *The Age of Revolution: 1789–1848*, Cleveland, OH: The World Publishing Co., 1962.

Holley, William and Jennings, Kenneth, *The Labor Relations Process*, 6th ed., New York: Dryden Press, 1997.

Josephson, Matthew, *The Robber Barons 1861–1901*, New York: Harcourt, Brace and Co., 1934.

Kadar, Sudhir, *Frederick Taylor: A Study in Personality and Innovation*, Cambridge, MA: MIT Press, 1970.

"Keep Your Profits," *Newsweek*, November 6, 1995, p. 98.

Ketchum, Lyman, "A Case Study in Diffusion," in *The Quality of Work Life*, Vol. 2, New York: The Free Press, 1975.

Kotker, Norman, Ed., *The Middle Ages*, Boston: Houghton Mifflin, 1968.

Kreitner, Robert, *Management*, 3rd ed., Boston: Houghton Mifflin, 1986.

Lacey, Robert, *Ford: The Men and the Machine*, Boston: Little Brown, 1986.

Laszlo, Ervin, *Introduction to Systems Philosophy: Toward a New Paradigm of Contemporary Thought*, New York: Harper & Row, 1972.

Laszlo, Ervin, *The Relevance of General Systems Theory*, New York: George Braziller, 1972.

Lewis, Pamela, Goodman, Stephen, and Fandt, Patricia, *Management: Challenges in the 21st Century*, New York: West Publishing Company, 1995.

Likert, Rensis, *New Patterns of Management*, New York: McGraw-Hill, 1961.

Lucas, Henry, The Renaissance and the Reformation, New York: Harper & Row, 1960.

Machiavelli, Niccolò, *The Prince*, New York: Mentor Books, 1952.

Maslow, Abraham, *Motivation and Personality*, 2nd ed., New York: Harper & Row, 1970.

Mason, Anthony, *Medieval Times*, New York: Simon & Schuster Books for Young Readers, 1996.

McGregor, Douglas, *The Human Side of Enterprise*, New York: McGraw-Hill, 1960.

Mill, John Stuart, *Autobiography*, New York: Bobbs-Merrill, 1957.

Naughert, Charles, *The Age of Renaissance and Reformation*, New York: University Press of America, 1997.

Olson, Sidney, *Young Henry Ford*, Detroit: Wayne State University Press, 1963.

Ouchi, William, *Theory Z*, New York: Avon Books, 1981.

Painter, Sidney, *Medieval Society*, Ithaca: Cornell University Press, 1951.

Peck, M. Scott, *People of the Lie*, New York: Simon & Schuster, 1983.

Polland, S., *A History of Labour in Sheffield*, London: Ashgate Publishing, 1960.

Richards, William, *The Last Billionaire: Henry Ford*, New York: Charles Schribner's Sons, 1948.

Robbins, Stephen, *Essentials of Organization Behavior*, 5th ed., Upper Saddle River, NJ: Prentice-Hall, 1997.

Roth, William, *Work and Rewards: Redefining Our Work Life Reality*, New York: Praeger Publishers, 1989.

Roth, William, *The Evolution of Management Theory: Past, Present, Future*, Delray Beach, FL: St. Lucie Press, 1993.

Roth, William, *Quality Improvement: A Systems Perspective*, Boca Raton, FL: St. Lucie Press, 1998.

Roth, William, "Work Ethics," in *National Productivity Review*, New York: John Wiley & Sons, 1998, pp. 1–4.

Russell, Bertrand, *A History of Western Philosophy*, New York: Simon & Schuster, 1945.

Sass, Steven A., *The Pragmatic Imagination: A History of the Wharton School 1881–1981*, Philadelphia: University of Pennsylvania Press, 1982.

Schlereth, Thomas, *The Cosmopolitan Ideal in Enlightenment Thought: Its Form and Function in the Ideas of Franklin, Hume, and Voltaire, 1694–1790*, London: The University of Notre Dame Press, 1977.

Schon, Donald, *Beyond the Stable State*, New York: Random House, 1971.

"Shot down Like Many Worthless Objects," *The Valley Gazette*, Lansford, PA, Sept. 1997.

Singer, E. A., *In Search of a Way of Life*, New York: Columbia University Press, 1948.

Spitz, Lewis, Ed., *The Reformation: Material or Spiritual?* Boston: D. C. Heath, 1962.

Spock, Benjamin, *Baby and Child Care*, 7th Ed., New York: Pocket Books, 1998.

Stayer, Ralph, "Managing Without Managers," *Harvard Business Review*, September–October 1989, pp. 76–84.

Stayer, Ralph, "How I Learned to Let My Workers Lead," *Harvard Business Review*, November–December 1990, pp. 66–82.

Tarrant, John, *Drucker: The Man Who Invented the Corporate Society*, Boston: Cahners Books, 1976.

Taylor, Frederick, *The Principles of Scientific Management*, New York: Harper and Brothers, 1911.

"They Call Their Boss a Hero," *Parade Magazine*, September 8, 1996, p. 5.

Thompson, James, Rowley, George, Schevill, Ferdinand, and Sarton, George, *The Civilization of the Renaissance*, New York: Frederick Ungar, 1959.

Thomson, David, *Europe Since Napoleon*, 2nd ed., New York: Alfred A. Knopf, 1962.

Time Magazine, "Special 1776 Issue," Vol. 105, No. 20, New York: 1975.

Time Magazine, "Special Bicentenial Issue," Vol. 107, No. 21, New York: 1976.

Trist, Eric, *The Evolution of Socio-Technical Systems: A Conceptual Framework and an Action Research Program*, Toronto, Ontario: Quality of Working Life Center, 1980.

Vinacke, W. Edgar, *Foundations of Psychology*, New York: American Book Co., 1968.

Walton, Mary, *Deming Management at Work*, New York: Perigree Books, 1990.

Whitsett, David A. and Yorks, Lyle, *From Management Theory to Business Sense: The Myths and Realities of People at Work*, New York: AMACOM, 1983.

Index